The Globalization of Nothing 2

To Sue, who is really something.

The Globalization of Nothing 2

GEORGE RITZER
University of Maryland

PINE FORGE PRESS
An Imprint of Sage Publications, Inc.
Thousand Oaks • London • New Delhi

For information:

 Pine Forge Press
A Sage Publications Company
2455 Teller Road
Thousand Oaks, California 91320
E-mail: order@sagepub.com

Sage Publications Ltd.
1 Oliver's Yard
55 City Road
London EC1Y 1SP
United Kingdom

Sage Publications India Pvt. Ltd.
B-42, Panchsheel Enclave
Post Box 4109
New Delhi 110 017 India

Printed in the United States of America.

Library of Congress Cataloging-in-Publication Data

Ritzer, George.
The globalization of nothing 2 / George Ritzer.
    p. cm.
Includes bibliographical references and index.
ISBN-13: 978-1-4129-4021-4 (cloth)
ISBN-13: 978-1-4129-4022-1 (pbk.)
    1. Globalization. 2. Globalization—Social aspects. 3. International relations.
4. Nothing (Philosophy) I. Title. II. Title: Globalization of nothing two.
JZ1318.R583 2007
303.48′201—dc22

                                        2006025927

This book is printed on acid-free paper.

07   08   09   10   11   10   9   8   7   6   5   4   3   2   1

Acquisitions Editor:	Ben Penner
Editorial Assistant:	Camille Herrera
Project Editor:	Tracy Alpern
Copy Editor:	Barbara Coster
Proofreader:	Sally Jaskold
Typesetter:	C&M Digitals (P) Ltd.
Indexer:	Sheila Bodell
Cover Designer:	Ravi Balasuriya

Contents

About the Author

George Ritzer is Distinguished University Professor at the University of Maryland, where he has also been a Distinguished Scholar-Teacher and won a Teaching Excellence Award. He was also awarded the 2000 Distinguished Contributions to Teaching Award by the American Sociological Association, and in 2004 he was awarded an honorary doctorate by LaTrobe University, Melbourne, Australia. He is perhaps best known for several editions of *The McDonaldization of Society* (translated into more than a dozen languages) and other related books, including *Expressing America: A Critique of the Global Credit Card Society* (1995) and *Enchanting a Disenchanted World: Revolutionizing the Means of Consumption* (1999, 2004). He edited the *Encyclopedia of Social Theory* (2005) and is the founding editor of the *Journal of Consumer Culture*. He recently completed editing the 11-volume *Encyclopedia of Sociology* (2007) and *The Blackwell Companion to Globalization* (2007) and is currently writing a new book, *The Outsourcing of Everything*, with Craig Lair.

Preface

This should have been a simple and easy revision coming so soon after the publication of the original edition of this book. I felt pleased with that edition and believed that this iteration would involve only minor changes. However, once I began taking the book apart to, as in automobile mechanics, check out each of its component parts, I discovered a number of problems under the hood. Above all, I found that I had really written two books. One, the book I had originally intended to write, was on globalization, especially glocalization and the companion term—grobalization—coined there for the first time. The second dealt with my sense of "nothing" and "something," as well as the something-nothing continuum. I discovered that I had to spend so much time developing and explaining the way those terms were used, highly counterintuitively, in the book that it ended up taking up more space than, and tended to distract one from, the discussion of globalization.

Therefore, the first thing I decided was that I needed to (re)write only one book that clearly focused on the main topic—globalization. Thus, this is now much more clearly a book about globalization, and that is made abundantly clear in the largely new first chapter that now offers an overview of globalization, of globalization theory, and of the unique ways in which those topics are addressed in this volume. It is also clear in the last four chapters of the book that deal, successively, with elective affinities in the globalization of nothing, implications for the approach developed here for theorizing the relationship between globalization and culture, implications for understanding the globalization of consumer culture and the opposition to it, and ways of coping globally with the key problem identified in this book—loss amidst monumental abundance.

This dramatic expansion of the attention devoted to globalization means that since I wanted, if anything, to shorten the book in order to make its basic argument clearer, the amount of space devoted to nothing and something had to be reduced. The original edition's two basic chapters on conceptualizing nothing (and something) have been retained, although modified and in one case (Chapter 2) renamed. That chapter is now titled "Nothing (and Something): Another New Conceptualization" (the first new conceptualization is glocalization-grobalization developed first in Chapter 1). Chapter 3 is the least changed chapter in the book, and its title remains the same—"Meet the Nullities"—and it continues to be devoted to introducing *non*places, *non*things, *non*people, and *non*services, as well as their companions—places, things, people, and services. Chapter 4 is new and brings together under the heading of "Nothing: Caveats and Clarifications" a number of issues that were scattered throughout the original edition of the book. Thus, nothing and something are now dealt with tightly, coherently, and briefly in three contiguous chapters.

In order to make the book shorter and more focused, several things have been deleted from this edition. First, the old Chapter 6 on consumption sites on the Internet has been eliminated, not because the issue was unimportant, but because it was much more about nothing and something than it was about glocalization-grobalization. Second, the Appendix has also been eliminated. I think there are very important issues there, and I refer readers to the original edition if they are interested in some of the larger philosophical and methodological issues associated with the conceptualization of nothing. However, I decided to drop it not only because interested readers could find it in the original edition, but also because, once again, it was about nothing and not globalization. Third, a number of specific discussions of nothing that were scattered throughout the book and that were not combined in the new Chapter 4 have also been eliminated.

Thus, overall, this is a shorter, tighter, and more focused book that deals focally and directly with globalization, at least as it relates to nothing and something.

The major additions to the book are almost all on the topic of globalization. Chapter 1 now offers a broad background on globalization and globalization theory in order to contextualize this book's contribution to that literature. Chapter 6 is almost entirely new and seeks to show the need for the idea of grobalization in globalization theory by carefully reviewing and critiquing works that purport to focus on glocalization, localization, and domestication. It is shown that grobalization is either explicitly or implicitly involved in those analyses even though it is either ignored or critiqued. Chapter 7 is made up of much new material, especially a discussion of consumer culture and its globalization as well as the role of branding in it. While some material carries over from the original edition, Chapter 8 is new in that there is additional coverage (e.g., of craft consumers and brand communities) and it is now focused on what can be done about the problem(s) identified in the book. I hope that readers come away from this revision with not only a new way of looking at globalization but also a sense of the problems posed by the grobalization of nothing and the need to find ways to deal with its pernicious aspects.

I would like to thank Becky Smith, developmental editor with Pine Forge Press, for undertaking the initial deconstruction of the original edition of this book. It was that deconstruction that allowed me to see a number of things that I had not seen before, especially the uncomfortable coexistence of two books within one. I added that and other insights provided by Becky to my own sense that the book had to be much more focused on globalization. The reconstruction of the book that follows is not quite what Becky had in mind, but I could not have done it nearly as well, or quite in the same way, without her help.

Finally, I need to thank Ben Penner, my editor at Pine Forge, for his belief in this book, indeed all my books with Pine Forge, and his material and intellectual help with this revision. He also found several excellent reviewers for this new edition—Dana Stukuls Eglitis, Celestino Fernandez, Karen Bettez Halnon, and a fourth anonymous reviewer. The former three have been, and continue to be, valued reviewers of various plans for, and iterations of, this book as well as of others of mine published by Pine Forge Press.

1

Globalization

A New Conceptualization

Every time one enters the World Wide Web (www), by definition (it is, after all, "worldwide") one enters the global world. Googling almost anything is likely to yield many sites from various parts of the world. With a few keystrokes one can purchase virtually anything from anywhere. Thus, one can download, often for a fee, music, text, and even pornography from anyplace in the world. Indeed, in some cases, especially pornography, the sources may be, and usually are, from anywhere (or everywhere) in the world.

A trip to the nearby local shopping mall is, whether the shopper knows it or not, a global experience. This is most obvious in the products on sale there. For example, I recently purchased three seemingly identical Russell T-shirts at a mall, and when I got home and examined the labels, it turned out that while all the shirts had the identical logo, and looked the same, each was produced in a different third world country. A visit to a consumer electronics store is also a global experience in the sense that virtually everything offered there is made somewhere else in the world. Even a casual examination of the goods for sale at virtually any shop at any mall will indicate that few things are being produced in one's own country (unless you happen to live, say, in China). It is literally the case that the world is on sale at your local mall.

Beyond the products for sale there, the mall itself is increasingly global. For example, many of the malls in my home area (suburban Maryland) and in the area in which I vacation in the winter (Sarasota, Florida) are owned and/or managed by an Australian firm, Westfield (it now has interests in more malls in the United States than in Australia, and also has malls in New Zealand and Great Britain). Furthermore, many specific shops are outlets of chains that may well be owned elsewhere. This is especially true outside the United States, since many of the world's largest chains are U.S. based. However, it is increasingly the case that global chains with roots outside the United States are coming to populate American malls. Examples include The Body Shop (Great Britain), Pollo Campero (Guatemala), H&M (Sweden), to say nothing of the freestanding Ikeas (Netherlands, by way of Sweden) that are increasingly common and visible throughout the United States.

The same is true if one is in the market for an automobile. One's local car dealer is increasingly likely to be offering automobiles produced by companies whose headquarters, if not manufacturing facilities, are elsewhere in the world. Thus, in many places in the world, one is likely to buy cars from companies headquartered in Japan, Korea, Germany, and in the not-too-distant future, China. If one is an American, one is increasingly less likely to buy a car from an American firm, and as a result, those companies are in deep economic difficulties, engaged in downsizing production facilities and workforce, and may be on the verge of bankruptcy. Furthermore, even if an American bought an "American" car, it is likely that many, if not most, of the components of that car were manufactured elsewhere.

O ur everyday lives, especially in the realm of consumption (the area covered in the above cases and from which most of the examples used in this book will be drawn), have become increasingly globalized. However, while for reasons of manageability and interest the main examples here will relate to consumption, the fact is that this is merely the tip of the iceberg. As one contemporary thinker has put it, we now live in a "global age."[1] Globalization is not only increasingly ubiquitous in our everyday lives but also of great relevance to, and of enormous significance for, many larger issues and problems, including inequality between nations and parts of the world (North-South), social class inequality, gender inequality, democratization, and so on. Virtually every nation and the lives of billions of people throughout the world are being transformed, often quite dramatically, by globalization.[2] The degree and significance of its impact is to be seen virtually everywhere one looks, most notably and specifically in the economic realm, in the activities of not only transnational corporations but also such global organizations as the World Trade Organization (WTO), International Monetary Fund (IMF), World Economic Forum (WEF), and World Bank, as well as of those organizations that oppose the actions of many of them such as Greenpeace, World Wildlife Federation, Amnesty International, the Clean Clothes Campaign, and the World Social Forum (WSF). That this is of great significance is made clear by the great importance of the former organizations, the level of protest against them by the latter organizations (and others), and the fact that the implications of both organizational actions and protests against them have reverberated throughout widely dispersed geographic areas and affected the everyday lives of large numbers of people almost everywhere.

Even more visible, although perhaps of declining significance in the face of the expansion of global organizations like those mentioned above—IGOs (international governmental organizations) and INGOs (international nongovernmental organizations)—that are more or less independent of nation-states, are the actions taken by such nation-states, especially the United States, on the global stage. In recent years, this is most obvious in military interventions and, as of this writing, the continuing U.S. military occupation of Iraq and Afghanistan. Of course, the United States claimed that those global actions were provoked by other global activities, mainly global terrorism, most notably the infamous September 11, 2001, attacks by al-Qaeda on the World Trade Center in New York and the Pentagon in Washington, DC.

All of this—changes wrought in everyday life and consumption, the operations of global economic organizations and of nation-states, the actions of, and reactions to, global terrorism, and much more—has led to increasing interest in globalization among laypeople, business leaders, politicians, popular writers, and scholars.[3]

In terms of scholarly work, there is now a vast and growing literature on globalization that is derived from many academic fields, including international relations, political science, anthropology, economics, and sociology. It is work in the latter field that will inform this analysis primarily. More specifically, it is theoretical work, mainly in and around sociology, that forms the base for this book. Indeed, in recent years we have witnessed the emergence of a distinctive body of work known as globalization theory.[4]

While this theory is multidisciplinary in nature, the primary emphasis here is on the utilization of sociological contributions to it, as well as a sociological take on theoretical work derived from other fields. Globalization theory has not only emerged in recent years as a result of efforts to better understand the kinds of social changes discussed above but also because of a series of developments internal to social theory, notably the reaction against such earlier perspectives[5] as modernization theory.[6] Among the defining characteristics of that theory were[7] its orientation to issues that were of central concern in the West, the preeminence it accorded to developments there, and the idea that the rest of the world had little choice but to become increasingly like it (more democratic, more capitalist, more consumerist, etc.). Other theories (e.g., world-system[8] and dependency theory[9]) emerged in reaction, at least in part, to such a positive view of the West (as well as of the North versus the South) and offered international perspectives that were critical of the West (and North) for, among other things, its exploitation of many other parts of the world. Nevertheless, they retained a focus on the nation-state and the West, albeit a highly critical orientation toward both.

While there are many different versions of globalization theory, there is a tendency in virtually all of them to move away from a focus on the nation-state, the West, and the North and to examine transplanetary processes that flow in many different directions, as well as those that are independent of any nation-state or area of the world.[10] Thus, Ulrich Beck (and many others) argues for a globalization theory (and for a social science—including sociology—in general) that adopts a "cosmopolitan"[11] orientation. That would involve a shift away from a focus on the West and North, and especially the nation-state, and toward a concern with transplanetary processes such as global "networks" and "flows" (see below).

Thus, there are good reasons, both external and internal to academic work, for the rise in interest in globalization in general, and globalization theory in particular, but globalization is by no means simple or unambiguous; it covers a wide range of very different phenomena. In dealing with some of that complexity, we need a basic definition of *globalization* as "the worldwide diffusion of practices, expansion of relations across continents, organization of social life on a global scale, and growth of a shared global consciousness."[12, 13]

Key Topics in the Study of Globalization

As it has come to be used, the notion of globalization encompasses a number of transplanetary processes that, while they can be seen as global in their reach, are separable from each other (at least for purposes of discussion). It is beyond the scope and intent of this book to deal with the full range of globalization processes and issues,[14] but at this point I can at least give the reader a sense of the breadth and complexity of this still burgeoning topic and literature.

Perhaps no topic has received more attention from those interested in globalization than the *economy* in general and especially the role played in it by *transnational corporations* (TNCs) such as Toyota, Microsoft, and Exxon. Most observers see TNCs as the most powerful players on the globe today, or at least one of the two or three most important participants.[15]

Politics is the other of the most important concerns of those interested in globalization, especially the role of the *nation-state* in that process.[16] There is a broad consensus that a wide variety of social changes—increasingly porous borders, the growing power of supraterritorial entities (United Nations [UN], European Union [EU], World Bank), and even subterritorial entities (direct relations between regions in different countries)—are eroding the power of the nation-state. However, even if we acknowledge the decline of the power of the nation-state, it remains a potent force in globalization.[17]

An increasing force in globalization is the wide array of INGOs and IGOs mentioned previously. INGOs, especially the World Social Forum, are seen as forming the beginnings of a global *civil society* that could serve as an alternative to global political and economic organizations.[18]

A new type of *city*, the "global"[19] (as well as the broader "world"[20]) city, is seen as emerging, and it has been the subject of considerable thought and research. Among other things, it is one of the subterritorial units engaging in global relationships that largely or totally bypass, or rather pass through, the nation-state (e.g., financial transactions involving directly the three global cities—New York, Tokyo, and London—that are the sites of the largest stock exchanges in the world[21]).

Globalization has naturally been of great practical interest to those in *business,* especially the emergence of new global markets and how to create, serve, and/or get larger pieces of those markets. A variety of ideologies have been developed to support the globalization of business, and those *ideologies* have come to be analyzed by observers and critics of global business, especially in its capitalist form.[22]

Technology, especially the emergence of a bewildering array of new technologies, is related to virtually all aspects of globalization. Indeed, globalization as it currently exists, to say nothing of what it will become in the future, could not have occurred without all sorts of technological developments. Among the interests and concerns in this regard are the satellites that have allowed the mass media to become a global force,[23] the computer and the Internet[24] (including the role they have played in the emergence of the global digital divide as well as other global inequalities[25]), and the advanced information technologies that are transforming many domains, including warfare (at least as it is engaged in by the United States and to a lesser extent other developed countries), from, for example, hand-to-hand combat between people to missiles being launched, often from great distances, from planes, ships, and even pilotless drones.[26]

Then there are such issues as the relationship between globalization and religion,[27] sport,[28] pop music,[29] and virtually every other aspect of the social world. For example, in early 2006 the first global baseball championship, the World Baseball Classic, took place involving teams from, among other places, South Africa, Cuba, the United States, the Netherlands, Japan, Korea, and China.

Great attention has been devoted to the relationship between globalization and a range of *social problems* such as *poverty* and *economic inequality* in general[30] as well as gross *inequalities* in the nature and quality of *health care*,[31] global *crime*[32] and *corruption*,[33] global sex[34] and the *international sex trade*,[35] *terrorism*,[36] as well as the often *negative* impact of globalization on *agricultural life*[37] and the *environment*.[38] All of these problems, and many others, have led to considerable interest in the *morality and ethics* of globalization,[39] to say nothing of a wide range of efforts to deal with these problems, including *resisting* globalization, at least as it currently exists.[40]

However, the aspect of globalization that will concern us most in this book is the globalization of *culture* in general,[41] especially the globalization of *consumer culture*.[42] A great deal of attention will be devoted in these pages to the worldwide spread of consumer culture in general, as well as the various products, services, and settings (e.g., supermarkets, fast-food restaurants) associated with it. Also of concern is the issue of whether global consumer culture poses a threat to both indigenous consumer cultures and the distinctive commodities associated with them.[43]

While the examples to be deployed in this book are from consumer culture, this is not so much a book about consumer culture but rather one about globalization. While a new way of thinking about consumer culture will be presented in Chapters 2–4, the main objective of this book, as indicated by the title of this chapter and as detailed in Chapter 5 and further developed in the last three chapters of the volume, is to offer a new way of conceptualizing and theorizing globalization. Before we can get to the distinctive conceptual and theoretical contributions of this book, I need to offer a sketch of extant theories of globalization.

Globalization Theories

Like much else in globalization studies, theorizing globalization is highly contested. Everyone seems to have his or her favorite theory. Furthermore, the study of globalization is multidisciplinary, with the result that the distinctive theories of many different disciplines are represented in the overall set of globalization theories.

I have recently distinguished between three broad types of globalization theory—economic, political, and cultural.[44] There are, of course, many other ways to categorize globalization theories,[45] and all have their strengths and liabilities.

Political Theories

A particularly important example of political theory is liberal theory (derived from the classical work of John Locke, Adam Smith, and others),[46] especially in the form of neoliberal thinking[47] (often called the "Washington Consensus"[48]). This comes in various forms, but all are undergirded by a belief in the importance of the free market and the need to allow it to operate free of any impediments, especially those imposed by the nation-state and other political entities. The belief is that the free operation of the market, in particular the capitalist market, will in the "long run" advantage just about everyone. This is a popular theory in international relations, political science, and business; it is embraced by many politicians (especially in the United States; hence the Washington Consensus) and informs the writing of influential journalists such as Thomas Friedman.[49]

Another political theory involves a "realist" view, popular in most of the same venues, that sees globalization as the outcome of the *power* relations among nation-states.[50] That is, states are seen as aggressively pursuing their own interests on the global stage (as well as within their own borders) and using their power to advance those interests. As the most powerful nation in the world today (the sole remaining superpower), the United States is seen as the world's major user (and abuser) of its power on the global stage. Thus, for example, the war in Iraq (begun in 2003) is seen as an exercise of global U.S. power, especially military power. The United States exercised that power to advance its own interests, which could be interpreted, positively, as defending its own well-being against the threat of weapons of mass destruction (never found), or negatively, as a ruse to protect and advance its own interests, especially its economic interests in protecting vital oil supplies in the Middle East.[51]

Then there are a variety of other theories derived from the field of international relations (as is realist theory) that look more broadly at relations among and between nation-states.[52] While still influential, these theories have lost ground in recent years primarily because they focus, given the nature of the field from which they emanate, on relations among and between nation-states. As a result, they tend not to concern themselves with the wide range of transnational processes that exist independent of the nation-state and are of growing importance.

The focus and plight of international relations is clear in a fascinating recent essay by Justin Rosenberg in which he argues that the transnational focus of most globalization theories is misguided.[53] He argues that such theories may have enjoyed a boom in the 1990s, but they are now, in his view, moribund. Instead, he argues for a renewed focus on nation-states and their interrelationship, specifically from a Marxian perspective and its focal concern with capitalism. Rosenberg is making this case from the point of view of international relations and seeking the renaissance of a field that has tended to be eclipsed by a variety of globalization theories that see the nation-state as eroding or even disappearing.

Economic Theories

One (political-)economic[54] approach,[55] world-system theory, gives us a very broad sense of the capitalist world primarily divided between "core" nations that exploit economically "peripheral" nations (with the "semiperiphery" somewhere in between).[56] World-system theory is a neo-Marxian approach in which the focus shifts from a traditional concern with the exploitation of the proletariat by the capitalist within capitalist societies to exploitation *among* societies that are part of the capitalist world-system.

While world-system theory remains locked into a focus on the economic relationships within the global system of states, other neo-Marxian economic sociologists focus on economic processes that exist largely independently of the state and, in fact, are likely to control it. For example, Sklair focuses on the relationship between transnational practices (TNPs), transnational capitalist class (TCC), and the culture ideology of consumerism.[57] Of greatest importance to Sklair within the economy, and to others more generally, is theTNC.[58] Basically, the global spread of capitalism is spearheaded by TNCs and their TNPs, the TCC operates on behalf of the TNCs and spreads political TNPs, and the culture ideology of consumerism, spread through cultural elites, prepares the way throughout the world culturally for the acceptance of the products produced by the TNCs. This approach is much more in tune with contemporary globalization theory because, unlike world-system theory and its focus on the state, the focus in these theories is on processes that are largely independent of the state. Such an orientation is also to be found in a very influential work, *Empire,* in which Hardt and Negri see the emergence of a basically stateless, decentered system of global capitalism.[59]

Also focusing on global processes, especially in the economy, is Manuel Castells and his important work on "network society."[60] He sees the emergence of a new form of capitalism, "informational capitalism." It is knowledge based and founded upon information technology. Because of this, it is readily globalized, exists through global networks, and is dominated by a new organizational form, the network enterprise (horizontal and flexible rather than vertical and inflexible), which is the forerunner of a global network society. More generally, he sees movement from a world dominated by "spaces of places" (e.g., states, old hierarchical organizations) to "spaces of flows" (e.g., the information, products, and people that flow through and between network enterprises). This is very much in accord with work in cultural globalization on global flows (to be discussed below). Thus, as this discussion has moved in the direction of some (largely) economic theories of globalization, we have drawn closer to our focal concerns in this book—consumption and culture.

While these, and many other, political and economic theories are important, at least as background and context, they are not the specific theories that provide the more proximate base for the analysis to follow. Since this book is primarily concerned with the globalization of consumer culture, our main concern will be with cultural theories of globalization. However, one might ask: Since consumption is part of the economy, shouldn't economic theories of consumption also be of great relevance to the ensuing discussion? They are, of course, but unfortunately most economic theories of globalization, like theory (and the social sciences) in general, have a productivist bias.[61] That is, they continue to focus on issues of production (manufacture, jobs, TNCs) rather than devoting much, if any, attention to consumption as an economic phenomenon (see the discussion of Sklair's ideas on the culture ideology of consumerism for an exception, although note that he too emphasizes production). While production certainly continues to be of great importance in the contemporary world, it is clear that, at least in the developed parts of it, consumption is becoming perhaps as important to the economy,[62] if not more important, than production. This can be seen, for example, in the fact that the largest corporation (based on gross revenues) in the United States today, number one on *Fortune* magazine's influential (2005) list of the 500 largest public corporations, is one devoted to consumption—Wal-Mart. Many of the older production giants have already disappeared (U.S. Steel) or are in deep trouble (General Motors, with revenues only about two thirds of Wal-Mart's, although it still ranked third on the *Fortune* 500 in 2005). However, that is not to say that economic theories of globalization are not important in themselves and for advancing our understanding of the globalization of consumer culture.

Cultural Theories

Jan Nederveen Pieterse has identified three major approaches in theorizing the cultural aspects of globalization, specifically the centrally important issue of whether cultures around the globe are eternally different, converging, or creating new "hybrid" forms out of the unique combination of global and local cultures.[63]

Cultural Differentialism

Those who adopt this approach argue that there are lasting differences among and between cultures that are largely unaffected by globalization or any other bi-, inter, multi-, and transcultural processes. This is not to say that cultures are not affected at all by any of these processes, especially globalization, but it is to say that at their core they are largely unaffected by them; they remain much as they always have been. In this perspective, globalization only occurs on the surface, with the deep structure of cultures largely, if not totally, unaltered by it. Cultures are seen as largely closed not only to globalization but also to the influences of other cultures.

The most famous, and controversial, example of this paradigm is Samuel Huntington's *Clash of Civilizations and the Remaking of the World Order*.[64] Huntington's view is that the world is, and has been, divided into seven or eight world civilizations (culture on a large scale) and that they remain culturally distinct. More important, in some cases the nature of their cultures (among other things) make it likely they will clash with one another. Famously, Huntington envisions an economic clash between the West (especially the United States) and the East (especially China) and a bloody military confrontation between the United States and Islam. Huntington's view need not detain us long, not only because it is so hotly debated and criticized, but also because it relates much more to larger cultural (civilizational) issues than it does to the specifics of consumer culture. On the latter, there are few, if any, who argue that the culture of any nation is closed to global consumer culture. Those nations that have been exposed to little of it are in that situation mainly because they are so underdeveloped economically that they are of little interest to global purveyors of consumer culture, and, for their part, they can afford little that those purveyors have to offer. Once those nations do develop economically, the forces of consumer culture will seek to gain entrée and those in most cultures are likely to welcome what they have to offer, if not seek it out.

Cultural Convergence

While the previous approach is rooted in the idea of lasting differences among and between cultures and civilizations as a result of, or in spite of, globalization, this paradigm is based on the idea that globalization leads to increasing sameness throughout the world. While thinkers like Huntington emphasize the persistence of cultures and civilizations in the face of globalization, those who support this perspective see those cultures changing, sometimes radically, as a result of globalization. The cultures of the world are seen as growing increasingly similar, at least to some degree and in some ways. There is a tendency to see global assimilation in the direction of dominant groups and societies in the world. Those who operate from this perspective focus on such things as "cultural imperialism," Westernization, Americanization, "McDonaldization," and "world culture."

Much of my previous work is of this genre, although I certainly understand that while there are forces bringing increasing sameness, or homogeneity, to much of the world, those forces are *not uncontested* and their impact on particular locales is often muted and/or altered in many ways by and in those locales. Nonetheless, I have focused on various forces that seek to export greater homogeneity to ever larger portions of the world. Under the heading of McDonaldization[65] (I will have much more to say about this, and Americanization, later in this chapter), I have dealt with efforts to bring a system, a set of operating principles (see below), to more and more parts of the world. In part, this is a result of the spread of the fast-food chains throughout the world and the fact that wherever they go, they operate according to the same basic set of principles. By the way, this makes it clear, contrary to many of my critics,[66] that McDonaldization is not about the globalization of homogeneous food products but rather about the globalization of a set of principles and a system of operation.[67] More important than the global spread of fast-food chains themselves is the fact that restaurants and restaurant chains (as well as many other businesses) in many parts of the world are adopting the principles of McDonaldization and operating on the basis of the same basic system.

I have also written about Americanization as bringing with it greater global homogeneity. One of my interests has been the global spread of the modern universal credit card, which was invented in the United States in 1950 and in recent decades has become a global phenomenon.[68] It is not just that Americans are increasingly touring the globe using the major American brands, Visa and MasterCard, but the citizens of many other societies are also using those very same cards and in much the same way.

Furthermore, the global spread of the credit card, and the increasing indebtedness that tends to be associated with it, has brought with it the American proclivity to go into debt, and to ignore savings, in order to consume at an ever higher level. Many other cultures have been, at least in the past, much more oriented to savings and much more averse to debt, but the arrival of the credit card has led many of them in the direction of higher levels of debt and a lower savings rate.

Another of my concerns has been what I call the "cathedrals of consumption," another American invention in the post–World War II years.[69] The fast-food restaurant (and the chain store) is one of the cathedrals of consumption, but others with roots in the United States include the shopping mall, especially the fully enclosed mall, the Las Vegas–style casino-hotel, theme parks à la Disneyland and Disney World, and the modern cruise ship. All of these, and many others, have been aggressively exported to the rest of the world, with the result that many people in many nations around the world consume in settings that resemble, if not being identical to, the originals created in the United States. In addition, because the settings are much the same, many around the world consume many of the same things (goods and services) and in much the same way.

Other scholars also deal with increasing global homogeneity, albeit in very different ways. For example, there are those who emphasize a process of increasing organizational isomorphism whereby organizations throughout the world have emulated one another, leading to the creation of very similar organizational forms.[70] Then there are those who emphasize the importance of a world culture (or world society) that results in various domains around the world coming to function in much the same way. Thus, there emerge global models or blueprints for those in various places in the world. Such models exist for, among other things, nation-states, business organizations, and educational systems around the world. To the degree that they follow the same or similar models or blueprints, they grow increasingly homogeneous.[71] Of course, adherents of this approach recognize, as do most others associated with other perspectives included under this heading, that heterogeneity continues to coexist with homogeneous forces. Furthermore, forces of homogeneity can themselves give rise to increased heterogeneity by, for example, stimulating indigenous responses to them.

Cultural Hybridization

The third approach emphasizes the mixing of cultures as a result of globalization and the production, out of the integration of the global and the local, of new and unique hybrid cultures that are not reducible to either the local or the global culture. From this perspective, cultural imperialism may be taking place, but it is producing largely superficial changes in other cultures. Much more important is the integration of these and other global processes with various local realities to produce new and distinctive hybrid forms that indicate continued or increasing heterogeneization rather than the homogenization that is emphasized in the cultural convergence approach. Hybridization is a very positive, even romantic, view of globalization as a profoundly creative process out of which emerges new cultural realities and continuing, if not increasing, heterogeneity in many different global locales.

The concept that gets to the heart of cultural hybridization, as well as what many contemporary theorists interested in globalization think about the nature of transplanetary processes, is glocalization. In fact, it is so important and widely accepted that one observer sees glocalization theory as one of the four basic modes for analyzing globalization.[72] *Glocalization* can be defined as the interpenetration of the global and the local, resulting in unique outcomes in different geographic areas.[73] Following Roland Robertson, the following are the essential elements of glocalization theory:

1. The world is growing more pluralistic. Glocalization theory is exceptionally sensitive to differences within and between areas of the world.

2. Individuals and local groups have great power to adapt, innovate, and maneuver within a glocalized world. Glocalization theory sees local individuals and groups as important and creative agents.

3. Social processes are relational and contingent. Globalization provokes a variety of reactions—ranging from nationalist entrenchment to cosmopolitan embrace—that feed back on and transform globalization; that produces glocalization.

4. Commodities and the media are *not* seen as (totally) coercive but rather as providing material to be used in individual and group creation throughout the glocalized areas of the world.

A discussion of some closely related terms (and related examples) will be of considerable help in getting a better sense of glocalization as well as of the broader issue of cultural hybridization. Of course, *hybridization* itself is one such term, emphasizing increasing diversity associated with the unique mixtures of the global and the local as opposed to the greater *uniformity* associated with cultural imperialism. A cultural hybrid involves the combination of two, or more, elements from different cultures and/or parts of the world. Among the examples of hybridization (and glocalization) are Ugandan tourists visiting Amsterdam to watch two Moroccan women engage in Thai boxing,

Argentineans watching Asian rap performed by a South American band at a London club owned by a Saudi Arabian, and the more mundane experiences of Americans eating such concoctions as Irish bagels, Chinese tacos, Kosher pizza, and so on. Obviously, the list of such hybrids is long and growing rapidly with increasing hybridization. The contrast, of course, would be such uniform experiences as eating hamburgers in the United States, quiche in France, or sushi in Japan.

Yet another concept that is closely related to glocalization is *creolization*. The term *creole* generally refers to people of mixed race, but it has been extended to the idea of the creolization of language and culture involving a combination of languages and cultures that were previously unintelligible to one another. In the realm of food, the Cajun cooking associated with the Creoles of Louisiana (themselves a mix of various racial and ethnic groups) is a good example of creolization. For example, the famous Cajun jambalaya involves a mixing of the paella brought to the area by the Spaniards with a variety of local touches and ingredients, especially the substitution of a wide array of seafood abundant in and around Louisiana for meat and sausage.

Finally, mention should also be made in this context of Arjun Appadurai's *Modernity at Large: Cultural Dimensions of Globalization* and its emphasis on global flows and the disjunctures among them.[74] These serve to produce unique cultural realities around the world; they tend to produce cultural hybrids. Appadurai discusses five global flows or *"scapes"—ethnoscapes* (involving flows of people), *mediascapes* (media flows), *technoscapes* (technological flows), *financescapes* (flows of money and financial instruments), and *ideoscapes* (flows of ideas). The use of the suffix *-scape* allows Appadurai to communicate the idea that these processes have fluid, irregular, and variable shapes and are therefore consistent with the idea of heterogeneization and not homogenization. The fact that there are a number of these scapes and that they operate independently of one another to some degree, and are perhaps even in conflict with one another, makes this perspective also in tune with those that emphasize cultural diversity and heterogeneity. Furthermore, these scapes are interpreted differently by different agents, ranging all the way from individuals to face-to-face groups, subnational groups, multinational corporations, and even nation-states. And these scapes are ultimately navigated by individuals and groups on the basis of their own subjective interpretations of them. In other words, these are "imagined worlds,"[75] and those doing the imagining can range from those who control them to those who live in and traverse them. While power obviously lies with those in control and their imaginings, this perspective gives to those who merely live in, or pass through, them the power to redefine and ultimately subvert them.

All of the above concepts—glocalization, hybridization, creolization, and scapes—should give the reader a good feel for what is being discussed here under the heading of cultural hybridization.

While this book is shaped by a variety of inputs from globalization theory, it is especially framed by the cultural paradigms, in particular cultural convergence and cultural hybridization. Its starting point is the hegemony of the latter paradigm, *especially* its primary idea of glocalization and the associated notion of heterogeneization. It is undoubtedly the case that glocalization is not only a reality, but an important one in the world today, and that it is associated with continued global heterogeneization. However, it seems to me that the cultural hybridization paradigm, and the concepts of glocalization and heterogeneization, tell only part of the story. The cultural convergence paradigm also has considerable utility and validity in thinking about globalization. While there is certainly continuing heterogeneization, and undoubtedly even new forms of heterogeneity, it is clear that there are *also* powerful forces leading to at least some increasing homogenization in the world. Similarly, just as glocalization is a useful idea, there is a need for another concept (to be developed below and throughout this book) to parallel it and to help us better understand globalization in general, and homogenization in particular. In sum, what is needed is not a choice between the cultural convergence and the hybridization paradigms but the integration of the two—the use of *both* to offer a better understanding of globalization in general.[76]

Glocalization and Grobalization

It is clear that the concept of glocalization gets to the heart of what many contemporary theorists and analysts interested in globalization think about the essential nature of transplanetary processes.[77] They all recognize that there is much more to globalization than that, but glocalization is often the pivot around which much of their thinking and empirical research revolves. However, as has been made clear above, there is a need for another concept (and perhaps much else that, e.g., encompasses cultural differentialism) that, together with glocalization, would give a more balanced view of globalization, that would represent *both* cultural convergence and cultural hybridization. That concept is grobalization, coined here for the first time as a much-needed companion to the notion of glocalization. *Grobalization* focuses on the imperialistic ambitions of nations, corporations, organizations, and the like and their desire, indeed need, to impose themselves on various geographic areas.[78] The main interest of the entities involved in grobalization is in seeing their power, influence, and in many cases profits *grow* (hence the term *gro*balization) throughout the world. Grobalization involves a variety of subprocesses— Americanization and McDonaldization,[79] as well as capitalism. They, and others, are central driving forces in grobalization, and they are of particular interest to me.

Theoretical Orientation

Grobalization and glocalization are rooted in competing visions of the contemporary world. Grobalization is a modern view emphasizing the growing worldwide ability of, especially, largely capitalistic organizations and modern states[80] to increase their power and reach throughout the world. Two of the preeminent modern theories—those of Karl Marx and Max Weber (and of their followers)—undergird this perspective. While Marx focused on the capitalistic economic system, Weber was concerned with the rationalization of not only the economy but many other sectors of society in the modern world. Both capitalism and rationalization were products of the Western world, and both were aggressively exported to the rest of the world, largely in the 19th and 20th centuries and to this day. That is, it could be argued that both have been, and are, examples of grobalization.

Marxian (and neo-Marxian) theory leads to the view that one of the major driving forces behind grobalization is the corporate need in capitalism to show increasing profitability through more, and more far-reaching, economic imperialism. At first, the expansionism is internal to a given nation, but as profit limits are reached, or profits even begin to erode, there is great pressure to expand to other nations. Many of the firms that succeeded in becoming international presences in the 20th century have become global businesses in the early 21st century. Another driving force is the need for corporations and the states and other institutions (media, education) that buttress them to support efforts at enhancing profitability by increasing their cultural hegemony nationally and ultimately throughout the world. Thus, from this perspective, the need for (especially) American corporations to show ever-increasing profits, and the related and supporting need of the United States and American institutions to exert ever-increasing cultural hegemony, goes to the core of grobalization. American corporations aggressively export commodities for their own profit, and the nation as a whole is similarly aggressive in the exportation of its ideas (e.g., free market, democracy) in order to gain hegemony over other nations, not only for its own sake but for the increased ability to market goods and services that such hegemony yields. Of special interest today are the various consumer systems, the "cathedrals of consumption" or "new means of consumption" mentioned above (also, see below), that the United States is now exporting to the rest of the world.[81] They reflect the fact that capitalism has come to learn that it is not enough to export its products, but it also must grobalize consumerism and create and support the desire to consume those products. Of course, the United States was never alone in any of this; capitalism has thrived in many countries, and they too sought to grobalize. However, the United States, especially its corporations, took the lead in this, and while it has been supplanted in many areas of production by other nations (e.g., Japan and consumer electronics and automobiles), it retains the lead in the grobalization of its cathedrals of consumption, as well as other mechanisms (credit, advertising, marketing, branding), designed to lead people throughout the world to consume in a similar way, and to a similar degree, as do Americans. This is reflected, for example, in the grobalization of such consumption giants as Wal-Mart, Disney, McDonald's, and Visa and MasterCard.

The second modern theoretical perspective informing our views on grobalization is the Weberian tradition that emphasizes the increasing ubiquity of rationalized structures and their growing control over people throughout the world, especially, given our interests, in the sphere of consumption. One of the defining characteristics of rationalization is efficiency. Weber saw the 19th- and early 20th-century bureaucracy as a highly efficient organizational structure, and in the realm of production it was soon joined by the assembly line, which greatly increased the efficiency of the production process. Both forms have, of course, been grobalized. More recent is the creation and dramatic expansion of highly efficient cathedrals of consumption—McDonald's and Wal-Mart are good examples—and they too have been grobalized. The Weberian approach attunes us to the "grobal" spread of these rationalized structures. That is, rationalized structures have a tendency to replicate themselves throughout the world (through, e.g., global organizations emulating successful others wherever they may be found[82]), and those nations that do not have them are generally eager to acquire them. That is, they grobalize both because of a desire to export them to other parts of the world in order to enhance profits and influence and because other nations are anxious to acquire them and the greater efficiencies that they bring with them. While American corporations, indeed the United States as a whole, can be seen as highly rationalized in both production and consumption, there are, as we will see, many other rationalized structures not only in the United States but increasingly throughout much of the world.

While modern theories like those associated with the Marxian and Weberian traditions are closely linked to the idea of grobalization, glocalization is more in tune with postmodern social theory.[83] As we have seen, modern theories like those of Marx and Weber are characterized by an emphasis on great overarching (and homogenizing) processes and changes (the spread of capitalism, rationalization), especially progressively increasing rationality (capitalism was viewed as a rational system by both Marx and Weber). Postmodern theory rejects a focus on such grand sweeping changes and processes, especially the ideas of increasing homogenization and rationalization (itself a major force in homogenization). Instead, postmodern thinkers focus much more on the local and its nonrational, irrational, non-homogenized characteristics. Such an orientation is in tune with the idea of glocalization, especially its emphasis on the local, diversity, hybridity, and at least partial independence from grobal processes. In conjunction with local realities, the globalization of so many commodities and ideas gives communities, groups, and individuals in many parts of the world an unprecedented capacity to fashion distinctive and ever-changing realities and identities. Rather than increasing penetration by capitalist firms and the states that support them, or by rationalized structures, this perspective sees a world of increasing diversity. Although all nations are likely to be affected by the spread of capitalism and rationalization, they are likely to integrate both with local realities to produce distinctively glocal phenomena.

Another key difference between modern and postmodern theories lies in the fact that the former tends to emphasize the idea of *explosion,* while the latter is closely tied to the notion of *implosion.* Thus, grobalization fits with the idea of explosion, since there has been an explosive growth and global expansion of grobal forms. In contrast, glocalization fits better with the idea of implosion in the sense that the global mixes with the local, causing both to implode into one another and creating a unique mix of the two, the glocal.

Given very different theoretical associations, it should come as no surprise that grobalization and glocalization offer very different images of the impact of transplanetary processes. After all, they tend to be aligned with the often antithetical principles of modern and postmodern social theory.

Application of Glocalization and Grobalization

The ideas of glocalization and grobalization can be used to analyze not only the cultural realm but also the economic, political, or institutional realms. Most generally, in the realm of *culture,* grobalization can be seen as a form of transnational expansion of common codes and practices, whereas glocalization involves the interaction, the implosion, of many global and local cultural inputs to create a kind of "pastiche" (yet another postmodern term), or a blend, leading to a variety of cultural hybrids.

Theorists who focus on *economic* factors tend to emphasize their growing importance and homogenizing effect throughout the world and are therefore in tune with the idea of grobalization. They generally see globalization as the spread of the neoliberal market economy throughout many different regions of the world. Joseph Stiglitz, a Nobel Prize–winning economist and former chairman of the Council of Economic Advisors, offered a stinging attack on the World Bank, the WTO, and especially the IMF for their roles in exacerbating, rather than resolving, global economic crises. Among other things, Stiglitz criticizes the IMF for its grobalizing and homogenizing "one-size-fits-all" approach (this is closely related to rationalization, especially its commitment to increasing predictability) that imposes itself on various nations and fails to take into account national differences.[84] The IMF in particular, and globalization in general, have worked to the advantage of the wealthy nations, especially the United States (which effectively has veto power over IMF decisions), and to the detriment of poor nations; the gap between rich and poor has actually *increased* as a result of globalization. While the IMF is supposed to help poor countries by providing them with economic aid, Stiglitz shows that it is often the case that the reforms that the IMF insists that poor countries undertake to fix their economic problems often end up making them worse off economically.

While those who focus on economic issues tend to emphasize grobalization, some glocalization is acknowledged to exist at the margins of the global economy. Examples include the commodification of local cultures and the existence of flexible specialization that permits the tailoring of many products to the needs of various local specifications. More generally, those who emphasize glocalization argue that the interaction of the global market with local markets leads to the creation of unique glocal markets that integrate the demands of the global market with the realities of the local market.

A *political-institutional* orientation also emphasizes grobalization. I have already mentioned one example of a grobalization perspective in the political domain ("world culture" or "world polity") that focuses on the worldwide spread of models of the nation-state and the emergence of isomorphic forms of governance throughout the globe—in other words, the growth of a more or less single model of governance around the world.[85] The most important example of this is the grobal spread of a democratic political system. One of the most extreme views of grobalization in the political realm is Benjamin Barber's thinking on "McWorld," or the growth of a single political[86] orientation that is increasingly pervasive throughout the world.

Interestingly, Barber also articulates, as an alternative perspective, the idea of "Jihad"—localized, ethnic, and reactionary political forces (including "rogue states") that involve a rejection of McWorld in the political realm. Jihad also tends to be associated with an intensification of nationalism and therefore is apt to lead to greater political heterogeneity throughout the world. The interaction of McWorld and Jihad at the local level may produce unique, glocal political formations that integrate elements of both the former (e.g., use of the Internet to attract supporters) and the latter (e.g., use of traditional ideas and rhetoric).[87]

Derived from this is another important difference between these two perspectives: the tendency on the part of those associated with glocalization theory to value it positively[88] and to be critical of grobalization as well as those who emphasize it. This is traceable, in part, to the association between glocalization and postmodernism and the latter's tendency to value positively the individual and the local over the totality—diversity over uniformity. This is also true of work in anthropology, for example, the essays in James Watson's *Golden Arches East: McDonald's in East Asia*.[89] These glocalized McDonald's are depicted positively, and they are used not only to counter the idea of grobalization but also to be critical, explicitly and implicitly, of it.

By way of summary, Figure 1.1 offers a systematic contrast between the ideas of glocalization and grobalization.

While all of the aforementioned focuses on the differences between glocalization and grobalization, the fact is that this is largely a conceptual distinction that allows us to think more clearly about globalization. *In the real world, there is always a combination, an interaction, of glocal and grobal processes.* Anywhere one looks in the world, one sees *both* the glocal and the grobal. In fact, as this book proceeds, it will become clear that a major concern is with the relationship between, perhaps even the interpenetration of, the glocal and the grobal.

Grobalization: The Major Processes

While there are many different subprocesses that could be discussed under the heading of grobalization (imperialism, colonialism, and neocolonialism), we will focus on the ones I have already touched on earlier—capitalism, McDonaldization, and Americanization—this time as they relate more specifically to globalization. While it is clear that all of these processes are important, their relative significance and impact will vary (to the degree that they can be separated) on a case-by-case basis (nation involved, export considered, etc.). As we will see, it is no easy matter to distinguish clearly and unequivocally among these processes. For example, at a more concrete level, Disney is

Glocalization Theory	Grobalization Theory
The world is growing more pluralistic. Glocalization theory is exceptionally sensitive to differences within and between areas of the world.	The world is growing increasingly similar. Grobalization theory tends to minimize differences within and between areas of the world.
Individuals and local groups have great power to adapt, innovate, and maneuver within a glocalized world. Glocalization theory sees individuals and groups as important and creative agents.	Individuals and groups have relatively little ability to adapt, innovate, and maneuver within a grobalized world. Grobalization theory sees larger structures and forces tending to overwhelm the ability of individuals and groups to create themselves and their worlds.
Social processes are relational and contingent. Globalization provokes a variety of reactions—ranging from nationalist entrenchment to cosmopolitan embrace—that feed back on and transform grobalization, that produce glocalization.	Social processes are largely one-directional and deterministic. Grobalization tends to overpower the local and limits its ability to act and react, let alone act back on the grobal.
Commodities and the media, arenas and key forces in cultural change in the late 20th and early 21st centuries, are *not* seen as (totally) coercive but rather as providing material to be used in individual and group creation throughout the glocalized areas of the world.	Those commodities and the media are seen as largely coercive.
Core concepts include hybridization, creolization, and heterogeneization.	Core concepts include capitalism, Americanization, and McDonaldization.

Figure 1.1   Essential Elements of Two Globalization Theories

a capitalistic organization, its origins clearly lie in the United States, and it is highly McDonaldized. Furthermore, even though I will discuss each of these general subprocesses separately, it is clear that they are not easily distinguished from one another; they are highly interrelated.

Capitalism

No force has contributed more to globalization in general, and grobalization in particular, both historically and especially today, than capitalism. As Marx fully understood over a century ago,[90] capitalist firms must continue to expand or they will die, and when possibilities for high profits within a given nation decline, capitalistic businesses are forced to seek profits in other nations.[91] Eventually, such firms are led to explore and exploit possibilities for profit in more remote and less developed regions. Thus, except perhaps for the earliest forms, capitalistic businesses have always had global ambitions; they have always been interested in grobalization (and contributed to glocalization). However, their impact has greatly accelerated in the past several decades.

During the Cold War that lasted much of the 20th century, there were powerful restraints on capitalism's grobal ambitions. Most important, there was a seemingly viable alternative to it—socialism/communism—and this served to temper capitalism's expansion. On the one hand, the Soviet Union and China, as well as nations within their orbit, were largely closed to incursions by the capitalists. The idea, posited first by Winston Churchill in 1946, that an iron curtain had descended between Soviet-controlled Eastern Europe and Western Europe, made the barrier to capitalism, and much else, perfectly clear. On the other hand, many other nations throughout the world, even if they were not behind the iron curtain, were influenced by the ideas, if not the military and political power, of the communist countries. As a result, they were at least ambivalent about participating in the capitalist system, if not overtly hostile to it. In these and other ways, capitalism's grobal ambitions were limited to some degree throughout much of the 20th century.

However, by the close of the 20th century and the beginning of the 21st century, with the death of the Soviet Union and the near-death of communism/socialism, as well as Russia and especially China behaving very much like capitalistic nations, almost all limits to the grobal ambitions of capitalistic firms were eliminated. As a result, it is only now that we are beginning to see the full flowering of grobalization in capitalism. After all, in Marx's day (the mid- to late 1800s), capitalistic businesses were comparatively small, and the important technologies (computers, the Internet, telecommunications, fiber optic cables, huge cargo planes and ships, containerization, etc.) that permit and encourage high levels of grobalization did not exist.[92] Today's enormous capitalistic firms, equipped with magnificent globe-straddling technologies,[93] are far better able to grobalize than their predecessors. *And,* they move into a world in which there is *no* viable alternative to capitalism. We live in an era in which, truly for the first time, capitalism is unchained and free to roam the world in search of both cheap production facilities and labor (China is now a prime site for both) as well as new markets for its products. As two neo-Marxian thinkers, Ellen Meiksins Wood and John Bellamy Foster, put it, "[H]umanity is more and more connected in the global dimensions of exploitation and oppression."[94] As a result, there are those who believe that the death of communism around the world will not spell the death of Marxian theory but rather serve to resuscitate it.[95] That is, Marxian analysis will be more necessary than ever, with capitalism free to exploit more and more geographic areas and peoples of the world. It could be argued that it is only now that capitalism exists as a truly global phenomenon and the implication of Marxian theory is that this sets the stage, for the first time, for the emergence of global opposition to it.[96] This idea is explicit, among other places, in Hardt and Negri's work on "empire." They depict a new world of decentered global capitalism that they see as creating the opposition to it—"multitude"—that will ultimately undermine and destroy it.[97]

Capitalism is clearly related to economic grobalization, especially in the areas of production as well as the central interest here—consumption. However, capitalism is also related to other aspects of globalization. Without adopting a simplistic (economic) base-(political) superstructure model,[98] it is clear that much grobalization in the political realm is affected to a large degree by the capitalistic economic system. Thus, the United States' much-avowed desire to see democracy grow throughout the world,[99] as well as many of its military adventures, are closely related to the needs of its capitalistic system. That is, democratic societies are more likely to become capitalistic, and they are more likely to be open to the incursions of capitalistic firms from other countries (especially the United States). And, in those cases where a society does not move on its own in the direction of "democracy," there is always the possibility of American military involvement (in Iraq and Afghanistan, for example) in order to nudge it, not so gently, in that direction. While the state clearly has its own interests, it just as certainly shares many interests with the capitalistic economic system to which it owes much of its existence and success. Political leaders are generally safe as long as the economy is performing well; however, their situation becomes precarious when the economy falters.

Similarly, organizational-institutional grobalization is also closely related to capitalism. For example, the proliferation of the franchise system of organization (this involves a franchiser [e.g., Subway] selling others [franchisees] the right to operate an outlet, although some control remains with the franchiser, which also usually gets a share of each franchisee's profits[100]) throughout the world is driven, in significant part, by capitalist economics. That is, some franchisers have grown fabulously wealthy as a result of this system, and it is not unusual to find franchisees who have become multimillionaires from the profits from one or several franchises. However, it is important not to reduce all of this to (capitalist) economics alone (some value the franchise system, or a specific franchise, in itself and not just for its profit potential).

We need not go into great detail here about capitalism, because so much has been written about it, its operations are so well known, and it is so obviously a form of grobalization. We turn now to two somewhat less well-known forms of grobalization, although we will have occasion to return under each of them to their relationship to capitalism (and to each other).

McDonaldization

This is the process by which the principles of the fast-food restaurant are coming to dominate more and more sectors of American society and an increasing number of other societies throughout the world. It fits under the heading of grobalization because it involves the *growing* power of this form and its increasing influence throughout the world. In terms of some of the issues raised earlier in this chapter, it expands globally because, for example, of the economic needs and imperialistic ambitions of the corporation, the fact that businesses and other organizations around the world seek to emulate it and its success, and because it becomes a valued global model. The basic concept, as well as its fundamental dimensions (see below), are derived from Max Weber's work on rationalization.[101] As we've seen, Weber demonstrated that the modern Western world was characterized by an increasing tendency toward the predominance of formally rational systems and that the rest of the world was coming under the sway of these systems. Thus, the process of McDonaldization, or at least its forerunner (increasing formal rationality and bureaucratization), obviously predates McDonald's as an institution.[102] However, that franchise (and the franchise system, more generally) is the exemplar (the bureaucracy was the model in Weber's approach) of the contemporary phase of rationalization.

The model's principles are efficiency, predictability, calculability, and control, particularly through the substitution of nonhuman for human technology, as well as the seemingly inevitable irrationalities of rationality that accompany the process.[103] Ultimately, it is these principles, as well as the associated irrationalities, that are being grobalized through the spread of McDonaldized systems.

- The first of these principles, as mentioned earlier in the discussion of Weber's theory of rationalization, is *efficiency,* or the effort to discover the optimum means to whatever end is chosen. The drive-through window is, of course, a highly efficient mechanism for allowing people to obtain their food. The work that transpires in the fast-food restaurant (e.g., grilling hamburgers, frying potatoes) is designed for maximum efficiency.
- Second, *predictability* involves an effort to ensure that products and services are much the same from one time or place to another.

- Then there is the emphasis in McDonaldized settings on *calculability*, on quantity rather than quality. Among other things, this means that fast-food restaurants want the food, as well as the experience of their customers, to be fast and cheap. Furthermore, they do not care much about the quality of the food or the experience, and they are not interested in doing much to make them better, more meaningful, and so on.
- McDonaldized systems also seek to exercise great control over customers and workers through the use of *nonhuman technology*. The drive-through window and the uncomfortable chairs are examples as far as customers are concerned, while numerous technologies (automatic French fry machines, soft-drink machines with sensors that shut off the flow when the glass is full, etc.) control employees' actions.
- Finally, McDonaldized systems are characterized by the *irrationality of rationality*, one of which is *dehumanization*. In a fast-food restaurant, counter people and customers are unlikely to know one another well, if at all. Their interaction is not only superficial but dominated by scripts that counter people must follow in relating to customers. For these reasons, and others, relationships in fast-food restaurants tend to be less human, to be dehumanized.

While the fast-food restaurant is the paradigm of this process, the process and its principles have, by now, affected most, if not all, social structures and institutions in the United States, as well as most nations (at least those that are reasonably developed economically) in the world. Thus, McDonaldization is restricted neither to the fast-food industry nor to the United States. Rather, it is a wide-ranging and far-reaching process of global change.

Recent work has tended to support the McDonaldization thesis. That process has been extended well beyond the fast-food restaurant and even everyday consumption to such areas as higher education ("McUniversity"),[104] politics,[105] religion,[106] and criminal justice.[107] Of course, not all systems (or nations) are equally McDonaldized; McDonaldization is a matter of degree, with some settings more McDonaldized than others.[108] However, few settings (or nations) have been able to escape its influence altogether.

In terms of globalization, the McDonaldization thesis[109] suggests that highly McDonaldized systems, and more important the principles that lie at the base of these systems, have been exported from the United States to much of the rest of the world. Many nations throughout the world, and innumerable subsystems within each, are undergoing the process of McDonaldization.

Capitalism is clearly closely related to McDonaldization. The spread of McDonaldized systems throughout the business world is motivated largely by the high profits they tend to produce. However, McDonaldization cannot be subsumed under the heading of capitalism. For one thing, even within the economic system, there are other reasons (e.g., the cultural importance and meaning of McDonald's [and other] franchises) for their spread. More important is the impact of McDonaldization on many aspects of the social world (church, education, etc.) that can be seen as independent, at least in part, of capitalistic interests.

While McDonaldization is traceable, most proximately, to the United States, and especially the founding of the McDonald's chain outside Chicago in the mid-1950s (predated by the original McDonald brothers' 1937 California restaurant), it is also not possible simply to subsume the process under the heading of Americanization. First, it has roots outside the United States, including the German bureaucracies analyzed by Weber at the turn of the 20th century. Second, the process has taken root by now in many nations, and at least some of them are in the process of exporting their own McDonaldized systems throughout the world, including back into the United States. McDonaldization can be thought of as a global process that is increasingly independent of any particular nation, including even the United States, and therefore is not reducible to a specific form of Americanization. As such, it is a particularly powerful grobalizing force. In the future, paralleling the history of mass manufacturing, we can anticipate that the center of McDonaldization will shift from the United States to other parts of the world.

McDonaldization is obviously a global perspective, but it is both less and more than a theory of globalization. On the one hand, McDonaldization does not involve anything approaching the full range of global processes. For example, many economic, cultural, political, and institutional aspects of globalization are largely unrelated to McDonaldization. On the other hand, McDonaldization involves much more than an analysis of its global impact. For example, much of it involves the manifold transformations taking place *within* the United States, the main source and still the center of this process. Furthermore, one can analyze the spread of McDonaldization (once it has arrived) *within* many other nations and even subareas of those nations. In addition, one can, as we have seen, look at the McDonaldization of various aspects of the social world—religion, higher education, politics, and so on—without considering the global implications for each. Thus, McDonaldization is not coterminous with globalization, nor is it solely a global process. Nonetheless, McDonaldization has global implications and can thus be a useful lens through which to examine changes taking place around the globe.

What is clear is that McDonaldization deserves a place in any thoroughgoing account of globalization. There can be little doubt that the logic of McDonaldization generates a set of values and practices that has a competitive advantage over other models. It not only promises many specific gains but also reproduces itself more easily than other models of consumption (and in many other areas of society as well). The success of McDonaldization in the United States over the past half century, coupled with the international ambitions of McDonald's and its ilk, as well as those of indigenous clones throughout the world, strongly suggests that McDonaldization will continue to make inroads into the global marketplace not only through the efforts of existing corporations but also via the diffusion of the paradigm.

It should be noted, however, that the continued advance of McDonald's, at least in its present form, is far from ensured. In fact, there are even signs in the United States, as well as in other parts of the world,[110] of what I have previously called *de-McDonaldization*.[111] There is, for example, the recent problems of McDonald's. Not too many years ago it lost money for the first time and, as a result, was forced to close restaurants, fire employees, scale back planned expansion, and even let its chief executive go. Internationally, McDonald's restaurants became (and still are) targets for various groups with grievances against the restaurant chain, the United States, and even globalization. In light of such international difficulties, McDonald's rethought its plans to expand in certain areas and cut back in places where it felt it was particularly likely to be an object of protest and attack.[112] These problems seem to be behind McDonald's as I write, but others are likely to appear. Thus, the continued growth of McDonald's is not inevitable, although the same cannot be said of the underlying process of McDonaldization.

Thus, at the moment and for the foreseeable future, McDonaldization will continue to be powerful, and it is clearly and unequivocally a grobal process. The whole idea behind McDonaldization is to create a formal model based on a limited number of principles that can be replicated virtually anywhere in the world.

Americanization

Americanization can be defined as the propagation of American ideas, customs, social patterns, industry, and capital around the world.[113] It is a powerful unidirectional process stemming from the United States that tends to overwhelm competing processes (e.g., Japanization) as well as the strength of local (and glocal) forces that might resist, modify, or transform American models into hybrid forms. Moreover, the notion of Americanization is tied to a particular nation—the United States—but it has a variable impact on many specific nations. It can be subsumed under the heading of grobalization because it involves a commitment to the *growth* in American influence in all realms throughout the world.

Americanization is inclusive of forms of American cultural, institutional, political, and economic imperialism. For example, we can include under this heading the worldwide diffusion of the American industrial model and the later global proliferation of its consumption model; the marketing of American media, including Hollywood films and popular music; the selling abroad of American sports such as NFL football and NBA basketball; the transplanetary marketing of American commodities, including cola, blue jeans, and computer operating systems; the extensive diplomatic and military engagement with Europe, Asia, and South America; the training of the world's military, political, and scientific elites in American universities (and other training centers); the expansion of the American model of democratic politics; and the development and use of the international labor market and natural resources by American corporations.

The reach of Americanization is great. A striking example involves a traditional, century-old Scottish soft drink, Irn-Bru (containing a bit of real iron). A 2002 report indicated that for the first time in its history, Irn-Bru had been surpassed as the most popular soft drink in Scotland. The new favorite (with 41% of the Scottish soft drink market)? Coca-Cola, of course! Said an entertainer, "It [Irn-Bru] really is a national icon, even the name itself conjures up something of Scotland to me. . . . I am sorry to hear it's been beaten—it was nice that Scotland was independent in a way for a time."[114]

Or, take the case of Hollywood films.[115] The American film industry has overpowered many national film industries in Europe (especially France and Great Britain) and elsewhere, to the detriment of national artistic expression. The blockbuster films of Angelina Jolie and Tom Cruise not only flow through an official distribution system, but videotape and DVD versions are also pirated and sold on the streets of third world cities. While several nations, including India and China, continue to produce large numbers of commercial films, even in these countries, American films are often featured on theater marquees. Similarly, many films that are less successful in America find a global market, and this can hold true for art films as well as action movies. The result is not simply a general familiarity with American movies and many other cultural products; those products tend to have an adverse effect on local products. Indeed, in France there has been a very public debate over the so-called cultural exception, which involves, among other things, the subsidization of its flagging movie industry.

Yet this is only one part of the Americanization of contemporary cinema. Another side is that the grammars of other national cinemas are being transformed for distribution and production in America. The Chinese, for example, have bemoaned the fact that their leading directors (including Zhang Yimou and Chen Kaige) make films that exoticize (or "orientalize"[116])

Chinese culture and history for Western audiences. An example is Taiwanese director Ang Lee's *Crouching Tiger, Hidden Dragon,* which won many international prizes but reportedly was unsuccessful in mainland China. In short, Chinese films are being tailored to American sensibilities in order to gain prestige and sales. American film culture has, at least in some senses, become world film culture. American cultural artifacts are an increasingly central element of global culture.

In addition, leading film directors (including Ang Lee) have been co-opted by the American film industry. For example, in 2005 Ang Lee directed an award-winning American film, indeed the quintessential such film, the cowboy movie (although it was unique in many ways, especially its gay theme) *Brokeback Mountain.*

Many of the Americanized forms exported to the rest of the world are attractive not just because of their American character and roots, but also because they have proven to be particularly malleable and adaptable to many other cultures and nations. They often can be detached from their American roots and reconstructed in many different ways in many other places. For example, while those around the world may watch many of the same American movies (and television), they are likely to interpret them very differently. To take a different kind of example, Orchard Road, the main shopping street in Singapore, is awash with huge indoor malls, but they are in a highly urbanized area and rely heavily on foot traffic and consumers who arrive by public transportation rather than by automobile.[117] Thus, many other countries have now adopted the shopping mall, and still others are likely to do so in the future. While malls in other parts of the world may have some, even many, indigenous shops and products, they are still clearly malls and very much in line with their American models and predecessors.

Americanization is clearly not only broader than McDonaldization, but as was pointed out above, recent developments in the latter process do not stem from the United States. What of the linkage between Americanization and capitalism? Clearly, there is a strong relationship here—the American economy is the unchallenged leader of global capitalism. But, of course, the two are not coterminous. On the one hand, many other nations are also capitalistic, and furthermore, still others (most notably, China) are moving strongly in that direction. On the other hand, there are forms of Americanization in, for example, the arts, education,[118] and basic sciences, that are, at least to some degree, separable from capitalistic interests.

Americanization is in some ways at a disadvantage relative to both capitalism and McDonaldization. As we have seen, the desire of capitalists to maximize profits leads them in the direction of aggressively exporting their products and systems to the rest of the world. For their part, McDonaldized systems are also impelled by the need to maximize profits *and* they are largely devoid of substance and therefore need do comparatively little in order to fit into other cultures. In contrast, Americanized systems are often rich in the substance of American culture that may make it difficult for them to be easily accepted elsewhere. At least in some cases, those elements must be modified or eliminated in order for them to succeed in other cultures. Furthermore, in different countries it is not always the same elements that must be extracted and modified, and this greatly complicates matters. That is, one culture may require the modification/removal of one set of elements, while another may demand a very different set be altered or eliminated. Overall, both capitalism and McDonaldization are purer grobalization forces than Americanization. In terms of power, it is capitalism that is probably the most powerful grobalizing force. While the impact of the United States has its ambiguities, and is not as powerful as capitalism, it is clearly an enormously powerful force throughout the world. The power of Americanization comes from its strength in all of the sectors—cultural, economic, political, and institutional—discussed earlier in this chapter. While capitalism affects all of these realms, its greatest impact is obviously in the economic realm. McDonaldization also is found in all of these sectors, but its most profound effects are cultural and economic. Americanization is not only a potent force in the latter realms, but its power extends much more into the political and institutional areas, including the military. The political and military hegemony of the United States in the world today accords it enormous power. While it is possible to discuss the role of capitalism and McDonaldization in politics and the military, there is far more to those realms than simply increasing profitability and increasing rationalization.

Glocal, Grobal, and Local

Most students of globalization, especially its cultural elements, have tended to see the defining conflict in that domain, where one is seen to exist, as between the global and the local. However, the perspective offered here is that the most important conflict is between grobalization and glocalization. There are several reasons for this important shift in perspective.

First, globalization does not represent one side in a central conflict. It is far too broad a process (and concept), encompassing, as it does, all transplanetary processes. It needs further refinement to be useful in this context, such as the distinction between grobalization and glocalization. When that differentiation is made, it is clear that the broad process of globalization already encompasses important subprocesses, some of which are in conflict. Since globalization contains the key poles in the conflict, it therefore is not, and cannot be, one side in that conflict.

Second, the other side of the traditional view of that conflict—the local—is relegated to secondary importance in this conceptualization. That is, the local, to the degree that it continues to exist, is seen as increasingly insignificant; it is less and less likely to be a key player in the dynamics of globalization. Little of the local remains that has been untouched by the global. It is either shaped by the global or its nature is altered by the fact that it is reacting against it. Thus, much of what we often think of as the local is, in reality, the glocal. As the grobal increasingly penetrates the local, less and less of the latter will remain free of grobal influences. That which does will be relegated to the peripheries and interstices of local communities around the world. The bulk of that which remains is much better described as glocal than local. (For more on this, see Chapter 6.)

In community after community, the real struggle is between the more purely grobal and the glocal. One absolutely crucial implication of this is that *it is increasingly difficult to find anything in the world untouched by globalization.* The major alternative in an increasing proportion of the world seems to be the choice between that which is inherently and deeply globalized—grobalization—and that in which the global and vestiges of the local intermingle—glocalization. This clearly implies the near-total triumph of the global throughout the world.

Ironically, then, the hope for those opposed to the excesses of globalization—and those excesses are traceable mainly to grobalization—seems to lie in an alternative form of globalization—glocalization. This is hardly a stirring hope as far as most critics of grobalization are concerned, but it is the most realistic and viable one available. The implication is that those who wish to oppose globalization, specifically grobalization, must support and align themselves with the other major form of globalization—glocalization.

Yet, glocalization does represent some measure of hope. For one thing, it is the last outpost of most lingering, if already adulterated (by grobalization), forms of the local. That is, important vestiges of the local remain in the glocal. For another, the interaction of the grobal and the remaining elements of the local produces unique phenomena that are not reducible to either the grobal or the local.

If the local alone is no longer the source that it once was for uniqueness, at least some of the slack has been picked up by the glocal. It is even conceivable that the glocal is, or at least can be, a more significant source of uniqueness and innovation than the local. Another source of hope lies in two or more glocal forms interacting to produce that which is distinctive in content.

Is it possible that globalization in both of its major guises—glocalization and grobalization—can give new life to the local? After all, if one of the reasons for the development of glocalization is that it is a counterreaction to grobalization, then the combination of the two forms of globalization can, at least theoretically, have the effect of alienating locals and forcing them to turn inward (assuming it is not too late) in search of alternatives to *both* forms of globalization. While grobalization can certainly offend locals (Victoria's Secret in nations dominated by religious fundamentalism), the bastardizations produced by glocalization can have much the same effect. Some locals will look at glocal forms arising around them—for example, in the case of McDonald's, McSpaghetti in the Philippines, McHuevo in Uruguay, McFalafel in Egypt, and Teriyaki Burger in Japan—and yearn for a return to the original local forms. It is unlikely, to put it mildly, that, for example, McDonald's falafel or teriyaki is going to measure up to indigenous versions. Thus, one local's reaction to McDonald's McArabia sandwich (chicken patties on flatbread) in Kuwait was, "It's not real Arabic taste."[119] Some may even be driven to ransack their past in search of traditional local practices that could be resuscitated in an effort to provide alternatives, and counters, to both the grobal and the glocal.[120]

While such scenarios are possible, and even likely, it is difficult to be hopeful about the revival of the local and its prospects for countering globalization. This pessimism is based on several factors. First, any local revival is, from the outset, implicated in globalization, since it is a reaction against it. Second, if it succeeds in attracting enough interest, firms, eventually those with global interests, will move in and seek to gain control over it. Finally, even greater success will bring it to the attention of entrepreneurial exporters who will aggressively seek to export it—to grobalize it (can we, e.g., anticipate a global trade in betel nuts if the chewing of them is revived in Korea?[121]). Thus, revivals of that which is local, especially those that are successful, are likely to be grobalized and thereby lose their local character.

While it may be doomed eventually to be co-opted completely by the forces of grobalization and glocalization, what remains of the local continues, at least at present, to play a role in the world as a source of both diversity and innovation. While one can envision a scenario in which diversity and innovation increasingly come from the glocal, it can never be quite as good a source of innovation as the local. After all, by definition, the glocal is modified from the very beginning by a variety of forces that seek to make it acceptable to a wide range of consumers, perhaps in many different locales throughout the world. In this way, linkages to the original place and thing are progressively lost as they are increasingly watered down to suit diverse tastes and interests. In contrast, the local, again by definition, has not been so modified, with the result that it is generally more unique and a source of greater diversity.

Because of this, it is possible to argue that the world grows increasingly impoverished as the local declines in importance and perhaps disappears. The paradox is that grobalization brings with it unparalleled development in some parts of the world at the same time that it impoverishes others culturally (and, according to Joseph Stiglitz, economically) by reducing or eliminating the role of the local.[122] This point leads nicely into a discussion (in Chapter 8) on the 2001 terrorist attacks on the United States, their relationship to the impoverishment of the local, and more generally the idea of "loss amidst monumental abundance" associated with the globalization of nothing.

This chapter has focused broadly on the issue of globalization. One major objective has been to underscore the centrality of the concept of glocalization to thinking on globalization. Another has been to show that while it is important, there is much more to globalization than glocalization. The other major objective has been to introduce a new concept, grobalization, to parallel glocalization and to help us better understand not only what glocalization omits but also the larger process of globalization. Thus, we are now in possession of a pair of concepts—glocalization and grobalization—that are central to the ensuing analysis. In the next chapter we turn to a delineation of the second pair of concepts—something and nothing—that are equally essential to this analysis. It will take us all of three chapters (2–4) to fully explicate what I mean by something and nothing. However, by the time we finish that explication, we will be in a position to juxtapose these two pairs of concepts in Chapter 5. It is there and in that juxtaposition that the reader will get a full sense of the distinctive contribution of this work to theorizing globalization, and that contribution will be explicated in the last three chapters of this volume.

2

Nothing (and Something)

Another New Conceptualization

Vast, fully enclosed shopping malls. Lots of glass, light, stainless steel, chrome, and granite. Hundreds of shops along lengthy corridors that crisscross at various points. Most of the shops are outlets of large chains, a fact that is made clear by their well-known signs and logos. Large numbers of people traipsing through familiar structures, along well-traveled corridors, and past shops with names well known to them. Some are just strolling, others window-shopping, while still others dart in and out of shops to make purchases, usually using credit cards.

Whether or not they shop in malls, consumers are increasingly drawn to more-or-less mass-produced and -distributed products and brands: Ikea sofas, L. L. Bean shorts, Sharper Image "boy toys," Victoria's Secret lingerie, Nike athletic shoes, Mickey Mouse ears, Dolce & Gabbana frocks, Gap jeans, and Hard Rock Cafe T-shirts.

In purchasing these things, in logoed shops, in or out of malls, consumers encounter employees who are less and less likely to be knowledgeable about what they sell and increasingly likely to interact with them in an impersonal, even highly scripted, manner. The shops are increasingly also on the Internet, where consumers are more likely to encounter "shopbots" than people.

Anywhere they go, consumers are increasingly unlikely to receive much in the way of service from such employees and, in fact, are likely to serve themselves or to interact with technologies like the Web site of an online retailer, the ATM, the self-service gasoline pump, or the Speedpass lane on the toll road.

All these vignettes exemplify nothing (as that term is used here). Given the discussion in Chapter 1, we can easily accept the idea of the increasing globality of the phenomena mentioned above, but to argue that they are nothing is clearly another matter altogether, since it is so counterintuitive and controversial. Judging by their thoughts and actions, most people seem to feel very differently—that all of the things discussed in these vignettes are quite something. Because the argument to be made here is so unique, at least as far as nothing is concerned, the bulk of this chapter, as well as of the ensuing two chapters, is devoted to a definition and delineation of the idea of nothing (and something; as we will see, it is difficult to discuss one without the other) as it is used and defined idiosyncratically in the following pages.

It is absolutely essential in understanding the discussion to follow, as well as the main theses of this book, that readers put aside their normal, everyday definitions of, and ways of thinking about, nothing (and something). Among the usual definitions of nothing are that which people believe lacks existence, significance, or value. (In contrast, something would normally be defined as that which people believe has existence, significance, or value.) Thus, the commonsense notion of nothing relates to beliefs, definitions, attitudes, and so on. That is, in the lay view, nothing is subjective. However, the definition of nothing (see below) employed here relates to the objective characteristics of a wide variety of social forms. As a result, what people think about these forms has no effect on, no necessary relationship to, the fact that they are objectively nothing. In fact, as we will see, it is often the case that what people subjectively define as something is what is in this book treated as nothing. Thus, in many, many ways, nothing as it is used here is in near-total opposition to the way people conventionally use that term. As a result, if readers do not make the definitional and broader mental switches required here, the conclusions they draw from this book will be totally different from, if not diametrically opposed to, those that I intend.

It is also worth noting that while we all know the conventional meaning of nothing, there are many other ways in which the term has been defined and used, especially in philosophy. There is a surprisingly large literature on the topic of nothing; we could even conceive of a field called "nothingology."[1] Indeed, some of our greatest thinkers—Immanuel Kant, Georg Hegel, Martin Heidegger, Jean-Paul Sartre, Jerry Seinfeld(!)—have offered important definitions and made key contributions to our understanding of nothing. However, the way nothing is used in this book not only has little relationship to the conventional definition but also to the way other thinkers have used the concept.[2]

Defining Nothing

The social world, particularly in the realm of consumption, is increasingly characterized by nothing. *Nothing* is defined as a social form that is generally[3] centrally conceived, controlled, and comparatively devoid of distinctive substantive content. Not only is this definition silent on how people define these social forms, but it also carries with it no judgment about the desirability or undesirability of such a social form (or about its increasing prevalence).[4] That is, a phenomenon that meets this definition of nothing is not necessarily problematic. Meeting the definition simply means that a social form is likely to have been thought up at some central locale, to be controlled from such a location (not necessarily the same one), and to lack distinctive content, that is, to be very much like others, perhaps many others, of its ilk. However, to be perfectly honest, I chose such a value-laden term as *nothing* because, as the reader will see, in the end this book does come to some highly critical conclusions about nothing and its globalization. However, we need to separate the term itself and its definition from the implied double meaning associated with the critique of it and its proliferation.

Let us use the credit card, specifically the steps involved in obtaining a credit card, as an example of nothing (and its expansion).[5] Clearly nothing, as that term is used here, is involved at least as far as the nature of the credit card offer extended to the consumer is concerned. This is clearest when an unsolicited offer for a credit card, usually with a predefined credit limit, arrives in the mail. In terms of the definition offered above, this is nothing, because the offer and its basic parameters were conceived and are controlled centrally and there is no distinctive content involved in this invitation—thousands, hundreds of thousands, perhaps millions of potential cardholders receive exactly the same letter of invitation in the mail. Even if potential credit card holders are grouped into categories based on, say, their credit ratings, those in each group receive the same invitation letter with the same credit limit.

Somewhat more is involved in a telephone call offering consumers a credit card. The call requires more complexity, since the telemarketer may need to respond to some idiosyncratic questions from the potential cardholder. However, there are often centrally conceived scripts for responding to all but the most unusual questions, and of course, the basic approach is highly scripted and great control is exerted by supervisors who may listen in on what employees using those scripts are saying. So even here, the process of offering a credit card is (largely) nothing, since everyone who is solicited in this way will hear much the same centrally controlled and conceived pitch with little or no room for individual variation.

Furthermore, the details of the offer, especially the all-important credit limit associated with the card, are determined by a computer program that bases its decisions on a set of objective criteria. All potential cardholders who fall within certain parameters will receive the same credit limit.

More generally, a credit card can be seen, in this context, as a relatively empty form. That is, in itself it is little or nothing—a small rectangular piece of plastic with a few names, numbers, dates, words, a logo, and maybe a hologram. There is little of distinctive substance inherent in the card itself (except for the cardholder's name and number)—little to distinguish one card from any others.[6] And, of course, the nature and design of the card is a product of the central offices of a credit card bank, as is control over how the card is used.

In terms of expansion, the modern credit card, and eventually the methods discussed above to solicit new cardholders, was invented in the mid-20th century in the United States, and since then the number in use has boomed not only here but in many other countries around the world. In the case of the United States, the number of major credit (bank) cards (e.g., Visa, MasterCard) in use increased from 213 million in 1990 to 419 million in 1999 and grew to a total of 566.8 million by the beginning of 2005.[7] The amount of high-interest bank card debt owed by American consumers grew from $2.7 billion in 1969 to $154 billion in 1990, $430 billion in 1998, and reached $805.5 billion by the end of 2005.[8] Finally, bank credit card spending rose from $213 billion in 1990 to $839 billion in 1998 and stood at $1,342.4 billion in the fourth quarter of 2005.[9, 10] Comparatively affluent Americans (and increasingly those from many other countries) are traveling abroad more often, and they are very likely to use their credit cards to pay for expenses incurred on such trips. Furthermore, large numbers of people in many other countries are now using credit cards and in much the same everyday way that Americans have for decades. Thus, the global expansion of this relatively empty form—one that gains much of its substance in actual use—exemplifies the main argument being made in this book.

As was made clear above, in spite of the negative connotations generally associated with the word *nothing*, the phenomena to be discussed under that heading are, in fact, viewed very positively, if not worshipped, by many people throughout the world. Thus, for example, while we may be critical of the nothingness of credit cards, the ways in which they are proffered, the indebtedness that many users incur because of overuse of the cards, and the world of hyperconsumption[11] that they play such a huge role in creating, there are clearly innumerable consumers who feel strongly about, if not love, their credit cards and delight in the unquestioned advantages (convenience, ability to consume without cash on hand or in the bank, etc.) offered by them. Similarly, as is clear in one of the vignettes that opened this chapter, name brands are generally associated with the trend toward the increase in nothing, and will come under critical scrutiny at various points in this analysis, but many people feel very strongly about their favorite brands—Coke, Nike, Rolex, Dolce & Gabbana, and so on (for more on brands and branding see Chapter 7).

Given these kinds of complexities, we need powerful analytical tools to analyze nothing as clearly as possible, study its expansion, and eventually render more balanced and nuanced judgments about it, as well as the implications of its increase. In fact, this chapter and the next two will be devoted to the development and use of a variety of conceptual and methodological tools that will allow us to grapple better with the substantive, and potentially value-laden, issues of concern here.

Defining Something

Among the things we need in order to get a better feel for nothing is a definition of something, as well as the ways in which the two terms can be distinguished from one another. I will devote much attention to refining our definition of these terms and iterating and elucidating their subdimensions and manifestations, but it is necessary at this point to offer a preliminary, orienting definition of *something* as a social form that is generally[12] indigenously conceived, controlled, and comparatively rich in distinctive substantive content. As was the case with nothing, something is an objective state and does not necessarily correlate with people's feelings about, or what they define as, something.

Having looked, albeit briefly, at nothing, in part through the example of the credit card, it is incumbent on me at this point to offer a brief parallel discussion of the something end of that continuum. If the credit card loan is a largely empty form through which what are, in effect, lines of credit are extended to consumers, then a line of credit negotiated personally between banker and customer is the parallel within the realm of something. Such a line of credit is, of course, a form (of lending money), but it is a form that is much more likely to be locally conceived and controlled and to be rich in distinctive substance. For example, a long-term relationship may develop between lender and borrower that may inform decisions on the need to borrow and the willingness to lend. Lenders are apt to have deep and personal knowledge of borrowers, and that knowledge has a profound effect on their decisions. In the course of a single negotiation, or better, in a number of such negotiations over a lifetime, a great deal of distinctive substance develops in this relationship. In this case, it is the richness of a personal relationship between customer and banker—its high degree of individualization—that helps make the personal line of credit something, at least in comparison to the credit card loan.

Personally negotiated lines of credit had (and still do, where they continue to exist) a number of advantages. Great care was taken in granting lines of credit, and bad decisions were less likely because loan officers knew their customers personally. If a loan came due and the debtor was unable to pay as a result of any number of unforeseen circumstances, the banker could consider these exigencies in the context of a long-term and personal relationship with the debtor and on that basis could choose to extend the deadline or even extend additional credit. Ultimately, of course, both borrower and lender could derive personal meaning from their relationship. However, we must not assume that such a method of obtaining personal lines of credit and such a personal relationship is necessarily unproblematic.

Of course, there are also liabilities associated with such relationships and such a method of extending credit. Among other things, they are time consuming, cumbersome, and expensive. Most important, as we have seen, the fact that lenders employ personal considerations in making their decisions means that they are quite likely to discriminate in favor of some borrowers and against others.[13]

A relationship is not necessarily a good one simply because it is local, rich in distinctive substance, and individualized. The converse is also true. A relationship is not necessarily problematic because it lacks much in the way of unique substance. For example, the likelihood of obtaining today's credit card loan is not affected by the personal feelings of loan officers (indeed, it is unlikely that a loan officer will be involved at all). Thus, a potential user is not likely to be turned down for a credit card because of the personal animus of a loan officer. The more general point, of course, is that just because an entity lies toward the nothing end of the continuum, we must not assume that it is necessarily bad, that the disadvantages outweigh the advantages. Conversely, that which exists toward the something end of that continuum is not necessarily good, that there are more advantages than disadvantages.

The Something-Nothing Continuum

It should be clear that neither nothing nor something exists, at least conceptually, independently of the other; each makes sense only when paired with, and contrasted to, the other. While presented as a dichotomy,[14] this implies a continuum from something to nothing, and that is precisely the way the concepts will be employed here—as the two poles of that continuum. The phenomena of focal concern in this book exist at or near the nothing end of the continuum; all phenomena exist somewhere between the extremes of the nothing-something poles of the continuum.[15] The distinction between nothing and something is far from being very clear-cut or refined. Furthermore, there is certainly no social phenomenon that can unequivocally and for all time be classified as either something or nothing. As pointed out in Chapter 1, all phenomena have elements of both something and nothing. To put it another way, all social phenomena can be positioned somewhere between the poles of this continuum. Of course, that is not to say that placement on the continuum is easy, precise, or uncontroversial. Furthermore, the whole idea of the continuum itself, as well as the binary opposition (something-nothing) that lies at its base, is highly controversial.

The social world, in particular the world of consumption, involves some combination of nothing and something wherever on the globe it may exist. Nothing may predominate in some times and places, while something may be preeminent at other times and places. Furthermore, nothing and something are not static categories; they are not cast in stone. Entrepreneurs are constantly trying to transform something into nothing in order to produce and sell more over greater expanses of time and place. Conversely, others, usually consumers, are often actively engaged in the process of seeking to transform nothing into something. That is, they might mark, score, or modify a phenomenon, thereby giving it at least a measure of local (really individual) conception, control, and distinctive content. Indeed, there is always a dialectic between something and nothing.

For example, money (currency) meets our definition of nothing. In the case of the United States, American currency is centrally conceived and controlled by the Department of the Treasury. All coins and bills of the same denomination are identical. Indeed, if they are not identical, we know that they must be counterfeit. However, as Viviana Zelizer points out in *The Social Meaning of Money*, people sometimes transform the money in their possession into something.[16] For example, they might put some aside in a jar, thereby earmarking it for specific purposes (e.g., a special dinner out). Of greatest interest is physically earmarking currency (e.g., decorating gift money), since this is a very material manifestation of transforming nothing into something. This leads Zelizer to conclude that in spite of the government's effort to make money nothing, "money is neither culturally neutral nor socially anonymous."[17] More generally, Zelizer argues that money is not unique, people do much the same thing with much else that they obtain in our consumer culture. For example, sewing a label with a child's name into a new coat serves to earmark it, as does purposely tearing or decorating a new pair of jeans. Earmarking takes objects that lie toward the nothing end of the continuum and moves them more in the direction of the something end by giving them a measure of local conception and control, as well as at least some distinctive content.

The conceptual tools to be developed here to help us analyze nothing should be equally useful in working the something end of the continuum, as well as everything in between. Indeed, it is hoped that this will be one of the great strengths of the concepts and continua developed here. Thus, more specifically, we should be able to use these concepts and continua to think about both credit card loans and personal lines of credit. Those tools should allow us to pinpoint the essential differences between them, as well as the many other forms that exist on the continuum from something to nothing as it relates to credit (and everything else in the realm of consumption).

The remainder of this chapter is, in a sense, devoted to further defining nothing, as well as something and the something-nothing continuum, in greater detail. The initial definitions developed above are obviously highly abstract, so the remainder of this chapter provides much more depth, detail, and concreteness by developing each end of the continuum, and the continuum itself, through a multitude of dimensions. What follows is an iteration and brief discussion of the five dimensions and subcontinua that are employed to help us better differentiate between nothing and something. Note that in each of the subcontinua discussed under the heading of the five dimensions, the first idea(s) relates to the something end of the continuum, while the second relates to its nothing pole (see Figure 2.1). The position of any given phenomenon on the broad something-nothing continuum is a composite of its positions on each of the subcontinua developed below.[18] Bear in mind that these are all continua and that any given empirical reality will fall somewhere between the two poles of each, as well as the more general something-nothing continuum.[19]

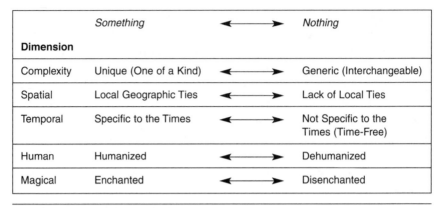

	Something	⟵⟶	Nothing
Dimension			
Complexity	Unique (One of a Kind)	⟵⟶	Generic (Interchangeable)
Spatial	Local Geographic Ties	⟵⟶	Lack of Local Ties
Temporal	Specific to the Times	⟵⟶	Not Specific to the Times (Time-Free)
Human	Humanized	⟵⟶	Dehumanized
Magical	Enchanted	⟵⟶	Disenchanted

Figure 2.1   The Something-Nothing Continuum, Its Five Dimensions and Subcontinua

The Complexity Dimension

This dimension and subcontinuum are premised on the idea that something is closely associated with uniqueness (being one-of-a-kind), while nothing is linked to a lack of uniqueness, to that which is generic (interchangeable).[20] That which is unique is highly likely to be indigenously created and controlled and to be rich in distinctive substance. That which is generic is likely to be centrally created and controlled and to be lacking in much, or even any, distinctive substance. A unique phenomenon is, by definition, different from every other one of its ilk.[21] That is, it has no like or equal. In order to be unique, something must have substance that differentiates it from all others. While something could, at least theoretically, be unique because it is totally devoid of substance, or because it has one or a small number of elements that distinguish it from all others, the view here is that unique phenomena almost always either have far more distinctive substance than generic phenomena or at least possess a number of distinctive substantive characteristics that set them apart from that which has few, if any, such characteristics.

Thus, a complex array of distinctive components or elements will tend to make something unique, while a (relative) dearth of the same is associated with the generic. The greater the number of distinctive components, the richer and the more complex the phenomena. And richer and more complex phenomena have a greater likelihood of being unique by dint of the fact that this complexity produces a phenomenon that is much more difficult to duplicate, let alone transform into a generic product. By contrast, phenomena with little in the way of distinctive substance are far more likely to be generic or to be transformed into generic phenomena.

Examples of the Complexity Dimension

Let us take as our examples a gourmet meal prepared by a highly creative and skilled cook[22] (unique) and a preprepared meal in a microwaveable package (generic) made in the factory of a large corporation. In this, we follow the usual pattern of discussing polar opposites, but the fact is that here (and throughout this chapter) we are discussing continua, with the result that most phenomena fall somewhere in the middle. For example, a home-cooked meal prepared by an unskilled cook using prepackaged ingredients would be in that realm (although toward the something end of the continuum), as would a microwave meal to which a few additional ingredients are added before serving (although this would be more toward the nothing end of the continuum).

A specific example of a microwaveable, prepackaged meal is Tyson Foods' Chicken 2 Go (there are many others), which includes chicken nuggets (a simulation of McDonald's highly successful Chicken McNuggets), French fries, and ketchup (in snack packs). The food is neatly packaged in a microwaveable tray with a clear lid. Each tray is designed to be a single meal and to be heated at work, at home, or elsewhere.

The gourmet meal is unique because it is created on the spot by the cook who controls every facet of its preparation, and it is composed of a complex array of distinctive ingredients and elements. That is, it involves creativity. This includes, but is not limited to, the selection, array, and quantity of raw ingredients and seasonings that go into the meal. It also includes the innumerable judgments made by the chef, the cooking utensils employed, the nature of the pots and pans, the degree and type (gas, electric, etc.) of heat used, the way the food is arranged on the plate, and the manner in which it is served. There are many options open to the gourmet cook, and the specific choices made make each meal unique.

The microwaveable meal is cooked centrally, and its later preparation is controlled by instructions printed on the package. It may have a similar (or even greater) number of seasonings and ingredients as in a unique meal, but it lacks the other components—there are no options, and no judgments or creativity are required of the "cook" (and, of course, virtually no skills are needed; it is even difficult to think of one who prepares a microwave meal as a cook), no tools other than the container that holds the food and the microwave are used, the temperature to be employed is predefined and only a microwave oven can be used, the food is prearranged in the container, and it is generally served in that container. Thus, there is simply much more of distinctive substance associated with a gourmet, or home-cooked, meal than a microwave meal, with the result that much more variation is possible in the former than in the latter. Thus, no two versions of veal parmigiana prepared by different skilled cooks (or even the same cook) are likely to be the same, while every package of microwaveable veal parmigiana is likely to be much like every other one. As a result, any given gourmet meal is likely to be unique, but even the idea, let alone the reality, of a unique microwave meal is a laughable oxymoron.

In addition to simply having much more distinctive substance, that which is unique may have one (or a few) overriding characteristic that sets it apart from the generic. In the case of the gourmet meal, it is the creativity, skill, and ability of the chef that is the primary factor distinguishing it from the microwave meal in which virtually no creativity is required to "cook" the meal. Another defining characteristic might be the use of fresh and natural ingredients in gourmet meals, while microwave meals rely on preprepared, often unnatural, ingredients. Then there might be the use of unique, even exotic, spices in gourmet meals, while the prosaic salt predominates in microwave meals. Microwave meals, and more generally that which is generic, tend to eschew anything that smacks of being exotic.

This overlaps with a related distinction between the one-of-a-kind and the interchangeable. The gourmet meal created by the creative cook is a one-of-a-kind event. Even if the cook tried to replicate the meal exactly at a different time or in a different place (and a truly creative cook would probably not even try), it would never be quite the same due to the complexities associated with variations in the mood of the chef, differences in the ingredients, a tad more or less of this or that seasoning, slight variations in the way the food is cooked and served, and so on. On the other hand, microwave meals of the same type are pretty much interchangeable; one meal is prepared just like every other one of that type and they all look and taste pretty much the same no matter when or where they are "cooked."

In a rather interesting twist on this, there are now cookbooks available—for example, *Top Secret Recipes: Creating Kitchen Clones of America's Favorite Brand-Name Foods*[23]—that allow at-home preparation of the same kinds of foods to be found in microwave packages or at the local fast-food restaurant. On the latter, one can consult Gloria Pitzer's (given the substance of her book, the similarities in our last names are too close for comfort) *Secret Fast Food Recipes: The Fast Food Cookbook*[24] if one is inclined to prepare such things as one's own Big Mac at home. Needless to say, closely following a recipe for such generic food products is highly unlikely, to put it mildly, to lead to the creation of unique meals.

In sum, no two gourmet meals composed of the same dishes, even if they are prepared by the same skilled cook, will ever be exactly the same, but every microwave meal, no matter who prepares it (or when they prepare it), will be just about the same. Thus, the gourmet meal can be placed at or near the unique end of this subcontinuum, while the microwaveable meal can be found toward the generic end of that continuum.

Further Ideas on Complexity

Not only does the unique gourmet meal tend to be a form rich in distinctive substance and the generic microwave meal tend to be a form largely devoid of such substance, but there is a long-term trend toward the ascendancy of the microwave meal, and the home-cooked gourmet meal is in decline (at least relative to the proliferation of the microwave meal). Of course, the microwave meal is but one example of the generic in this realm. Others include predecessors like Campbell's soup, boxes of Kraft Macaroni and Cheese, and Swanson's frozen TV dinners, as well as more recent innovations like Snack Packs and Lunchables (another Kraft product, although a subdivision—Oscar Mayer—is listed on the package).

Lunchables may look like microwaveable food, but unlike the latter, they require no "cooking"; they can be eaten, as is, directly from the package. The typical Lunchables includes a few slices of some meat (e.g., ham or turkey), cheese, and a few crackers neatly arranged in the three compartments of a sealed container.[25] Schoolchildren (the main clientele for Lunchables, although there are now "mega" Lunchables for adults and even "hungry" children) no longer need to put up with the surprises associated with a unique[26] lunch to be found in the brown bag brought from home. Instead, they can look forward to a generic Lunchables in which the only surprise is likely to be which heavily processed meat or cheese is to be found in the appropriate compartment of that day's container.

The key point is that Lunchables is yet another step in the direction of the progressive replacement of the unique by the generic in the domain of food. Not only are we likely to see further strides in this direction in the future, but the same general trend is occurring in virtually every other domain in the world of consumption.

There are advantages to both the unique (in this case, the pleasures involved in eating a gourmet meal) and the generic (e.g., the low cost, efficiency, predictability of a microwave meal or Lunchables; for some, the sameness of all Lunchables is highly rewarding).

There are disadvantages associated with both the unique (high cost, availability of gourmet meals mainly to societal elites or to those with the luxury of the time to cook them) and the generic (mediocre quality of microwave meals). While this is generally true, it is also the case that home-cooked meals can be quite low in cost, and the seemingly inexpensive microwaveable meals,

Lunchables, and the like are usually quite costly when one carefully calculates what one is really getting in those containers. The consumer pays for the expensive packaging, there is a lot of it—plastic container, plastic wrap, sauce packets, labels, and so on—and some of it may not even be biodegradable. The minuscule portions of meat and cheese could be purchased far more cheaply on their own than as part of the Lunchables package. As is always the case, there is a high cost associated with prepackaged food (and many other things) in contrast to what the cost would be if one packaged it oneself.

As with something-nothing in general, the unique-generic continuum can be analyzed using all of the other conceptual tools being developed in this chapter. For example, anticipating the next section (and conceptual tool and dimension), that which is unique—the gourmet meal—tends to have local roots (e.g., use of fresh, local ingredients; the skills of individual cooks in their own kitchens), while that which is generic—the microwave meal—tends to lack such roots; it tends to be from anywhere and everywhere (e.g., ingredients from many different areas; skills built into instructions on the package and accessible to everyone, everywhere).

The Spatial Dimension[27]

Phenomena that are found at or near the something end of the continuum are likely to have strong spatial ties to local geographic areas, while those at the nothing end of the spectrum have few, if any, such spatial ties. As we have seen, this is linked, albeit imperfectly, to the unique-generic continuum with phenomena that have local ties more likely to be unique (they will be different from similar phenomena with ties to other localities) and those lacking in such ties more likely to be generic (sharing characteristics with other, perhaps many other, phenomena of the same type in many different locations). Thus, it is argued that phenomena with local ties are more likely to internalize the rich complexity and the distinctive substance of the local environment. Conversely, those without such ties are likely to be lacking in such complexity and distinctive substance.[28] This, of course, is closely related to the issue of the presence or absence of centralized conception and control. That which is local tends to lack such centralization, while that in which local ties are absent tends to be centralized.

Examples of the Spatial Dimension

Our examples in this case are a piece of handmade pottery from, let's say, a small town in Mexico and pottery that is mass-manufactured in a variety of geographic areas for a world market. The piece of handmade pottery is, at least in part, something, for the reason discussed above—it is unique, one of a kind. In contrast, any given piece of mass-manufactured pottery, no matter how good it is, is nothing, because it is generic and each piece of a given type is interchangeable with every other piece. Beyond that, however, the handmade piece is something, because it reflects many characteristics of the local area from which it emanates. For example, the clay may be a very distinctive local variety, it may be fired in particular ways, the ovens and even the fuel may be idiosyncratic, the pottery may reflect designs indigenous to a very particular area of Mexico (or even to a specific craftsperson) that differ from designs developed only a short distance away (or by a different craftsperson), and it may depend on a series of skills that are specific to the artisans of that area or even to a single artisan.

In this section I focus on the local pottery of the Oaxaca area of Mexico.[29] Some years ago an American who was an apprentice there described the highly local nature of its pottery (note how well it illustrates several of the preceding points):

> So I work in Coyotepec—no throwing wheels or gas/electric kilns used here. And the clay comes from up the hill in baskets on burros.
> I've also got some potter friends in Atzompa—another nearby pueblo. Almost every house there has a stone kiln in the yard. They make a distinct type of pottery there (from Coyotepec) and use wholly different techniques and different clay—two villages probably 20 miles apart.[30]

While some of the pottery skills employed in these pueblos might be derived from general sources such as books, courses, seminars, and the like, even then they are likely to be modified greatly by the procedures of a local group of artisans or even the individual potter. The following is a good description of some of the procedures employed in producing Oaxaca's local pottery:

> From clay, fire, and hands full of knowledge passed from mother to daughter in an unbroken lineage that fades into the days of another age comes to life the pot. It is formed without a wheel and shaped with simple tools: a piece of gourd, a strip of leather, and the deep experience of patient time. It is warmed in the morning sun and fired in an open bonfire. What emerges from the flame is the creation of simple perfection and grace, the work of masters.[31]

Mass-manufactured pottery is likely to be lacking in all these respects.[32] It is centrally conceived and controlled and may be produced in exactly the same way in several, even many, different factories in various parts of the world. A very common clay is likely to be used, or it may even be the case that many different clays from different areas will be used depending on available supplies. Clays might even be mixed to create varieties that lack distinctive ties to any geographic area.[33] A single firing technique (e.g., one that is the most efficient and least expensive) is developed, and it is used over and over. The designs are likely to be generic, and even when they are derived from local, unique designs, they are likely to become generic as a result of being used over and over in many geographic locations. Furthermore, original unique designs are likely to be modified, usually simplified, so that overly complex elements (much of the substance) are removed, as are components with only local meaning or components that might be considered bothersome or even offensive by some potential consumers elsewhere in the world. The skills involved are likely to be a series of well-known and simplified steps that can be used in many different production facilities in many different locales; the skills have no ties to any specific geographic area or to the people indigenous to such a locale. Unskilled or semiskilled workers are likely to predominate with few, if any, artisans in evidence.

Of course, this distinction can be applied, as well, to the preceding example of the gourmet/microwaveable meal. The gourmet meal is likely to be linked to a specific geographic area where, for example, some of the ingredients might be local and obtainable, at least fresh, only there (e.g., the use of locally gathered truffles in a Parisian gourmet restaurant or, in a less elite example, of herbs raised in a window box in a Bronx apartment). While we tend to think of generic Mexican food, especially fast-food tacos (typical of the Mexican food sold in the United States and bearing little resemblance to the tacos sold on the streets throughout Mexico), the fact is that there is great regional diversity in gourmet Mexican food. In fact, Oaxacan cooking is especially fashionable these days. Said a cook featured on PBS, "I had taught Mexican cooking, and when I came to Oaxaca I had to relearn everything I knew. . . . Most ingredients are toasted, roasted or fried before cooking."[34] In contrast, the microwaveable Mexican meal has no ties to any specific area, it can be bought and cooked anywhere that electricity and microwave ovens are available and affordable, and it is likely to be composed of ingredients from many different places and to follow a generic recipe designed to appeal to the broadest possible range of consumers.

Further Ideas on Spatiality

That which has local ties tends to be a form rich in distinctive substance, especially that which is specific to and defines that area (e.g., the piece of Atzompa or Coyotepec pottery), and that which lacks such ties is more likely to be a form largely lacking in substance (e.g., mass-produced pottery). There is, of course, a long-term trend away from the predominance of the local (e.g., all types of crafts) and in the direction of that which has few, if any, such ties (e.g., all types of mass-manufactured products). A sense of this change is made clear by the potters of Oaxaca:

> In the waning days of this century the pottery of Oaxaca is disappearing. Tin, plastic, and aluminum are impatiently filling the place of clay. Today the potters still work, the pottery lives. But the question arises, how many more mothers will be able to pass the ways of clay, fire, and hands down to their daughters?[35]

There are advantages associated with local pottery (e.g., maintenance of traditions, sustaining local crafts), but the eradication of local ties in mass-manufactured pottery also has its advantages (e.g., a more general appeal, greater availability, lower prices).

There are disadvantages associated with both local pottery (e.g., limited availability) and mass-made pottery that lacks local ties (e.g., an absence of touches and nuance that can come only from a local craftsperson).

As with all the others, this continuum can be analyzed using the other conceptual tools outlined in this chapter. For example, once again anticipating the next section, local pottery tends to be linked to a specific time period, while mass-manufactured pottery tends not to be specific to the times (or to be time-free[36]) in the sense that term is used here (see below). Thus, as is made clear in one of the preceding quotations, the pottery of Oaxaca has a specific historical lineage, while the mass-produced pottery cannot be tied to any such period of time.[37]

The Temporal Dimension

We can differentiate not only among phenomena that are, or are not, specific to a given locale but also specific to a given time period. Those that are specific to a time period would tend to be distinctive (and more likely to be something), while those that are not specific to the times (time-free) would tend to lack distinctiveness (and more likely to be nothing). (Of course, nothing is ever really time-free, that is, totally free of the influence of the period in which it was created. This is indicated, in part, by my preferred use of "not specific to the times." In fact, everything is influenced by the time period in which it was created. The point is that at the not-specific-to-the-times [time-free] end of the continuum, the influence of that time period is far less consequential than at the specific-to-the-times end of that continuum.) Those phenomena that are particular to a time period (and, as we saw in the case of Oaxacan pottery, that time period can be quite long) would tend to be loaded with the substance of that slice of time, while those that are not specific to the times would tend to lack such substance. In fact, the need to be relatively time-free requires that virtually all substance that might have related to any particular time frame be removed or at least muted.

That which is locally conceived and controlled (e.g., Oaxacan pottery) tends to be specific to the times, while that which is centrally conceived and controlled tends to be time-free. Local producers naturally reflect the time in which they live or a longer sweep of time of which they are part and are only the most recent reflection. Centralized producers are more likely, because of their desire to maximize sales and profits, to be motivated to produce that which is not specific to the times, since such entities are likely to appeal to the widest possible audience. However, as we will see in the following example, even centralized producers can, either purposely or inadvertently, produce products that come to be seen as embedded in a particular time period.

Examples of the Temporal Dimension

Certain automobile styles have become timeless classics, and paradoxically one of the reasons they have achieved that status is that they reflect very well the era in which they were manufactured; they "say" something about that era. Take the American muscle car,[38] for example, the 1969 Pontiac Firebird. Muscle cars, of course, are big, powerful cars that are especially noted for motors with a great deal of horsepower. They are products of an era in which the United States was astride the world both economically and militarily, and the continued interest in classic cars of this period, as well as in more contemporary versions of such cars, reflects the fact that the United States continues to occupy such a position in the world.[39] I hasten to add that the 1969 Pontiac Firebird, and indeed all muscle cars, were mass-manufactured to be time-free. However, there was something about them, perhaps totally unintended by the designers and manufacturers, that strongly reflected the era from which they emanated.

In some cases, automobile manufacturers seek to bring back models that hearken back to a particular time period. For example, Ford's reintroduction of the retro-designed Thunderbird (some even call it the retro-bird[40]) was designed to tie it not only to early versions of that car—the first ones were manufactured in 1954—but even earlier road cars. Says Ford: "It's a truly modern rendering of the original American Dream Car."[41] More generally, some of the appeal of the convertible stems from the fact that it is a self-conscious descendant of early horse-drawn carriages, since "[i]n the beginning, all cars were open."[42] A more recent source of today's convertibles is the open touring cars of the roaring 1920s, which said something about the openness and abandon of that period (important new convertibles were introduced in the late 1920s). However, sales of convertibles in the United States declined, and in 1976 Cadillac announced that it was building the last American convertible (European manufacturers continued to produce convertibles). But, in 1982, the American convertible reappeared as the Chrysler LeBaron, and since then several American (and international) convertible brands have been produced. Their current popularity is traceable, at least in part, to the historical lineage of which they are only the latest manifestation.

These examples make it clear that while most automobiles are manufactured to be time-free, some (muscle cars, convertibles) come to be defined as timeless, at least in part, because fans see them as having ties to a particular time period. However, these examples also make it clear that manufacturers can self-consciously create automobile models—the retro-Thunderbird—that are linked explicitly to a particular period of time, to a longer tradition of which they are part.

There are innumerable examples of classic automobiles, and among other things, they tend to be cars that reflect something important about a given time period. One could say much the same about classics in many other realms. Such perennials would fall toward the something end of the continuum, while those things that are not intimately associated with a particular time period—those things that are relatively time-free—are more likely to be found at the nothing end of that continuum. Thus, a relatively generic car—one that has little to distinguish itself and that takes little, if anything, that is distinctive in character and styling from the era in which it is built—will be highly unlikely to become a classic, to become something. Examples would be many of today's low-end cars such as those produced by Korean manufacturer Kia and the coming influx of low-priced cars to be manufactured in China. Low-end cars of American manufacturers—say, the Chevrolet Aveo—are in a similar position.[43] Such cars are generic machines with generic designs that, among other things, take little from, and say little about, the era in which they were built. Thus, while the Web page for the Thunderbird embeds the car in a historical tradition, Kia's offers no such vision but instead focuses on pragmatic issues such as price, warranty, and special offers. History is strewn with long-forgotten brands of generic automobiles, but the truly unique ones, those that said, and perhaps still say, something about a given time period, continue to be of interest and even to have books written about and clubs devoted to them.

It is safe to predict that some of today's cars—even some of today's relatively inexpensive cars—will become the classics of tomorrow, and one of the reasons they will achieve that position is that they say, or will come to be seen as saying, something about the early years of the 21st century. Another way of putting this is that these cars—like the muscle cars and the Thunderbird described above—are likely to become cultural icons.

Of course, while I have focused on centrally conceived and produced products in this discussion, it is the indigenous products that are far more likely to reflect a specific time period and to do so to a much greater degree. Such products are quite simply deeply embedded in specific periods of time (and place) and must reflect them, at least to a large degree. On the other hand, those involved in the centralized conception and control of products often seek, quite consciously and usually successfully, to extract them from identifiable periods of time (and place). However, at times, even they are interested in trying to produce things that are portrayed as being enmeshed in a given time period.

Further Ideas on Temporality

That which is specific to a given time period (e.g., the muscle car) tends to be a form rich in distinctive substance (especially the reflection of a particular era), and that which is time-free (e.g., today's Kia) is more likely to be a form largely lacking in distinctive substance. Once again, there is a long-term trend from the predominance of that which is specific to a given time period (e.g., a classic in any one of many domains) to that which is not specific to the times (e.g., the vast majority of mass-manufactured[44] products, and, after all, virtually everything is made that way these days). In the case of automobiles, there are various cars—the Ford Thunderbird, the convertible—that have a measure of success because they have come to be linked to a particular time period, but the vast majority of cars sold, and the best-selling models, all are rather relatively time-free products. Indeed, it could be argued that broad success requires that products be as time-free as possible. Linkage to any specific time period may attract some buyers, but the unique characteristics associated with it are likely to be unattractive to, or even repel, most potential buyers. Thus, the vast majority of manufacturers feel impelled to emphasize the production of the most innocuous, time-free automobiles (and other products), since it is in that direction that the greatest sales potential lies.

There are advantages associated with that which is timebound (those who identify with the time period represent a ready clientele), but the time-free have advantages as well (appeal to a far wider and larger audience with no particular allegiance to any time period).

There are disadvantages associated with both that which is specific to a given time frame (limited interest) and that which lacks such specificity (an absence of "soul," of content that is a reflection of a particular time period).

Needless to say, the specific-to-the-times/not-specific-to-the-times continuum can also be analyzed using the other tools outlined in this chapter. As has become the pattern, anticipating the next section, the Chrysler LeBaron convertible, and before that another iconic car—the Ford Mustang— were very much the products of a giant of the era in the automobile industry, Lee Iacocca.[45] These automobiles are more the product of human beings and human relationships than they are of dehumanized bureaucracies and bureaucrats (more likely the source of automobiles like the Kia and the Aveo). Of course, this is even more true of the specific-to-the-times products that emanate from local communities where one can see an actual craftsperson who produces the product in question.

The Human Dimension

That which is something tends to be associated with deep and highly meaningful human relationships, while nothing is linked to the relative absence of such human relationships: to dehumanized relationships.[46] Those things that are enmeshed in strong human relations are likely to have a great deal that is substantively distinctive associated with such relationships (e.g., the detailed personal and interpersonal histories associated with them). On the other hand, dehumanized phenomena are far less likely to permit the development of substantial personal relationships among those involved. Overall, that which is characterized by human relationships is more likely to be something, while that which is lacking in such relationships is more likely to be nothing.

Examples of the Human Dimension

The exemplary contrast here might be the small teaching college and the Internet university. The small teaching college is largely an American phenomenon characterized by relatively small classes and professors whose prime responsibility is teaching and not research (the reverse is the case in large state and elite universities such as the University of Michigan and Yale University). The Internet university (University of Phoenix is a major example[47]) offers the possibility of obtaining a degree wholly, or in large part, online.

The Internet university is, by its very nature, centrally conceived and controlled. In contrast, a small teaching college is characterized by largely local conception and control. Such a college is, almost by definition, characterized by close, even intimate relationships between the people involved (although online contacts of various types are increasing in these settings). This is likely to be true not only of relationships between professors and students but also between the students (and professors) themselves. It is these highly personal relationships that are likely to place the small teaching college toward the something end of the continuum. Furthermore, it is likely to have many of the other characteristics of something discussed above. It is more likely to be a setting with which people identify strongly and, in some cases (especially the faculty), remain associated with for a long time. Even though students are likely to stay for only four or five years, they are more likely than students of Internet universities to identify strongly with the college during the time that they are there. Furthermore, they are more likely to retain that identity and therefore to return for class reunions, be involved in alumni associations, and so on. (Can an Internet university even have something resembling a reunion or an alumni association? After all, a reunion implies the personal relationships that the Internet university never had in the first place.) They are also likely to be strongly tied to a place (e.g., the small teaching colleges of New England such as Amherst or Smith) and a particular time period (there are likely to be efforts to retain historic architecture and long-standing and sometimes seemingly outmoded traditions). And, of course, each teaching college is likely to be quite unique.

The online university is almost diametrically opposed to the small teaching college and stands, therefore, toward the nothing end of the continuum. Almost by definition, it will be impossible to develop personal relationships in such universities either between teachers and students or among the students. As an Internet site, it is by definition a place of flows—information, students, and professors logging on and off, and so on—and highly unlikely to become a locale in which such flows slow down and even stop for a time (see Chapter 3 for a discussion of the relationship between locales and flows). Educational sites on the Internet are likely to appear and disappear with great rapidity. Furthermore, those who visit these sites are apt to have the most ephemeral of contacts as they dip in and out at a rapid rate. Internet universities certainly have, and offer, no sense of place, unless it is their specific Internet addresses. And, they have no historical ties (at least as yet), unless it is to the general era of the arrival of the personal computer and the Internet. Internet universities are likely to resemble closely one another, with the result that not one of them is likely to have much in the way of uniqueness.

Further Ideas on Humanity

The forms that involve deep human relations tend to be rich in distinctive substance (e.g., a small teaching college and the innumerable interpersonal relationships that develop while one is a student there), and those that are dehumanized and dehumanizing tend to be forms largely devoid of such substance (e.g., the Internet university in which it is literally impossible to develop such relationships). Furthermore, there is a long-term trend away from that which involves humanized relationships to that which is dehumanized. More specifically, while there will continue to be a place for the small teaching college (especially for elites who can afford it), it is likely that an increasing number of students will be educated in, and obtain degrees from, Internet universities. In addition, even those students who remain in traditional colleges and universities will get a lot more of their education via the Internet. Indeed, at least some of those colleges and universities will become increasingly involved in making their educational resources available—for a (high) price—on the Internet.

There are advantages to both the forms with deep human relationships (e.g., the satisfactions of relating to people one knows well in a small teaching college, the greater learning possibilities that exist in face-to-face relationships between teachers and students) and the dehumanized forms (e.g., the freedom and the efficiencies associated with lack of personal involvement with others in the Internet university).

There are disadvantages associated with both that which has strong human relationships (e.g., entanglements with people one might rather avoid at a small college, the hostility of particular professors) and that which is dehumanized (e.g., an absence of meaning or soul at Internet U.).

Again, the humanized-dehumanized continuum can be analyzed using the various tools being developed here. For example, anticipating the next section yet again, small teaching colleges tend to be quite enchanted, while Internet universities are apt to be highly disenchanted. For many, being a student in a small teaching college can be something approaching a magical experience, but little in the way of enchantment is likely to be involved in a student's relationship with an Internet university that, because of its very nature, must be highly rationalized and therefore, by definition, disenchanted.

The Magical Dimension

This final continuum tends to bring together much, or even all, of that which has come before in this chapter and dealt with under the headings of the other four dimensions.

Examples of the Magical Dimension

That which is something tends to have an enchanted, magical quality, while that which is nothing is more likely to be disenchanted, to lack mystery or magic. Thus, the foods delivered from Domino's, in the Lunchables youngsters (and some adults) devour, and the microwaveable packages that constitute dinner are unlikely to have much in the way of enchantment associated with them. Think of that wonderfully rationalized Lunchables package with its neat compartments and its uniform slices of meat and cheese. It is hard to think of any food more rationalized, and less enchanted, than this. And, of course, to most observers, its taste is consistent with its packaging. Indeed, some may prefer to eat the packaging than the food inside.

On the other hand, homemade gourmet meals may well have an enchanted quality about them. Taking a wide range of ingredients and seeing them transformed into a gourmet meal is likely to seem quite magical. The novel *Like Water for Chocolate* offers wonderful examples of the enchantment associated with food preparation and the consumption of lovingly made home-cooked meals. (Similarly, the movie *Chocolat* features handmade candies that have enchanting qualities.) At one level, there is the magic associated with the various steps involved in the preparation of food, including "peeling the garlic, cleaning the chiles, and grinding the spices"[48] and then seeing them come together in the creation of homemade sausage.

At another, there is food like chilies in walnut sauce acting as an aphrodisiac, creating "heat in her limbs, the tickling sensations in the center of her body, the naughty thoughts."[49] In contrast, one does not experience the magic of creating a Domino's pizza, and it is hard to imagine eating one of those pizzas having an impact like that of those chilies in walnut sauce or, more to the point, anyone writing a novel depicting such a pizza as an aphrodisiac. Even if it was to be written, a novel titled *Like Water for Lunchables* is unlikely to attract much of a readership.

Once again, we can see the way in which all of the preceding continua relate to this, perhaps culminating in an overarching, enchantment/ disenchantment continuum. The unique—as in the home-cooked sausages described above—is much more likely to seem enchanted than the generic— yet another Domino's pizza—which clearly seems to be associated with, and has many of the characteristics of, disenchantment. This is directly linked to the fact that foods like homemade sausage are local products and such sausages are likely to vary greatly from one locale to another. It is the local nature of the ingredients and the particular way in which they are combined in a given locale that gives such foods much of their magic. Needless to say, Domino's pizza has no such local ties; it is pretty much exactly the same wherever it is produced and eaten, and this contributes to its disenchanted character.

A similar point can be made about the issue of time. Using ingredients that are specific to a given time period is more likely to produce enchanted products than using those that are not specific to the times. For example, the use of ingredients that are seasonal—say, summer fruits and vegetables—is more likely to produce enchanted dishes than is the case with using ingredients available year-round. A medley of summer fruits or a salad made up of summer vegetables is more likely to seem magical than salads made with apples available year-round (and often stored for long periods and deteriorating over time) or a medley of potatoes, onions, and other vegetables available throughout the year. Similarly, a fresh summer fruit salad is likely to seem more enchanted than one served during the winter and made with frozen or canned fruits.

It is human beings who are likely to create magical phenomena of all types; it takes a creative cook to create a magical dish. Disenchanted dishes are likely to be the result of dehumanized processes (e.g., following instructions and heating up meals in the microwave). A similar point applies to the consumption of food. Eating an enchanted meal at home or in a gourmet restaurant can be a very human experience, whereas eating in a fast-food restaurant, or worse in an automobile after one has obtained one's food at a drive-through window, is likely to be a dehumanized and dehumanizing experience.

Of course, that which is conceived in some centralized setting and which is tightly controlled (Lunchables is a perfect example) is highly unlikely to be enchanted; indeed, it is almost by definition disenchanted. And that which is conceived and controlled locally (and the chilies with walnut sauce dish discussed above is an excellent example of that) is far more likely to have at least some enchanted qualities.

Further Ideas on Magic

Those enchanted chilies with walnut sauce are loaded with distinctive substance, while that disenchanted Domino's pizza is lacking much in the way of distinctive substance. There is a long-term trend away from meals characterized by enchanted foods to those composed entirely of disenchanted foods like microwave meals and Domino's pizza. The decline in meals made (especially from scratch) and eaten at home and the corresponding rise in premade dishes brought home from the local market, home delivery of pizza, and meals eaten out in fast-food (and other chain) restaurants are all indicators of this dramatic change in our eating habits.

Enchanted foods have their advantages (a magical dining experience), but so too do disenchanted foods (the ease of obtaining that pizza).

And both have their disadvantages. Homemade chilies with walnut sauce are available to only a few. Home-delivered pizzas are available to many, but they could hardly be seen as offering the kind of magnificent dining experience associated with those chilies.

Finally, and returning to the first dimension and set of conceptual tools since no new ones follow, the enchanted tends to be unique (homemade sausages vary from area to area, time to time, and even family to family), whereas the disenchanted tends to be generic (Domino's pizza is the same from one time and place to another).

Globalization and the Dimensions of Nothing

While I have not said much about globalization to this point in this chapter, I need at least to touch on this issue here (it will resume center stage in Chapter 5). The central point is that those phenomena that stand toward the nothing end of the general something-nothing continuum, as well as that end of each of the specific subcontinua discussed in this chapter, are far more likely to be grobalized than those that stand at the something end of both the five subcontinua and the something-nothing continuum. Thus, returning to the specific examples discussed above, the microwave meal (and Lunchables), mass-produced Mexican pottery, generic automobiles, higher education on the Internet, and fast-food pizzas are all nothing, as well as important grobal phenomena. The parallel examples in the realm of something—the gourmet meal, handmade Mexican pottery, muscle cars, small teaching colleges, and those exotic chili dishes—do not have nearly the global presence of their counterparts in the realm of nothing. Nonetheless, it is a reflection of the power of grobalization that even the various forms of something have a global reach. In some cases—muscle cars, for example—that global reach is quite extensive. It is clear that it is the various forms of nothing that are, and by a wide margin, the more significant players and forces in the grobal marketplace. I deal with this, and why it is the case, later in this book.

On the other hand, those things that stand at the something end of the general continuum, as well as each of the five subcontinua, are far more likely to be glocal than grobal phenomena. Their basic characteristics make it likely that some of their local elements, likely modified by globalization, continue to affect them and make it far less likely that they can be grobalized. That is, they retain local creativity, spatial and temporal elements of the local, characteristics of the people who live in that locale, and magical elements linked to the local. These characteristics not only serve to make it more likely that they will remain glocal but also highly unlikely that they can be grobalized (unless they are systematically transformed by, say, a mass manufacturer from something to nothing). I have much more to say about the issue of the relationship between the grobal-glocal and something-nothing in Chapter 5, but before we can get to that we need still further clarification of something and, especially, nothing.

3

Meet the Nullities

*Non*places, *Non*things, *Non*people, and *Non*services

As we saw in Chapter 2, there is a general something-nothing continuum, as well as five subcontinua involving five major conceptual dimensions of nothing and something. In addition, we can identify several broad types of phenomena that can be analyzed using both the something-nothing continuum as well as the five subcontinua. Those phenomena—what I call the *nullities*—are *non*places, *non*things, *non*people, and *non*services. To give concrete examples of each, people around the world are spending more time in *non*places (the shopping mall, the Las Vegas casino) and with *non*things (Old Navy T-shirts, Dolce & Gabbana dresses), *non*people (the counter people at Burger King, telemarketers), and *non*services (those provided by ATMs, Amazon.com).

Of course, as with something-nothing and the five dimensions of nothing, each of these concepts implies a continuum with *places, things, people,* and *services* as the opposing, *something* poles. To be on the "non" end of any of the four continua, phenomena must meet our definition of nothing and tend to be centrally conceived and controlled forms lacking in distinctive substance. Those entities that are to be found at the other end of each continuum must meet the definition of something and be locally conceived and controlled forms that are rich in distinctive substance.

Thus, in terms of the examples used in Chapter 2, a *thing* is a traditional personal loan, a *place* is the community bank to which people can still go to deal with other *people*—bank employees—in person and obtain from them individualized *services* (see Figure 3.1). On the other hand, a credit card invitation is a *non*thing, a contemporary credit card company—one that may be little more than a telephone center—is a *non*place, the highly programmed and scripted individuals who work there are *non*people, and the often automated functions can be thought of as *non*services. Clearly, nothing in general, as well as the specific nullities of concern here, only make sense when they are seen as part of these continua and in relationship to something and its various forms. This means, once again, that we are dealing with relative concepts, and one has no meaning without a sense of the other.

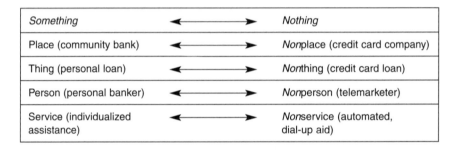

Something	←——————→	Nothing
Place (community bank)	←——————→	*Non*place (credit card company)
Thing (personal loan)	←——————→	*Non*thing (credit card loan)
Person (personal banker)	←——————→	*Non*person (telemarketer)
Service (individualized assistance)	←——————→	*Non*service (automated, dial-up aid)

Figure 3.1   The Four Major Subtypes of the Something-Nothing Continuum (With Examples)

*Non*places (and Places)

The idea of a *non*place is rooted in cultural geography[1] and the distinction between a space and a place. It is the idea of a *non*place that lies at the base of my conceptualization of, and thinking about, the other three nullities—*non*things, *non*people, and *non*services.

Social Geography

It is useful to begin with the work of Edward Relph, who, in a number of books, most notably *Place and Placelessness*,[2] developed a series of ideas on the issue of the relationship of place to placelessness. To Relph, places are loaded with distinctive substance: "Places . . . are full with meanings, with real objects, and with ongoing activities. They are important sources of individual and communal identity, and are often profound centres of human existence to which people have deep emotional and psychological ties."[3] Placelessness, then, is "an environment without significant places and the underlying attitude which does not acknowledge significance in places. It reaches back into the deepest levels of place, cutting roots, eroding symbols, replacing diversity with uniformity."[4] Relph sees a dangerous and powerful long-term trend away from place and in the direction of placelessness, from that which is rich in distinctive substance to that which is lacking in such substance, from something to nothing.

While a *non*place would be another way of describing what Relph conceives of as placelessness, of far greater and more direct use to our analysis of such settings is the work of Marc Augé, especially *Non-Places: Introduction to an Anthropology of Supermodernity*. To Augé, *non*places are "the real measure of our time."[5] I would generalize this to say that it is nothing that is, in many ways, the true measure of our time! In this book I seek to extend the idea of *non*places to *non*things, *non*people, *non*services, *and most generally to nothing.*

Augé argues that places and *non*places are intertwined today and that these days the possibility of being a *non*place is never far from any place. Augé defines a *non*place as "a space which cannot be defined as relational, or historical, or concerned with identity."[6] Augé is clearly anticipating many of the dimensions employed in this analysis; indeed his work is an important source of many of them.

While Augé describes places as involving fantasy and myth, he is more positively inclined to them than *non*places and the historical trend in their direction. Furthermore, many of the terms he uses to describe *non*places— *solitary, fleeting, similitude, anonymity, lacking in history,* and so on— communicate a critical attitude toward them. (I will discuss my own critique of nothing, especially as it relates to consumer culture, at various places in this book, especially in Chapters 6 through 8.)

The distinction between places and *non*places is closely related to Manuel Castells's[7] view that we are moving from a world characterized by "spaces of places" to one dominated by "spaces of flows."[8] Spaces of places tend to be unique settings characterized by rich geographic ties and an array of characteristics with deep ties to specific points in the locale's history, while areas defined by flows tend to be generic, to lack geographic ties, and to have a time-free quality. Given their constant and ubiquitous fluidity, it is very difficult for spaces of flows to become something. Spaces of places are more likely to be something because they have the stability to develop a distinctive substantive base, but flows lack such stability and therefore tend to be relatively devoid of such substance.

We can take as an example of spaces of places a well-established local residential community in which houses are a hodgepodge of different styles, each of which is built by a different builder, or even by the owners themselves. A more elite version of this is, say, a community in which each house has been built to the owner's specifications and is therefore different from every other house. That is, the array of houses is not centrally planned or controlled by developers and builders. Those who live in such communities are more likely to have lived there for long periods of time and to have deep ties to them. These communities are likely to be integral parts of the larger geographic settings in which they exist and to have an organic relationship with their environments. They are also likely to be products of a specific time period and to continue to have deep ties to it. Given all these characteristics, such communities are likely to be quite unique and, most generally, to be positioned close to the something end of the something-nothing continuum.

The contrast—that is, those communities that can be considered spaces of flows—are the myriad tract houses and planned communities that followed in the wake of the construction of the paradigmatic Levittown[9] in the post–World War II era (see also the discussion of the English planned village of Milton Keynes in Chapter 4). The houses in such communities are built according to a limited number of designs, so that many houses are identical to many others. The entire community is conceived by a central source (usually a developer) and once in existence is subjected to centralized control (especially today's gated communities). In the main, these communities have not been created to last, and the houses built in them are constructed of inexpensive materials so that they are unlikely to survive nearly as long as the houses built in more traditional communities. Residents move in and out of these communities rapidly and rarely settle in for long periods of time. Thus, there is an ephemeral quality to these communities, as well as to the houses and people in them. Much the same setting, style, and configuration of housing are likely to be repeated in many different places, with the result that it seems hard to differentiate among such communities. In addition, they often seem to be imposed on the local geographic area rather than being an organic part of it. Finally, the communities and houses are purposely rather time-free;[10] they seem to lack ties to a specific time period (or a given geographic location). Such settings can be thought of as "nowhere."[11]

Great Good Places and McDonaldized Settings

Another conceptual distinction that is useful in getting a sense of the difference between a place and *non*place is that between a *great good place* and a *McDonaldized setting*. We can illustrate this distinction with examples of a diner as a great good place and a fast-food restaurant (of course) as a McDonaldized setting.

Before discussing the diner as a great good place, some introduction to it is necessary, since readers in many parts of the United States and the world may be unfamiliar with it. Diners were quite popular in the United States in the early part of the 20th century but began to decline at about the same time the modern fast-food restaurant boomed. They usually took the narrow and elongated form of railroad dining cars or trolley cars. They were usually independently owned small restaurants serving inexpensive and basic meals to customers, many of whom were regulars. They can be seen as precursors to fast-food restaurants, although they were usually not part of chains and the food was usually idiosyncratically cooked from scratch by short-order cooks. However, diners are not merely of historical interest. They continue to exist as independent entities in many parts of the country, and there are now some small chains of diners, such as Mel's Diner in Florida (founded in 1989 and now with 11 restaurants).[12] More important, diners are an important cultural icon, and we have occasion below to discuss, for example, some of the movies, most notably *Diner,* that have featured this type of restaurant.

A diner can be seen, in most cases, as a specific type of what Ray Oldenburg calls a "great good place"[13] or a "third place" (in contrast to first [home] and second [work] places). Oldenburg's examples of great good places include German beer gardens, English pubs, French cafés, American taverns, coffeehouses, and book shops. Also included under this heading are settings that have largely disappeared from the American scene such as "soda fountains, malt shops, candy stores, and cigar stores."[14] Interestingly, Oldenburg does not explicitly include a diner under the heading of a great good place, but it will be my example because of the ways in which it fits the category as well as the interesting and revealing ways in which it does not, the fact that although it still exists, it may be going the way of the malt shop, and because the diner has been the subject of a large amount of research and writing.

To Oldenburg, great good places are "informal gathering places."[15] There are a variety of characteristics that make for a great good place, including the fact that it is a neutral ground for all, it is a leveler in that virtually everyone is welcome because of the absence of formal criteria for either admission or exclusion, it is easily accessible and readily available, the setting is unpretentious, the mood is playful, there are many regulars, and conversation is the main activity within these settings. Great good places may be seen as homes away from home, giving us roots, a sense of possession and control, an environment where we can be regenerated and restored, a place where we have great freedom, and a setting of great warmth. One regular at Trena's (an African American tavern that is a good example of a great good place) says the following: "If you can't reach me at Trena's, then try calling me at home. But you're more likely to catch me here [Trena's]."[16] Ann Sather, a local Chicago restaurant, is another good example of a great good place:

> Regulars make up about one-third of the customers at Ann Sather, Tunney [the current owner] said. "I spend a lot of time in the front-of-the-house and try to remember names." That goes a long way. "We train our servers to be that way, too," he added. "We have so many regulars that they have developed friendships just by being there at the same time," he added. "It's a warm and friendly atmosphere where they feel comfortable eating alone, too."[17]

Being a visible, hands-on owner makes it easier for Tunney to create that sought-after sense of community. "That's the personal touch for which there really is no substitute," he said.[18]

While a highly McDonaldized fast-food restaurant *could* become a great good place, there are major impediments (see below for a discussion of some of them) to it taking on the basic characteristics of such a place. Nonetheless, there are certainly times when every fast-food restaurant does, at least for short periods of time, function much like a great good place. Furthermore, this may be regularized when, for example, seniors are allowed to use the restaurant one morning a week for their bingo games. And there is evidence that in other cultures, fast-food restaurants are much more likely to function like great good places than they do in the United States.[19] While fast-food restaurants *can* be transformed into great good places, it is difficult to do so and, as a result, rarely occurs.

Think, for example, of the increasingly popular drive-through windows that are designed to keep people out of the restaurant and to prevent informal groups, especially of regulars engaged in lively and playful conversation, from developing in it. Then there are the famous chairs that are designed to be so uncomfortable that people want to leave soon after they sit down. The bright colors grow ever more off-putting the longer people remain in the restaurant. Or there is the spartan, even antiseptic, environment that is hardly conducive to staying long enough to create a great good place. Let's be clear: fast-food restaurants, at least in the United States, do not want to be great good places and strive mightily to avoid being such places. Among the many reasons is the fact that a great good place attracts those who linger over their food and/or drink; fast-food restaurants do not want those who linger and, in fact, would rather their customers never enter the restaurant at all (that's why drive-throughs are so commonplace).

Thus, it is clear that there are major differences between great good places and McDonaldized settings. To put it in the terms of this chapter, the former are places (and lie toward the something end of the continuum), while the latter are *non*places (and can be positioned more toward the nothing end of the continuum).

Nonplaces and Places: The Five Dimensions

Given this general background, let us turn now to a discussion of each of the five dimensions and continua as they relate to the *non*place-place continuum. However, instead of discussing the continua in general terms, in each case I will focus on a specific example of a *non*place[20] and contrast it to a place (I will do the same and focus on specific examples in ensuing discussions of *non*things, *non*people, and *non*services). In the case of the *non*place-place continuum, the specific contrast will, once again, be between a diner[21] (more likely to be a place) and a fast-food restaurant[22] (more likely to be a *non*place).

Complexity: Nonplaces and Places

The nothingness of *non*places like fast-food restaurants is manifest first in the fact that they are generic rather than unique and interchangeable, rather than one of a kind. In contrast, virtually every diner is different, often in quite profound ways, from every other one. This is the case even though for many years, and especially in the two decades after the end of World War II, large numbers of diners were prefabricated by a relatively small number of manufacturers and many were identical to one another in both external design and interior structure.[23] However, most owners seek to create at least superficial structural differences in order to distinguish their diners from competitors. There are many common elements in almost all diners—the counter, the griddle, the cashier station, and so on—but these are all likely to be arranged slightly differently and to include elements that are likely to be found in few, if any, other diners.

However, while there are strong physical similarities among many diners, they are not nearly as similar as the exterior structure and interior design of fast-food restaurants, especially in their early years. Furthermore, there is no parallel in diners to the golden arches in front of McDonald's restaurants. But what is truly unique about the diner is the ambiance created by owner and employees and the interaction between them and customers, as well as that between customers, especially the regulars. Furthermore, as chains of fast-food restaurants grew and became powerful competition to diners, the latter had to respond, if they hoped to survive, by taking on more of the characteristics of a great good place.

One indicator of the profound difference between these phenomena is the fact that while fast-food restaurants have proven to be ideal for the development of chains of generic, interchangeable units, diners have proven far less amenable to such a business structure, with the result that efforts to form chains of diners have been notably unsuccessful.[24] Yet, there is nothing inherent in the diner, or anything else for that matter, that makes it impossible to create a chain. Indeed, there have been, as we have seen, efforts to create chains of diners. In fact, McDonald's itself has dabbled in the diner business and would endeavor to create a large chain of such diners if it thought it could be successful. The basic elements of a successful diner could be isolated, predefined, prefabricated, and replicated in many different settings. One could even envision a time in the future when society goes through a retro craze and a chain of diners becomes a huge success. In fact, there are currently chains of restaurants like Applebee's ("Neighborhood grill and bar," "Everything a neighbor ought to be"[25]) that try to present themselves as some sort of throwback to an earlier period of time when the neighborhood bar and grill (like the diner, a great good place) thrived. However, Applebee's can be found in more than 1,800 "neighborhoods" in 49 states and in other nations.[26] Furthermore, most of its so-called neighborhoods are on well-traveled roads and highways where the only "neighbors" are likely to be other chains. The people who eat in these places are likely to have arrived by car, perhaps to have driven quite some distance, and are very unlikely to know any of the other patrons in the restaurant. It is highly unlikely that any of them are their neighbors in the traditional sense that term is used. In spite of its efforts to convince us otherwise, it is hard to think of, or treat, an Applebee's restaurant as a great good place.

Basic to the whole idea of a franchise is the centralized conceptualization of the chain as a whole, as well as of every unit in it. Furthermore, McDonald's used (and continues to use) inspectors as a form of centralized control to ensure that franchises live up to its standards and guidelines. In contrast, since they are usually individual, stand-alone operations, diners are subjected to neither centralized conceptualization nor control.

A diner seems like a throwback to an earlier time in our history, while a fast-food restaurant, even though some of the early ones go back to the 1920s (A&W Root Beer stands), seems much more time-free. The boom in fast-food restaurants began with the first of the McDonald's chain in 1955, while the heyday of the diner, which had begun several decades earlier, was beginning to wane at that point, in part because of the rise of the fast-food restaurant.[27]

Diners, perhaps because they are reminiscent of an earlier time, seem to have an image in people's minds of being highly idiosyncratic. When they want to go to a diner, people tend to want to experience one that has its own distinctive characteristics. Even if they want to imbibe the generic in the fast-food restaurant, they do not want that in the diner. Thus, the patrons who are drawn to diners are more likely to prefer those that are idiosyncratic, perhaps the more idiosyncratic the better, and to shun those that are, or seem to be, part of chains. Furthermore, they may well be the kind of relatively unusual people whose presence serves to make diners even more idiosyncratic, more like great good places. Of course, it is also likely that there are some who enjoy going to generic fast-food restaurants on some occasions and idiosyncratic diners on others.

Spatiality: Nonplaces and Places

The complexity continuum (unique-generic) is closely related to the second *spatial* continuum dealing with the presence or absence of local geographic ties. The *non*places of concern here—for example, fast-food restaurants—tend, of course, *not* to have local geographic ties and *not* to be localized in place (or time). In contrast, a great good place like a diner is likely to be deeply embedded in the local geography. As the founder of the Silver Diner said, "People think of the diner not as a chain, but as a *neighborhood* restaurant" (italics added).[28]

If McDonaldized settings were to vary greatly from one locale to another and to blend into the local environment, those who are searching them out would find it difficult, or impossible, to find them. (I had this experience in Bangkok a few years ago when I came upon a vaguely recognizable restaurant. After careful examination, I found the iconic "Big Boy" statue, but it could easily have been missed by a passerby. The restaurant had adapted so much to its local environment that it was virtually impossible to tell that it was a Big Boy restaurant.) Furthermore, even when McDonaldized settings are found, they would not, if they had become highly localized, offer the experiences that consumers had come to expect. There is some evidence that *non*places do change to some degree over time and do adapt somewhat to local realities, but the fact is that they must retain a high level of predictability to survive, and localization in terms of place (and time) tends to reduce such predictability. Thus, McDonaldized settings have a vested interest in *not* having local ties,[29] or at least not very many of them, and in order to survive must avoid being pushed in the direction of becoming too enmeshed in any given locality.

In contrast, the local diner is not expected to have this level of predictability from one locale to another. In fact, it is expected to be unpredictable. Of course, some predictability is required—certain types of food, availability of all meals and snacks during the day, comparatively low prices, a train- or trolley car–like structure, and so on—but it need not have near the degree of predictability of a chain restaurant. Indeed, patrons are often attracted, and look forward, to some distinctive characteristics and are apt to prize a diner in one locale over another (and certainly over a fast-food restaurant) for its distinctiveness. Of course, that distinctiveness works only when it is part of a setting with the requisite predictable elements.

The unpredictability of the diner is only relative to the predictability of the chain restaurant. To those who work or eat there, a diner would be highly predictable. However, that predictability is *locally produced*, while the predictability of a chain restaurant is, at least in part, centrally produced in accord with a corporate blueprint. Thus, the short-order cook at a diner may prepare scrambled eggs the same way every time, but the method chosen and its repetition is produced by that particular cook or the manager-owner of the diner. In contrast, the griddle person at a chain restaurant may also cook scrambled eggs the same way every time, but that is a product of corporate training, guidelines, guidebooks, and close surveillance and supervision.

Since a diner is usually the idiosyncratic product of a local business-person, it is likely that it will grow out of, and reflect, the nature of the local environment. Although it has ties, if only informal ones, to the larger culture of diners, each diner springs, in the main, from a local community and is likely in many ways to reflect that environment. For example, one might expect a diner in the northwestern United States to reflect something of the character of that area (say, e.g., having its walls covered with the kind of wood paneling found in a lodge, or pictures of animals, fish, or greenery indigenous to the area). It would differ from those in the Southwest (where kokopellis[30] [see Chapter 4 for more on this] might be a common decoration), Texas (with lots of cowboy pictures and paraphernalia), or the Southeast (with reminders, perhaps, of Miss Pittypat's porch[31] from *Gone With the Wind* [1939]). While much of the food—waffles, scrambled eggs, burgers—would be the same, there would also be regional variations such as more salmon in the Northwest, huevos rancheros more likely in the Southwest, and grits more common in the South. And the manner of dealing with customers (southern hospitality or a more no-nonsense approach in the Northwest) would reflect similar regional differences. This list of local geographic ties could obviously be extended in many different directions.

Any given fast-food restaurant is far less likely to reflect the local environment and far more likely to reflect the structural demands and expectations of the corporate entity of which it is part. If there are differences, they are more likely to spring from the increasing demands from central office for some diversity than they are from local realities. In fact, burned by the critics of their architectural homogeneity and their imposition of a uniform style on widely divergent localities, some fast-food chains have been endeavoring to build more architectural diversity into their systems. There is a huge difference between creating a local diner out of elements derived from the locale and strategically using a few local elements to give a chain restaurant the feel of the area. While the latter may defuse opposition and allow the chain restaurant to seem to fit better into the local community, it falls far short of making it a genuine part of that locality.

Temporality: Nonplaces and Places

The third, or *temporal,* dimension (specific to the times/relatively time-free) is also related to the issue of predictability, although it plays itself out very differently in this case. The diner should have at least some elements that indicate that it is a predictable throwback to an early part of the 20th century, while a chain restaurant should be predictably time-free.[32] The diner was very much a product of not only a place but also its time (roughly the 1920s through the 1960s). It grew out of a specific epoch and remains wedded to it. Over time, because it changed little, it became increasingly anachronistic, and as a result, many diners were forced to close their doors. The dilemma for the diner is that if it had changed dramatically and become more contemporary, it would have lost that which defines a diner in people's eyes, especially those who are likely to frequent it. For example, if the diner surrendered the traditional look of an early 20th-century railroad or trolley car and took on the appearance of, say, a 21st-century rocket ship, it would be very difficult for most people, especially devotees, to think of such a setting as a diner.

Similarly, a diner is associated with the era of made-to-order food. Thus, patrons expect to order their food and have it prepared specifically for them, perhaps even watching from the counter as the short-order cook whips up some scrambled eggs or waffles. They would likely be repelled by a diner that sought to modernize by offering preprepared food in shrink-wrapped, Styrofoam containers. Consumers would also expect to be served, usually by a waitress, either at the counter or at a table. And they would expect to have someone clean up after them. In contrast, as a paradigmatic *non*place and purposely constructed in that way, a McDonaldized chain restaurant is designed not only not to be space specific but also *non*time specific: time-free.[33] True, there is something vaguely modern about such settings. In fact, however, this was more true of the early versions of, say, McDonald's where the abundance of glass, steel, and so on gave one the feeling of something related to the then-new era of supersonic planes or even space travel. However, over the years much of that has been lost. A given McDonald's might include some very local and traditional elements, some brick to suggest the past and some stainless steel to suggest the future. In other words, in the main they are designed to be time-free, abstract enough to last well into the future without seeming to be old-fashioned.

Closely related to the issue of temporality is that of permanency-impermanency. In contrast to the aura of permanency surrounding places, there is a kind of ephemerality associated with *non*places. Of course, they all are in a real sense ephemeral. Given the short lifespan of most small businesses, most great good places, including diners, are not likely to survive very long (there are notable exceptions), and they may well be outlived by *non*places such as McDonaldized chains. However, at least some great good places seek to surround themselves with an aura of permanency, with the image that they have been there for a long time and will continue to be there for the foreseeable future. For example, business at the Silver Diner increased when the chain reintroduced low-priced "blue-plate specials," associated nostalgically with the early history of the diner. Of course, chains of *non*places seek to create such images as well. Thus, McDonald's, past its 50th anniversary, increasingly presents itself as a tradition, and Johnny Rockets wants to be seen as a reincarnation of a 1940s hamburger and malt shop. Nonetheless, any given McDonald's (or Johnny Rockets) restaurant, and more generally any *non*place, feels more ephemeral than the typical diner, or great good place.

Also related to temporality (and many of the other dimensions) is the idea that *non*places tend to be characterized more by flows, while places are more concrete geographic settings. A great good place like a diner is a distinctive setting to which customers are not only expected to go but to linger for a time. The physical setting is designed to welcome them, to make them comfortable, even embrace them. Thus, diners are seen as "homey meeting places" where customers are "welcome to come in and drink bottomless cups of coffee."[34] It is clear that customers will be expected to leave eventually, but while they are there, the physical setting is designed to make them feel welcome. A diner's customers are in transit, but the feeling is that they have paused in their movements, at least briefly, so that they can enjoy a particular setting and what it has to offer. To put it another way, and more generally, a great good place is designed to be a safe haven that offers a respite from the ever-present flows within which people increasingly find themselves.

In contrast, a *non*place is an integral part of the larger space of flows where visitors rarely, if ever, feel as if they have arrived anywhere (at least for any length of time). In McDonald's, people flow through the restaurant, rarely staying for very long. Of course, the drive-through lane is a near-perfect example of this as people and their cars flow through them barely stopping long enough to pay for, and obtain, their food. And this, in turn, is part of a larger flow of people from, for example, work to home, one leisure setting to another, and so on.

Starbucks is very interesting in this context since it tries to present itself as a place rather than a *non*place, as a place where the flows can stop and people can relax in those big comfy chairs and couches and sip their coffee while checking their e-mail. While this is true for a few customers lucky enough to find a place to sit, the vast majority of those who get their coffee at Starbucks have no time or interest in relaxing there. Rather they are lining up, either in the store or drive-through, to get their coffee quickly and efficiently and then continuing on their way to wherever it is they are going. Starbucks is an integral part of the spaces of flows; it is a *non*place masquerading as a place. There would, of course, not be nearly enough room if the majority of Starbucks' coffee drinkers actually wanted to linger in the shops. In fact, the shops would grind to a halt if that happened. Contrary to its carefully created public image, Starbucks must have almost all of its coffee customers keep on moving down the road if it is to survive. It would quickly go out of business if the only customers it handled were those able to drink their coffee in the shops.

Another interesting aspect of Starbucks in this regard is its impact on traffic flows, especially during the morning rush hour. Many commuters have come to adjust their driving routes to work so that they can get their morning caffeine fix at Starbucks (or a competing chain). This has altered traffic patterns, with some unanticipated routes now jammed with traffic while others that were planned to handle lots of traffic experiencing a decline during the morning rush hour. Thus, there are now too many stoplights, with unnecessarily long delays, in some places, while in others there are insufficient traffic lights, producing traffic jams. Relatedly, Starbucks has played a key role in the increase in importance of cup holders in automobiles. Drivers can now simultaneously remain in the flow of traffic *and* maintain the flow of caffeine into their systems. Furthermore, other fast-food restaurants as well as food producers are creating other kinds of products—soup, salad, and so on—for those cup holders, thereby adding still other things that are part of the spaces of flows rather than the spaces of places.

Humanity: Non*places and Places*

Places are more likely to be characterized by human relationships, while *non*places are more likely to be dehumanized. All of the characteristics of places discussed above—their unique, one-of-a-kind character, their ties to a specific place and time—serve to make it more likely that deeper and more personal human relationships will develop in places such as diners. Being in a unique setting is likely to lead people to want to linger longer and to return. The same is true of settings that are place- and time-specific. This rootedness gives visitors the comforting feeling that this is a place to go, because they can anticipate returning over and over. And there is a well-defined physical space in these settings, a space where one at least gets the feeling that one is welcome and able to pause, if only for a time, before moving on. And all these things are conducive to the development of human relationships with those who work in these settings as well as with other customers.

In contrast, dehumanized relationships are more likely to occur in generic, interchangeable *non*places like fast-food restaurants, characterized by their lack of ties to specific geographic locales and time periods and the sense that one is simply flowing through them. One Silver Diner customer makes the differences between diners and fast-food restaurants on this dimension clear: "It's [Silver Diner] an easy place to tell people to meet you. The food is good, and the people are nice. . . . I'll kid with them, and they kid with me. It's an easy place to drop in and chat. If they go in a McDonald's, you don't get a chance to know the wait staff."[35]

Social relationships may develop and be repeated over and over in a chain restaurant, but if they occur, it is usually in spite of efforts to discourage or even prevent them. In contrast, a diner is likely to encourage such relationships because they are likely to lead to repeat business.

Magic: Non*places and Places*

Finally, the diner (and places in general) is much more likely to seem enchanted than the fast-food restaurant (and *non*places more generally), which, after all, is the paradigm of rationalization and therefore disenchantment.[36] In a way, all the preceding continua serve to enchant diners and disenchant fast-food restaurants. Diners are more likely to internalize elements of a specific place and time, as well as the magic of being embedded in such contexts. In contrast, the placelessness and time-freeness of fast-food restaurants serve to contribute to their rationalized character lacking in much, if any, magic. As more substantial locales, diners have the base on which to build enchantment, whereas the constant movement associated with fast-food restaurants makes it nearly impossible to create any sense of magic. Almost all enchantment flows out of human relationships, and their greater likelihood in diners makes diners more apt to seem magical than fast-food restaurants. Along the same lines, people are much more likely to feel that what they identify with (diners, in this case) is more likely to seem magical than what they do not identify with (fast-food restaurants).

There is little question that diners, and more generally places, tend to seem more enchanted than fast-food restaurants and, more generally, *non*-places. One need look no further than the way the two have been treated in the movies. The setting for the movie *Diner* (1982) is a place to which the characters return over and over. It clearly has an enchanted, nearly religious quality as far as they are concerned. On the other extreme, in *Falling Down* (1993), the fast-food restaurant is a metaphor for a cold, unfeeling world, and the gun-toting "hero" (portrayed by Michael Douglas) is depicted as venting his rage against such a disenchanted world on the restaurant and its employees.

However, the movies also provide examples of the ways in which some of the earlier forms anticipated problems that were exacerbated in later forms. For example, in *Five Easy Pieces* (1970), Robert Dupea—a character played by Jack Nicholson—attempts to order toast in a diner.

Dupea: I'd like a plain omelet, no potatoes, tomatoes instead, a cup of coffee, and wheat toast.

Waitress: (She points to the menu) No substitutions.

Dupea: What do you mean? You don't have any tomatoes?

Waitress: *Only* what's on the menu. You can have a number two—a plain omelet. It comes with cottage fries and rolls.

Dupea: Yeah, I know what it comes with. But it's not what I want.

Waitress: Well, I'll come back when you make up your mind.

Dupea: Wait a minute. I have made up my mind. I'd like a plain omelet, no potatoes on the plate, a cup of coffee, and a side order of wheat toast.

Waitress: I'm sorry, we don't have any side orders of toast . . . an English muffin or a coffee roll.

Dupea: What do you mean you don't make side orders of toast? You make sandwiches, don't you?

Waitress: Would you like to talk to the manager?

Dupea: . . . You've got bread and a toaster of some kind?

Waitress: I don't make the rules.

Dupea: OK, I'll make it as easy for you as I can. I'd like an omelet, plain, and a chicken salad sandwich on wheat toast, no mayonnaise, no butter, no lettuce. And a cup of coffee.

Waitress: A number two, chicken sal san, hold the butter, the lettuce and the mayonnaise. And a cup of coffee. Anything else?

Dupea: Yeah. Now all you have to do is hold the chicken, bring me the toast, give me a check for the chicken salad sandwich, and you haven't broken any rules.

Waitress: (spitefully) You want me to *hold* the chicken, huh?

Dupea: I want you to hold it between your knees.

Waitress: (turning and telling him to look at the sign that says "No Substitutions") Do you see that sign, sir? Yes, you'll all have to leave. I'm not taking any more of your smartness and sarcasm.

Dupea: You see this sign? (He sweeps all the water glasses and menus off the table.)

Thus, diners had aspects of a *non*place (and had their *non*people like the waitress above) and those who reacted with hostility to such characteristics were not unknown. However, the reaction of the Jack Nicholson character (Dupea) to the diner pales in comparison to that of the character played by Michael Douglas in *Falling Down*. This can be seen as reflective of the fact that the diner falls closer to the place and the fast-food restaurant the *non*place ends of the continuum discussed in this section.

*Non*things (and Things)

It is clear that one can make a strong case that we are witnessing the proliferation of *non*places, but what of the *non*things that are usually offered in them? Following our general definition of nothing, a *non*thing is centrally created and controlled and is lacking in distinctive substance. It is clear that *non*places tend to offer *non*things, but increasingly the latter are not restricted to *non*places—even places are now likely to offer *non*things (more on this later). Thus, *non*things are far more pervasive than *non*places, and this is even more the case because there are obviously infinitely more things than there are places. *Non*things are also a much more intimate and pervasive presence in our lives than *non*places. Furthermore, we may go in and out of *non*places, but at least some *non*things have the possibility of being with us literally all the time. Our bodies are covered by an array of *non*things, and even when we go to bed at night, we are likely to be surrounded by *non*things (Sealy Posturepedic mattresses, Martha Stewart sheets and pillow cases, Chanel perfumes or colognes, etc.), even if we sleep in the nude and therefore without Victoria's Secret, Ralph Lauren, or even Mickey Mouse sleepwear.

There are innumerable examples of *non*things in the contemporary world, such as the burritos at Taco Bell, Benetton sweaters, jeans from the Gap, even elegant and very expensive Gucci bags. Since generic products are centrally conceived and produced over and over in the same way thousands, millions, or even billions of times, any one of these products can be said to be lacking in distinctive substance. Staying with the fast-food restaurant for the time being, we can use the Big Mac as our example of a *non*thing and the contrasting thing will be a Culatello ham. The latter is a distinctive product of a particular region of Italy and is produced on small farms in the area. It is cured over long periods of time hanging from the rafters of a small building (with dirt floors) devoted to that purpose. There is no large corporation conceptualizing the nature of these hams or controlling how they are produced on these farms. Not surprisingly, Culatello ham is one of those products championed by the Slow Food movement (more on this in Chapter 8) as an alternative to such fast food as the Big Mac.[37]

Nonthings and Things: The Five Dimensions

Complexity: Non*things and Things*

First, of course, any given Big Mac lacks anything distinctive that would serve to differentiate it from any other Big Mac; one is basically the same as any other sold anyplace in the world. All Big Macs have essentially the same ingredients and are the same size, shape, and weight. There is nothing unique or very complex about any given Big Mac; they are all more or less interchangeable. In contrast, no single Culatello ham is exactly the same as any other. Size, shape, and weight will vary depending on the pig from which it is taken, the butchering process, and the vagaries of the curing process, as well as differences between curing houses. Overall, every Big Mac will be generic, while every Culatello ham will be unique.

Spatiality: Non*things and Things*

The Big Mac is a product from nowhere. While it, and its ancestor the hamburger, may have achieved its greatest success in the United States, it has roots in Germany (Hamburg) and England (Salisbury steak). However, the Big Mac or similar variations on the hamburger (e.g., the Whopper) has long since lost any geographic identity as it has come to be sold, among innumerable other *(non)*places, in McDonald's restaurants in approximately 130 nations throughout the world. In contrast, the Culatello ham is not only from Italy but from a very specific region of the country. It is a product that is intimately tied to that region and its distinct culture and history. While some of it is exported, it is likely that most of it is consumed by locals in or near where it is produced.

The local farms that produce Culatello hams seem far from the flows of consumer products throughout the world. The hams hang in the local curing houses for long periods of time before they are deemed ready for consumption by locals or for sale outside the area. Of course, when the Culatello ham enters the world market, it becomes part of a global flow of consumer products, but it is such a minimal part of that flow that it hardly seems that way. In addition, it takes consumers much longer to work their way through a Culatello ham than a Big Mac.[38] In contrast, the Big Mac is inherently very much a part of that flow and has very little, if anything, to do with places where that flow seems to slow down or even stop for a time. The consumer does not know where, for example, the beef in the Big Mac comes from. In fact, it is part of a global flow of frozen beef patties that is hard, if not impossible, to identify with a specific locale. It is in the interest of fast-food chains to set it up in this way so that they are free to use beef from anywhere, from everywhere, from nowhere.

Temporality: Non*things and Things*

However, the third dimension of our analysis does not seem to work quite as well in terms of attempting to differentiate things from *non*things. *Both* the Big Mac, at least in its most basic form—the hamburger—and the Culatello ham can be linked to a particular period of time. While the Big Mac is clearly a product of mid-20th-century America, the hamburger has centuries-long ties to predecessors like its forerunners from Germany and England. Similarly, the Culatello ham has deep roots in the history of Italy and the region from which it comes. Thus, neither the hamburger nor the Culatello ham is time-free.

While both the Big Mac and the Culatello ham have long traditions, the latter has the far greater aura of permanency, whereas the Big Mac seems more ephemeral. The Culatello ham is rooted in a specific tradition, has existed in that tradition for centuries, and will likely last as long as the tradition exists. In contrast, in spite of its roots in earlier hamburgers and Salisbury steaks, the Big Mac is clearly one of the innumerable products of 20th-century America, and we have many examples of such products (e.g., McDonald's Hula Burger) that have become popular for a time, only to be abandoned when they are no longer profitable.

We can envision a time when McDonald's will cease selling the Big Mac because it is no longer a popular, profitable product. In contrast, even if Culatello hams were no longer profitable products, the local producers would continue to make them, at least for themselves and their neighbors.

Traditionally, it is those things with patina (a thin coating or a color change resulting from age) that are the most desirable and bring the highest prices.[39] It could be argued that because it is embedded in an ancient tradition, and is the result of a long curing process, the Culatello ham has patina and is therefore likely to have staying power and to bring a far higher price than a product like the Big Mac that is clearly totally lacking in patina. The latter is produced in order to be consumed almost immediately. In fact, fast-food restaurants often have rules about how long products like Big Macs can remain unsold before they must be discarded. Of course, there are better examples of things with patina, such as antiques. In fact, people are willing to pay a far higher price for certain things just because they have patina. Thus, many people are willing to pay much more for an antique (often something) than for a contemporary factory-made alternative (likely nothing), and similarly, some (at least those who know about the distinctiveness and quality of such ham) will pay more for a Culatello ham than for virtually any other type of ham.

Humanity: Non*things and* Things

The Culatello ham is very much a human product. Individual pigs are raised on small farms, they are butchered by hand, and each ham is hand carved from the pig. Each ham is cured on small farms by individual producers over a long period of time, and when they are deemed ready, they are sold, bartered, or eaten by the producer. There is a very personal relationship between producer and Culatello ham. No such personal relationship exists between producer and the Big Mac. Furthermore, as Eric Schlosser has shown in *Fast Food Nation*,[40] the demand of the fast-food industry for massive quantities of hamburger has, among other things, led to the McDonaldization of the slaughterhouse business.[41] The latter, of course, was already a highly rationalized business a century ago with its pioneering assembly-line methods for butchering animals. However, as Schlosser shows in great detail, the pressure produced by the demands of the fast-food industry has led to an extraordinary increase in their degree of rationalization. Those who work in such slaughterhouses are poorly paid, dehumanized workers who, to say the least, have no time to develop any bonds with the steer they slaughter or the meat products they butcher. In contrast to the personal relationship between the Italian farmers and their pigs, consider the following description of the relationship of one type of worker to the steers that pass by on today's "disassembly" lines:

> For eight and a half hours, a worker called a "sticker" does nothing but stand in a river of blood, being drenched in blood, slitting the neck of a steer every ten seconds or so, severing its carotid artery. He uses a long knife and must hit exactly the right spot to kill the animal humanely. He hits that spot again and again.[42]

Producers and consumers are likely to develop a stronger sense of identity with a thing like Culatello ham than a *non*thing like the Big Mac.[43] Those who produce Culatello hams certainly strongly identify with them—they may well be at the center of their lives. Those who put together and sell Big Macs (or who slaughter the steers whose meat becomes the centerpiece of the Big Mac) are unlikely to have a similar sense of identity with them. Even consumers of the Culatello ham are likely to have at least some identity with it and to strongly prefer it to the alternatives, but this is far less likely to be true of the consumer of the Big Mac, who may be just as likely to eat a competing product (Burger King's Whopper, for example) as a Big Mac.[44]

Magic: Non*things and Things*

Finally, there is clearly much more enchantment associated with the Culatello ham than the Big Mac. As the signature product of the paradigmatic site—McDonald's—of disenchantment (and rationalization), the Big Mac is a model for a *non*thing lacking in magic. In contrast, the Culatello ham exists on the other end of the continuum and is a good example of a thing that has magical qualities, at least for those who produce and are devoted consumers of it.

Thus, the dimensions of something-nothing do a good job of distinguishing between the Culatello ham and the Big Mac and more generally between things and *non*things.

*Non*people (and People)

The places (and *non*places) and things (and *non*things) analyzed above require analysis of the human relationships (or their relative absence) that serve to make them something, nothing, or everything in between. Thus, settings become places or *non*places (or somewhere in between) because of the thoughts and actions of the people who create, control, work in, and are served by them. Objects are turned into things or *non*things by those who manufacture, market, sell, purchase, and use them. And even human beings (and their services) become people or *non*people (and *non*services) as a result of the demands and expectations of those with whom they come into contact.

The idea of a person (or people) is clear enough, but that of a *non*person (or *non*people) is another matter. How can a person be a *non*person? In 1959, Erving Goffman wrote about the "non-person" (e.g., the taxi driver who is treated by passengers as if he or she is not present),[45] but to most this is a counterintuitive notion. Of course, a *non*person is a person but one who does not act as if he or she is a person, does not interact with others as a person, and perhaps more important is not treated by others as a person. For discussion purposes, my specific example in this section of a *non*person is a Disney "cast member," especially one who dons the costume of one of the Disney characters (Snow White, Mickey Mouse, etc.),[46] while our person is a bartender in a traditional tavern.

*Non*people and People: The Five Dimensions

Complexity: Non*people and People*

Bartenders in traditional taverns tend to be unique, one-of-a-kind characters. They have distinct personalities, are likely to be personally well known to customers (especially regulars), and they get to know their clientele quite well. Their relationships with customers, as well as relationships among the latter, are likely to grow quite dense and complex. Beyond perhaps the bar owner (if different from the bartender), there is no centralized organization conceiving of what bartenders should say and do and controlling their actions. This is clearly not true of the Disney cast member. The Disney Corporation is very powerful and is notorious for the control that it exercises over employees. Any number of people can and have donned the Mickey Mouse or Snow White costume and have wandered about the park greeting visitors. Those who play these parts are interchangeable. And while each might invest his or her performance with some creativity and individuality, what each does is scripted and choreographed, so that it matters little which particular individual happens to be wearing the costume. There is little that is distinctive or complex about what any cast member in such a costume says or does, with the result that it is easy to replace any given individual worker, and in fact, several different people might don the same costume on the same day. Any given bartender is harder to replace, and when such a change occurs, the nature of the performance and of relationships to customers is likely to change a great deal. Thus, a bar might lose considerable business when a favorite bartender leaves, but business at Disney World goes on without a blip when one person replaces another in that Mickey Mouse suit.

Spatiality: Nonpeople and People

Taverns and their bartenders tend to have deep ties to, for example, a local urban neighborhood. Bartenders are likely to come from that neighborhood or, if not, to develop ties within it over time. Ties may also be developed to particular groups within a neighborhood. Thus, an Irish pub, even when it is not in Ireland, is likely to draw much of its clientele from the residents of a local community with Irish roots. In contrast, of course, there are no local geographic ties as far as Disney World (wherever it exists—United States, France, Japan, or Hong Kong) and its employees are concerned. Employees are likely to be drawn from all over the world. Its clientele is national and international rather than local, and it is far more linked to the world than to the local community. Employees are also not likely to remain on the job for very long, and this inhibits their ability to develop ties to the local community. Furthermore, the area around Disney World with its many highways and modern hotels is so transient that it is unlikely to produce much in the way of a community. In fact, Walt Disney was so upset about the transient world of motels and fast-food restaurants that sprang up around Disneyland in California that in planning Disney World in Florida, he quietly and anonymously bought up a huge land mass in order to insulate Disney World from this. However, Disney World itself is such a transient world, and it led to the dramatic growth of nearby Orlando, which is both part of that world and dedicated to serving the transients who trek to Disney World and surrounding theme parks. Thus, traffic jams in and around Orlando are now a common occurrence.

Temporality: Nonpeople and People

Although there are types that are more long-lasting, the local bartender tends to be tied not only to a specific place but also a particular time. Since individual bartenders are constructing their own reality during their own life course and historical time period, that reality is unique to that time and will differ from those created by bartenders with different life experiences and spans and who live in different time periods. In contrast, the Disney characters (Mickey Mouse and Snow White) inhabited by cast members are time-free. Furthermore, even when they play more human roles, the scripts that inform their performances tend not to be time-specific.

Contrary to initial expectations, some Disney characters are, at least in some ways, surrounded by a greater sense of permanency. Characters like Mickey Mouse date back to the early 20th century, while others such as Snow White have ancient or even mythical roots and therefore have a powerful aura of permanency—we know that not only have they existed since our own childhood (if not seemingly forever), but they will be with us into the indefinite future. However, we also know that the specific individuals who wear particular costumes are highly impermanent, will be gone in short order, and will be replaced as soon as they move on. We also know that they will alternate with others who wear the same costume. We realize that the human cast members (those without the costumes that conceal the fact that they are people) are only temporary inhabitants of those positions.

Because our paradigmatic bartenders work in places like the neighborhood tavern, there tends to be greater stability associated with their position. They are more a fixture in a place than part of a flow of members of the labor force freely moving into and out of transient positions. Of the regular bartender at Trena's (the African American tavern mentioned above), "The bartender is an integral part of the social atmosphere in neighborhood taverns. Monique is no exception. As the regular bartender . . . she creates Trena's social atmosphere."[47] In contrast, Disney workers operate in one of the contemporary settings most defined by flows of all types, with the result that there tends to be little in the way of stability associated with their work, and as individuals they do little to create a sense of stability.

Humanity: Nonpeople and People

Clearly, the bartender is expected to develop personal relations with customers (and vice versa), especially those who are regulars, and assist them in developing relationships with one another. Said one bartender (Kenny), "I get paid to talk to people," and he concluded, "You come in here by yourself and walk out knowing 10 people." According to this bar's manager, "Kenny's a tremendous bartender. . . . No matter how busy he is, he's never too busy to be friendly."[48] In contrast, the relationship between those who don a Disney costume and visitors to the theme park approaches the highest level of dehumanization. While they may talk to, and act friendly toward, park visitors, Disney cast members, often occupying *non*human roles and costumes, are highly unlikely to develop personal relationships with visitors, and the reverse is even more the case. Similarly, even the highly scripted cast member without a costume is more likely to interact in a *non*human manner than the bartender who is more likely to be on his or her own in creating "recipes"[49] for dealing with customers on a day-to-day basis, let alone in dealing with more problematic situations for which there are no recipes (in contrast, Disney employees are more likely to have scripts even to deal with such situations). Of course, the whole notion of being a "cast member" implies a scripted, dehumanized relationship with those one interacts with on the job.

Bartenders are more likely to identify with their jobs and the specific taverns in which they work. This is true, in part, because they are far more likely to be in specific jobs and settings for longer periods of time than Disney employees. Because of that fact, the latter are unlikely to identify strongly with the characters they play or with the Disney enterprise as a whole. Even if they do manage to develop such identities, they are not likely to endure, because the career of the typical Disney cast member does not last very long.

Magic: Non*people and People*

Finally, genuine enchantment is far more likely to develop between bartender and customers than between Snow White and visitors to Disney World. In fact, the theme park is one of the key sites in which simulated enchantment is produced, and the relationship that exists between cast members and visitors is but one example of that. However, the efforts to produce simulated enchantment are highly rationalized and are therefore better described as being disenchanted. The irony is that Disney World proclaims itself the "Magic Kingdom." There is, of course, magic there, but it is of the simulated and disenchanted variety. Little militates against "genuine" magic more than simulation and disenchantment.

Reflecting the latter dimension, indeed all of the dimensions employed here, bartenders are far more likely to become cultural icons than are Disney cast members.[50] Thus, in the 1950s one of TV comedian Jackie Gleason's best-known characters was Joe the Bartender. A local barkeep, Joe always had a song and friendly word for his customers, especially the regulars. A central character in the blockbuster TV show *Cheers* was the bartender. First, it was Coach, but when the actor who played that role died, he was replaced by Woody. It is difficult to imagine the faceless *non*person who plays a Disney character becoming a cultural icon. Indeed, if anything about them is iconic, it is the costumes they wear, and this serves to reinforce the view of them as *non*persons.

*Non*services (and Services)

The idea of *non*service closely parallels the preceding discussion of *non*people and is hard to disentangle from it. Ultimately, of course, it is *non*people who are more likely to provide *non*services, although it is increasingly likely that even people provide services that approach the nothing end of the continuum. And, of course, *non*services are more likely to be offered in *non*places and to involve *non*things, but as is true in the preceding point, *non*services are also increasingly likely to be found in places and to involve things. In this case, I will use as examples the services provided by waiters in gourmet restaurants and those on one of today's huge and spectacular cruise ships.

*Non*services and Services: The Five Dimensions

Complexity: Non*services and Services*

Waiters in gourmet restaurants generally offer more complex and creative service that varies with the needs and demands of particular diners. While control is exerted by owners and headwaiters, there is generally no centralized control, because gourmet restaurants tend to be one-of-a-kind operations. In contrast, since cruise ships are huge operations, usually part of increasingly enormous and centralized organizations, there is great control over waiters on those ships. What such waiters do and how they do it is likely the subject of corporate directives, guidelines, and handbooks. As a result, waiters on such ships offer basic service that varies little from one set of diners to another. Furthermore, while serving large numbers of people at a given meal, such waiters are unable to give customers much, if any, individual attention. Thus, each diner gets essentially the same service. In contrast, of course, the waiter in an elite restaurant is dealing with a small number of diners and is able to interact with each diner in a unique manner. To put this another way, the interactions between cruise ship waiters and diners tends to be interchangeable, while those between gourmet restaurant waiters and diners tend to be one-of-a-kind experiences. Of course, this is one of the reasons that eating in gourmet restaurants is so expensive and, conversely, why so many find a cruise an affordable vacation.

Spatiality: Non*services and Services*

The cruise ship lacks any specific geographic ties—wandering as it does from port to port—so the services provided by waiters onboard are literally from (and in) nowhere. In contrast, those offered by the waiter in a gourmet restaurant (except those, like Wolfgang Puck's, that have grown into small chains) tend to be more embedded in local settings and linked to the expectations associated with them.

Temporality: Non*services and Services*

The time continuum is more problematic here. Just as there is a spaceless quality to service on the cruise ship, it is also the case that there is a time-freeness to it. The diner and the waiter on the cruise ship seem to be adrift in a world without time. However, the cruise ship is a very modern creation, and therefore the services provided on it do, in this sense, seem to be embedded in a particular time period. Furthermore, there is a history here of fine service on transatlantic and cruise ships, and the service offered aboard today's ship is part of that sweep of history. While the service of a waiter onboard ship is diverse in terms of the time dimension, the services provided by the waiter in a gourmet restaurant seem clearly tied to a long history of service, especially to an earlier time in history when such services were more the norm, at least for society's elites. They not only appear to be little different than those offered, say, a century ago but also unlikely to change very much in the future.

The services offered by the waiter in a gourmet restaurant have an aura of permanency about them. Not only do they seem unchanged and unchanging, but the settings in which they occur—gourmet restaurants—have a similar feel of permanency, even though specific gourmet restaurants (although not the broader type) come and go. On the other hand, the dining services on a cruise ship are occurring on a ship on the move and during a time period—usually a week—that is soon to end and not likely to be repeated, at least on that particular ship.[51] In the case of the gourmet restaurant, there is always the possibility that one can return for another meal, perhaps even involving the same dishes, prepared in much the same way, and served in the same manner by the same waiter.

More of a *non*place, the cruise ship is a space on the move, as is everyone associated with a given cruise. As a result, the dining services offered seem to be just one more flow in a larger set of flows. Specifically, modern cruise ships are famous for the round-the-clock, *non*stop availability of food, and any given meal may seem to be merely a part of a continuous flow of food. In contrast, the services offered by the waiter in a gourmet restaurant, while certainly part of a similar set of flows, occur in a place and have a strong sense of "placeness." Maybe it is little more than a flow with a different pace, but flows associated with the gourmet restaurant seem glacial and therefore more rooted in place than those found on the cruise ship. Another big difference is traceable to the fact that while waiters in gourmet restaurants are likely to see at least some customers over and over, the cruise is a one-time experience for most people, with the result that the waiter is likely to see them only during a single cruise.

Humanity: Nonservices and Services

Waiters in gourmet restaurants are more likely to identify strongly with what they do, the services they offer, the (often regular) customers they serve, and the settings in which they work. As a result, diners may identify a very specific kind of service with a given restaurant and even with a particular server. A very human relationship is likely to develop between a waiter in a gourmet restaurant and diners, especially regulars. In contrast, waiters and diners on cruise ships, because they are part of so many different flows, are far less able to develop any of these identities and personal relationships, at least to any great degree.

Magic: Nonservices and Services

Finally, the service at a gourmet restaurant is likely to have a magical quality about it, whereas the service provided by waiters on cruise ships, like the cruise ships themselves, is likely to be more simulated enchantment and therefore more disenchanted. In terms of the former, a good example would be one of Paris's great gourmet restaurants, especially during truffle season. Soon after diners are seated, and periodically during the evening, staff members circulate around the restaurant with a basket laden with truffles. Diners are allowed to gaze at this magical (and hugely expensive) food and to inhale its aroma. The expressions on diners' faces indicate that this is clearly a magical moment. One is unlikely to experience such a moment, or such service, on a cruise ship, where the emphasis is on serving huge numbers of people lots of food quickly and efficiently.

In sum, the something-nothing continuum, and its various subcontinua, works very well, albeit in a few cases imperfectly, in distinguishing services-*non*services. Not only are the various continua useful, but so are the cases in which the expected distinctions do not quite pan out as expected. This serves to give us a more nuanced picture of the nullities of concern here and their distinctions (or lack thereof) from services with more substance.

Relationships Among the Nullities

While each of the four types of nothing have been discussed independently, the fact is that there is a powerful tendency for the types to vary together.

That is, the development of nullities in one domain (say, *non*places) tends to foster their development in the other domains (*non*things, *non*people, and *non*services).

For example, it is largely in *non*places that one finds *non*things, *non*people, and *non*services. Since *non*places are expanding, so too are the other nullities. For example, once-unique department stores, and small chains of such stores, have been swallowed up by huge conglomerates and, as a result, have come to look increasingly alike. Federated Department Stores Inc. now includes such formerly independent department store minichains as Bloomingdale's, Macy's, and the Bon Marche. In other words, and following this book's grand narrative, once something, department stores have increasingly moved in the direction of nothing. More specifically, the men's departments of such stores that once looked and operated like distinct haberdashery shops now look increasingly alike as they are divided up into similarly looking and logoed[52] boutiques featuring much the same clothing of most of the same leading designers—Nautica, Calvin Klein, Polo, and so on. Because department stores now tend to be part of chains, they are characterized by centralized buying and by general contracts negotiated with designers and manufacturers that lead all department stores in the chain to offer many identical products and product lines. In addition, personalized service has given way to increasingly impersonal relationships between clerk and customer, and even to an ever-greater pervasiveness of a do-it-yourself, *non*service, system for customers. Fewer people work in these departments, and those who do are likely to act more like *non*people. The example of the contemporary department store makes clear the fact that the increase in nothing in one domain serves to support its increase in other domains.

The simple fact is that it is difficult for things, people, and services to survive in *non*places; they do not seem to fit there. First, people who consume in *non*places are generally looking for *non*things. They do not expect to find things (e.g., a custom-made suit, a truly unique piece of handmade pottery) in *non*places; they may even be jarred by the presence of things in *non*places. The result is that things are increasingly unlikely to be found in *non*places. Thus, if the work of a craftsperson such as a potter from Oaxaca, Mexico, were to find its way into Target or Wal-Mart (clearly an unlikely possibility), it would not be likely to sell well and would quickly be withdrawn from the shelves. Given the low-price image of Wal-Mart, those who shop for pottery there are generally looking for low-cost, mass-produced items. They are unlikely to be interested in, or willing to pay, the higher price for handmade Oaxacan pottery.

Second, consumers do not expect to encounter employees who act like full-fledged people in *non*places. They expect either to serve themselves or to receive minimal assistance from *non*people. Encountering an employee who is a person in such a setting would be disconcerting and might even drive the consumer away. For their part, those employees who want to act like people rather than *non*people would be discouraged by management (because, e.g., it is too time-consuming and labor-intensive) as well as by the negative reactions of consumers to their behavior (many do not want to deal with people in *non*places). The likelihood is that those employees who want to act in this way would quickly be driven to leave such settings in search of those where their actions are more appreciated. The problem is that with the progressive disappearance of places, there are fewer and fewer settings available to them. The long-term result, at least logically, would be the complete disappearance of people (as opposed to *non*people), at least in many areas of the service sector of the work world.

Third, and relatedly, customers do not expect service, and the clerk who offers it is not likely to be rewarded by the consumer. That is, customers are likely to brush off, or even react negatively to, offers of assistance. More important, the personalized service that is offered is not likely to lead to higher sales and may even have an adverse effect on sales. The result is that services are likely to cease to be offered, and as pointed out above, the employees offering them are apt to leave the *non*place sooner or later.

Of course, much the same argument can be made with whatever nullity one begins. The pervasive existence of *non*things leaves less and less of a role for places and makes for their progressive replacement by *non*places. *Non*things seem out of their element in places. The increasing tendency for people to become *non*people on the job, and for consumers to prefer to deal with *non*-people, makes it unlikely that places will survive, because there are no people to work in such settings, and, in any case, consumers prefer to deal with *non*-places and *non*people. And the increasing preference for *non*services, even do-it-yourself services, tends to drive places out of existence, leaves those who desire to be people fewer settings in which to work, and tends to drive away things that need to be sold by people in places offering full-scale services.

Thus, there is a kind of vicious, self-reinforcing process here in which *non*places, *non*things, *non*people, and *non*services tend to mutually reinforce one another, leading to their increasing pervasiveness in the social world. Of course, places, things, people, and services survive, but it is more on the margins of the social and economic world. They tend to continue to exist for the elites who can afford the high premium that has now come to be associated with that which was in the past a low-cost reality for almost everyone. However, they also continue to exist for those of more modest means in the form of rural roadside fruit and vegetable stands, craft fairs, co-ops, and the like. While those who are troubled by the increasing prevalence of nothing might be given hope by such phenomena, it is clear that these tend to be throwbacks to the past that, at best, offer highly limited and difficult-to-find alternatives to nothing.

If there is a vicious circle of the kind described above, is it possible to choose a starting point, a development that set the whole process in motion? In one sense, it is probably impossible to find such a point of origin,[53] but if one were forced to choose, it would have to be in the realm of things, specifically their mass manufacture. Thus, as good a starting point as any would be Henry Ford and the first automobile assembly line, especially perhaps the mass production of the classic *non*thing, the Model T Ford, which was available, at first, in only one style and in only one color—black! Of course, over the years Ford found a way of producing many different styles and colors of automobiles, but they were still mass-manufactured and continued to approach the *non*thing end of the continuum.[54]

The problem of allowing for diversity, but still producing *non*things, has long since been solved by improving technologies that allow for the mass manufacture of products that seem highly diverse. This is known as the process of *sneakerization*,[55] where, for example, dozens, perhaps hundreds, of types of athletic shoes can be produced but still be mass-manufactured and able to retain economies of scale. Indeed, even customized production that would seem to produce what are, by definition, things is being transformed into *mass customization*,[56] whereby even seemingly customized products can take on at least some of the qualities of *non*things.

In any case, if we take the mass production of *non*things as our starting point, it is clear that expanding production of such *non*things led to an increased need for *non*places in which they could be sold. True, *non*things could be, and were, sold in places, but there was a clear and growing disjuncture between the two. *Non*things seemed out of place, and increasingly so, in places. This disjuncture gave impetus (of course, other factors were involved) to the development of *non*places—for example, supermarkets, chain stores, franchises, discounters—where the increasing number of *non*things seemed to fit perfectly.

Then, of course, people began to seem odd and out of their element selling *non*things in *non*places. In any case, their skills were no longer needed; *non*people do as good a job selling *non*things, they work for less, and most generally they constitute a better fit with selling *non*things. People were no longer needed because *non*things sold themselves, or better yet were presold by massive advertising campaigns. Thus, no selling was required in a supermarket because consumers simply bought what they needed, compared prices on their own, and, most important for our purposes, purchased name- (or house-)brand products presold by massive advertising campaigns that sought to create invidious distinctions between the product advertised and competing products (soap is an excellent example). Furthermore, people had fewer and fewer settings to turn to for such work, as they were not only replaced by *non*persons but also by self-service, where even the *non*person was no longer required.

Finally, of course, the process of *non*things leading to *non*places and then *non*people led to *non*services. Service was no longer needed to sell *non*things, it was no longer needed and did not fit very well in *non*places, and *non*people, again by definition, did not, perhaps could not, offer anything but *non*services. The supermarket and later the fast-food restaurant are, of course, classic examples of *non*places where *non*service is the norm.

I do not want to take this argument too far and suggest some lawlike changes resulting from the mass manufacture of *non*things. Furthermore, developments in the other nullities were more or less simultaneous with the rise of large numbers of *non*things, and the development of all of them may have been, at least in part, the result of external changes of various sorts. For example, it is likely that the sheer increase in the population and the difficulties involved in serving ever-greater numbers of people led to the increase in *non*things,[57] as well as the other nullities discussed in this chapter. Finally, there were surely changes within each domain that led to the rise of *non*places, *non*people, and *non*services. For example, rising labor costs may have forced the substitution of *non*people for people, with an accompanying shift to more *non*services. Furthermore, technological advances like automated telephone technology led to the elimination of many phone operators, with the remaining employees serving more as *non*people.

While it has historically been the case that mass manufacture was the starting point of this process, it may now be the case, with the shift from production to consumption, that it is mass consumption that is the new point of origin. The prime example is Wal-Mart, which is now so big and so powerful that it dictates terms to producers rather than vice versa. It tells them what it wants, how much it needs, and what it is willing to pay.

It is also the case that phenomena at the something ends of the four continua of concern here tend to occur together, and the presence of one makes the others more likely. Without going into much detail or into all the permutations and combinations, if you start with, say, things, that is, phenomena that exist at the something end of the continuum, then you are likely to need places in which to sell or offer them, people with the skills and sophistication to deal with and sell them, and to offer an array of services to consumers interested in acquiring things.

This suggests a way of reversing the seemingly inevitable trend in the direction of nothing in all of these realms. That is, either founding places, or creating things, or training people, or offering services has the potential of introducing something into the circle, and once established, it will require the creation of something in the other realms as well.

An Illustrative Excursion to the Movies

A powerful illustration of the various types of nothing discussed in this chapter is to be found in the movie *One Hour Photo* (2002). Robin Williams plays Sy Parrish, the operator of a one-hour photo lab within the confines of a fictitious big-box store named Savmart (a thinly disguised send-up of Wal-Mart). The Savmart store is clearly depicted in the movie as nothing. It is certainly part of a great chain that has been constructed on the basis of a model that was created by a central office that also manages what goes on there on a day-to-day basis. Like the chains on which it is modeled, it is likely that one Savmart looks much like every other one. There are great long aisles with endless shelves loaded with products lacking in distinctive substance. There is a pervasive coldness in the store atmosphere (and in the attitude and behavior of the store manager) that is abetted by the abundance of white and icy blue colors. In case anyone misses the point, there is a dream sequence in which Parrish envisions himself standing alone in one of the store's great aisles amidst a sea of totally empty shelves. The red of the blood that begins to stream from his eyes is sharply distinguished from the whiteness that surrounds him. The pain in his face is in stark contrast to the coldness that envelops him. Savmart is clearly a *non*place, as is the photo lab housed within it.

Employees who operate the one-hour photo stand (and Savmart more generally) are expected to be *non*persons. The makeup, the nondescript clothes, the shoes that squeak when Sy walks the store aisles, and his unassertive and affectless demeanor all combine to make it seem as if Sy Parrish is the ideal *non*person required of his position. Sy has worked at the photo stand for a long time; he is virtually a fixture there. Indeed, like store fixtures, he acts, and is to be treated, as if he is not there. He is expected to interact with his customers rapidly and impersonally. This is made abundantly clear in the uncomfortable reactions of customers when Sy deviates from being the ideal *non*person by attempting to interact with them in a more personal manner.

The photo lab is offering a *non*thing—rapidly and automatically developed photographs. Those who oversee the development of the film and then hand over the photographs are not supposed to take a personal interest in them or to take a role in the process by which they are developed. This is clear when Sy calls in a technician because the Agfa photo machine is producing pictures that are slightly off and the technician becomes enraged for being called in on such a minor matter. The technician knows that few employees, let alone customers, recognize, or care about, minor variations in the quality of photos from such a *non*place as the photo lab at Savmart.

Finally, Sy is supposed to provide a *non*service. That is, he is expected simply to accept, in a very routine fashion, rolls of film handed him by customers, to have them developed as quickly and efficiently as possible, and to hand them back to customers in exchange for payment. However, Sy cares about the photos and their quality, at least as much as the automated technology will allow. He wants to provide the best possible service, especially to his favorite customers. Of course, he is not supposed to have favorites (that would be something), and this is where the movie grows interesting, because Sy, for his own personal reasons, has sought to turn nothing into something. Indeed, the movie can be seen as a cautionary tale on what happens when efforts are made to transform the nothing that pervades our everyday lives into something.

Sy is quite taken with one particular family that he regards as ideal (Sy's personal life is totally empty; indeed, he buys a photo of a woman at a street market and later shows it off, claiming that it is of his mother). When the mother and son of that family come in with some film to be developed, it is clear that he is fond of them, and he acts like, and wants to be treated by them as, a person. He also treats them as people, and even though it is late in the day, he agrees to have the photos developed before the close of business. In other words, he offers them personalized service! Furthermore, when he learns that it is the boy's birthday, he gives him a free instant camera claiming (falsely) that it is store policy to give children such gifts on their birthdays. In acting like a person (he also demonstrates personal knowledge of the family and asks personal questions), Sy is seeking to turn these *non*-places (one-hour photo, Savmart) into places. And the *non*things that he works with—automatically developed photos—are obviously transformed into things by Sy.

It turns out that Sy has an unnatural interest in this family and is routinely making an extra copy of every photo he has had developed for them. Furthermore, he is papering his otherwise desolate apartment with these photographs. When another woman brings in a roll of film to be developed (he inappropriately—for a *non*place and from a *non*person—asks if he knows her from somewhere), he remembers her from one of his favorite family's photos on his wall. It turns out that she works with the husband of that family, and when, late at night, he examines her developed photos, he discovers that the two are having an affair. Enraged, Sy sets out to end the affair, first by "accidentally" putting a photo of the lovers in with a set of photos developed from the camera he gave the child. When, after viewing that photo, the wife does not seem to react in the desired way by confronting the husband and throwing him out (Sy spies on the family that night and witnesses a normal dinner free of confrontation), Sy follows the lovers to a hotel (also depicted as a *non*place), where he has a confrontation with them, using his camera as a "weapon." While Sy ends up being arrested, the affair seems at an end, and it is at least possible that the "ideal" family will be restored to its "proper" state. One lesson seems to be that "somethingness" lurks beneath the nothing that pervades our lives. Another is that the norm in our society and in our lives is pervasive nothing, and those who violate it are at least slightly abnormal and do so at great risk to themselves.

We have now explored the five dimensions of nothing (and something) in Chapter 2 and the four main types of something and nothing (in this chapter). However, more needs to be said about our basic concepts (something and nothing), and it is to that further analysis that we turn in Chapter 4.

4

Nothing

Caveats and Clarifications

I have now spent two chapters devoted primarily to clarifying what I mean by nothing, as well as how it relates to something and the something-nothing continuum. However, nothing is an elusive and complicated idea. Thus, I will devote yet another chapter to it seeking to better understand it and the related ideas that lie at the heart of this analysis.

Conceptual Aids in Understanding Nothing

Three additional ideas may help the reader get a better feel for the elusive concept of nothing (and, by implication, for something).[1] We can begin with the idea of an *empty manifold*. A manifold involves the centrally conceived and controlled repetition, perhaps over and over, of some phenomenon. Most, if not all, forms of nothing are composed of such a multitude of units, and furthermore, each of those units is largely or totally empty. A fast-food restaurant is a largely empty manifold in that its form can be repeated throughout the United States and the world, while the nature of its contents (hamburgers, fried chicken, pizza) can vary greatly between chains, between parts of a country, or from nation to nation. Similarly, shopping centers can be seen as empty manifolds, with each highly similar iteration filled with variable content (the Gap, Banana Republic, Old Navy). That the fast-food restaurant and the shopping mall are both nothing, at least in the sense of empty manifolds, is relatively easy to see in such physical settings.

Another term that relates to, and enhances our understanding of, nothing is *grid*. That concept communicates much the same idea as a (empty) manifold, that is, a series of parallel lines (like each of the 10-yard lines on a football field; a *grid*iron) repeated over and over with "nothing" between the lines. Thus, the endless repetition of a chain of fast-food restaurants can be seen as forming a kind of grid, as can their dispersion throughout a given geographic area. Indeed, fast-food chains such as McDonald's and Starbucks give careful study to the geographic placement of their settings and, in at least some places, set them up in a gridlike fashion.

The idea of a *template*, while related to that of a manifold and a grid, emphasizes something a bit different about nothing. Here we are talking about some sort of basic pattern or mold that is conceived and used centrally to create each new form. Since the same pattern is used over and over, each iteration of the form is more or less exactly the same as every other. Thus, all popular, branded commodities are clearly based on templates, and in almost all cases, each iteration is, for all intents and purposes, exactly like every other one (say, cans of Coca-Cola, each type of Nike athletic shoe, every Whopper, etc.). Places that stand toward the nothing end of the continuum are certainly created on the basis of templates, although they are now more variable in their construction (at least on the surface) and less obviously like every other setting of a given type than they have been in the past.

In spite of these contemporary variations, a basic template undergirds the creation of every setting such as a fast-food restaurant. And there are even templates used to train and constrain the people who work there and the way they offer services (e.g., those created and used at McDonald's Hamburger University as well as by graduates of that university who come to own or manage a McDonald's restaurant).

Terms like (empty) *manifold*, *grid*, and *template* help us to get a better understanding of nothing. At the same time, naturally, they enhance our sense of something as that which is *not* a product of a manifold, is *not* created on the basis of a grid or in a gridlike manner, and is *not* based on a template used to churn out many nearly identical copies.

Closely related to the idea of nothing, and more specifically manifold, template, and grid, is the idea of simulations, most closely associated with the work of the French postmodernist Jean Baudrillard.[2] To Baudrillard, a *simulation* is a copy of a copy for which there is no original. It could be argued that *all* forms of nothing are also simulations. That is, it is originals that have distinctive content (and are something), but copies—simulations—are by definition lacking in such content; they are nothing! Furthermore, it is precisely simulations that tend to be centrally created and controlled. Baudrillard's assertion that the world is being increasingly characterized and dominated by simulations is consistent with this book's grand narrative about the global proliferation of nothing.

Some Paradoxes

Given the further elaboration of the idea of nothing, it is time to make a number of things clear about this phenomenon, including the fact that *nothing is nothing* (and, relatedly, that something always has its elements of nothing).[3] It is also true that, wherever it occurs, nothing is still nothing; something becomes nothing and begets more nothing; and a lot of nothing is still nothing. What does all this seeming double-talk mean?

Nothing Is Nothing

First, the idea that nothing is nothing means that no phenomena exist at the furthest extreme of the nothing end of the something-nothing continuum. That is, all phenomena have at least a touch, a tad, of something. (Even a physical vacuum is not completely empty![4]) As alluded to above, this also means that no phenomena exist at the extreme something end of the continuum; all have at least some degree of nothing associated with them. That is, even a paradigmatic example of something—say, a great good place—has elements (say, the provision of electricity or of packaging for take-out orders) that are conceived and controlled centrally and that are lacking in distinctive content.

Second, there are always at least some people who find meaning in phenomena that are relegated by this analysis to the farthest reaches of nothing. In fact, as has already been mentioned, and will be discussed later, much of what is regarded here as nothing, or at least as lying toward that end of the continuum, is of great importance to large numbers of people. And, again on the other side, that which appears to virtually everyone to be quite something will, to at least some, seem to be nothing, or at least pretty close to it.

Third, some people (Sy Parrish, for example) struggle mightily to transform that which seems like nothing into something, and it is possible that their efforts will succeed, at least in their minds, to some degree. Conversely, there are those who, in their dealings with something, work equally hard to turn it into nothing.

For these and other reasons, while nothing is discussed throughout this book, the paradoxical point should be borne in mind that *nothing is truly nothing*! In fact, that should be obvious from the fact that an entire book is being devoted to . . . nothing. If nothing was truly and completely nothing, this book would be simply a series of blank pages.[5] It is clear to me, at least, that phenomena at the farthest reaches of the nothing end of the continuum have at least a bit of something, that the emptiest forms of nothing have the potential to be transformed into something.

Wherever It Occurs, Nothing Is Still Nothing

Wal-Mart (we discussed the fictional counterpart, Savmart, at the end of Chapter 3) is another paradigmatic form of nothing in that it is highly centralized and controlled from Bentonville, Arkansas, as well as from regional offices and warehouses. In fact, one of the great revolutions wrought by Wal-Mart is the methods and advanced technologies it developed to control what goes on in each of its stores. This is especially true of inventory, which is closely monitored by advanced technologies, and stores and shelves are restocked automatically when inventories dip to a certain point. And each Wal-Mart looks pretty much the same and has pretty much the same array of products in more or less the same places. That is, each Wal-Mart is lacking in distinctive content.

At one level, there are thousands of Wal-Marts in the United States and elsewhere in the world, but the fact that a lot of them are widely dispersed geographically does not alter the fact that they are nothing. In fact, the more of them there are, and the more spread out they are, the greater the need to place them ever closer to the nothing end of the continuum. They need to be more similar and to be subject to even more central conception and control to ensure that each of the Wal-Marts in such a large and far-flung empire operates in much the same way.[6]

It is abundantly clear that the arrival and spread of nothing tends to sound the death knell for many forms of something. Perhaps the best example is the arrival of a Wal-Mart in a small town, often on its outskirts, and the resulting decline and even demise of downtown small businesses. Not only is Wal-Mart nothing, and abundantly stocked with nothing, but the small businesses that are likely to lie more toward the something end of the continuum tend to disappear. Furthermore, so does the distinctive downtown business district and the community it supported. Instead of congregating there in the midst of something, people drive (often great distances) to the great nothingness of Wal-Mart. Of course, the Wal-Mart tends to lead to the development of a whole series of satellite businesses, many of which are likely to be chains of one kind or another. The nothingness of this largely suburban or even exurban environment replaces the somethingness, or at least the possibility of it, in the life of the center of the small town.

The impact on the large city is not nearly as profound. Wal-Mart remains a largely small-town and suburban phenomenon, but others of its ilk (e.g., superstores such as Bed Bath & Beyond, Linens-N-Things, Best Buy, and Borders) are increasingly found in big cities. Of course, other forms of nothing of concern here, especially the fast-food restaurant, have long since found their way into even the largest cities. A city like New York or London was, and is, the site of virtually every form of something one can think of. Such cities have not been immune to the spread of nothing, but they are so large and diverse that the impact of the spread of nothing is diffused and may itself give birth to new forms of something. One can rue the passing of various forms of something in, say, New York—the cafeteria, the Jewish delicatessen, the Italian grocery, the Irish pub, and so forth—but there are also many new bodegas and small restaurants serving things like jerk chicken that have tended to replace them. True, there are now also many fast-food restaurants, superstores, and the like in New York, but they seem to coexist with many forms of somethingness. Furthermore, it is there that one sees the simultaneous expansion of new forms of somethingness—for example, the rise of an enormous variety of ethnic restaurants from all over the world.

Nevertheless, it is hard to escape the view that the world's great cities have all witnessed the explosive growth of nothing, with the result that there is much more in each of these cities that closely resembles what is to be found in the others.[7] This tends to leave at least some visitors with a sense that some of the forms that made a given city distinctive (something) have been supplanted by various forms of nothing. Thus, the cities themselves seem to have moved in the direction of nothingness even though in a broader sense they may be more diverse than ever before; they offer a greater variety of somethingness.

For example, in the last few years London has witnessed the opening of numerous Starbucks coffeehouses, especially in the downtown areas most likely to be seen and visited by tourists. Thus, the areas around Piccadilly Circus and the West End (the theater district) are awash with Starbucks coffee houses. Such a uniform chain is one of the prime examples of nothing, and its proliferation in the most visited areas of that city tends to give it the feeling of nothingness. However, the proliferation of Starbucks is not restricted to the tourist areas. The Fleet Street area, populated by businesspeople, lawyers, and the like, seems to have at least as great a concentration of Starbucks as London's tourist areas. However, London is a huge and highly diverse city that has, at least until now, been able to absorb chains like Starbucks and still retain its distinctiveness.

Tokyo has long had American fast-food chains of various types but is now witnessing an influx of more specific, often upscale chains, largely from New York City.[8] Among the chains that have recently migrated to Tokyo are Dean & DeLuca, Grand Central Oyster Bar, and H&H Bagels. Nathan's Famous hot dogs, something when it originated in Coney Island in 1918, has moved to the nothing end of the continuum and now has about 200 outlets in the United States. It has joined the invasion of Tokyo, and Japan more generally, and plans still further expansion there. Starbucks has been a strong presence in Tokyo since 1996 and in Japan more generally, where it now has about 600 outlets. Like London, Tokyo (as well as Japan in general) can absorb this influx, at least for the foreseeable future, without surrendering its basic character.

A more midsize city, say, in the midwestern United States, is another story. Those cities are more likely to resemble the small town described above than they do New York, London, or Tokyo. It is in those cities that nothing is more likely to replace something. Furthermore, in comparatively new cities of this ilk, or ones that have experienced their growth relatively recently, there were likely to be few forms of something in existence prior to the explosion of nothingness. Thus, it was not a matter of nothing replacing something; nothing had the field virtually all to itself. The forms of nothingness did not need to compete with, or overcome, parallel forms of something, and that made their spread throughout midsize American cities that much easier.[9]

A similar point applies at the societal level. That is, as societies grow more affluent, they have increasing interest in acquiring what the wealthiest countries have, and much of that can be included under the heading of nothing. For their part, the affluent nations (the centers of nothingness), especially the states that represent them and their most powerful companies, are deeply interested in exporting the goods, services, and ideas that reflect and manifest nothing to whatever country will accept and pay for them (and often even to those that are not so eager to accept them). There are countries that are largely, perhaps even totally, ignored, perhaps because of their hostility or lack of openness to these things, but in the main every nation is at least a potential market for nothing. As nations that once fell below some economic (and perhaps political) threshold achieve a minimal level of economic success, they are likely to be bombarded with many things, including large amounts, and an incredible variety, of nothing. Of course, this is not one-sided. The people of such nations have seen these things in the media, and they generally crave what is swamping the more developed world. Furthermore, there are indigenous entrepreneurs eager to meet this demand, and to stoke it further, because of the great profits that are likely to await them.

The result is that an ever-increasing number of nations and areas of the world are coming to be penetrated by nothing, and the more affluent they become, the greater the nothingness. Nothing, wherever it occurs (small town, metropolis, nation, or even globally), is still nothing.

Something Becomes Nothing and Begets More Nothing

One of the tendencies in this discussion has been to categorize phenomena as either something or nothing. However, such categorizations can and do change over time. For one thing, at their creation, various forms are likely to be local, decentralized, and heavily laden with content—to be something (e.g., the original McDonald's restaurant created by the McDonald brothers in California). However, over time, especially if the objective is to have the forms grow dramatically, there is a tendency to centralize conceptualization and control further and to denude them of as much of their content as possible so that they can proliferate more rapidly and extensively.

For example, the founder of Kentucky Fried Chicken, the "real" Colonel (Harlan) Sanders, was very proud of his chicken, especially the gravy and secret seasonings originally made at home by his wife. In fact, his goal was to create such delicious gravy that people would have little interest in the chicken. However, when Sanders sold his business in 1964, the new owners dramatically altered the gravy in order to cut costs, simplify the product, and speed up the time it took to prepare. Sanders expressed his outrage to his friend Ray Kroc (founder of the McDonald's chain): "That friggin' . . . outfit . . . they prostituted every goddamn thing I had. I had the greatest gravy in the world and those sons of bitches they dragged it out and extended it and watered it down that I'm so goddamn mad."[10]

At the same time, as content is reduced or eliminated, the form is elaborated in ever-greater detail so that it can be re-created and used easily in diverse settings by many different people. Thus, for example, the company manual, frequently many volumes in length, grows to explain more and to take more contingencies into account. An organization develops more and more subgroups, departments, and divisions to handle various matters. Specialized personnel are hired and trained to handle increasingly detailed issues and transactions. Nothing tends to beget other forms of nothingness.

A Lot of Nothing Is Still Nothing

Another of the paradoxes pointed up by this analysis relates to the fallacy that quantity, especially large quantities, is related to quality.[11] At the individual, collective, and societal levels, there seems to have emerged a widespread belief that more is better (supersizing everything is one contemporary example[12]). However, if much of what is being produced and distributed in the world is at the nothing end of the continuum, then more of nothing, even a lot of nothing, does not necessarily translate into something. Indeed, it could be argued, paralleling Gresham's law as it relates to money,[13] that increases in nothing tend to leave less and less room for something. Thus, not only does a lot of nothing not add up to something, but the increasing quantity of nothing leaves less space for something.

We see increasing numbers of people eating more meals at fast-food restaurants, wearing Gap clothes, and staying at Holiday Inns. But eating more meals at fast-food restaurants, or supersizing everything we eat, does not transform the meals or the food into something. Furthermore, while we may now be able to do and acquire lots of nothing, that tends to leave little time, money, and desire for something. So, lots of nothing is still nothing, and its acquisition tends to inhibit our ability to find and consume something.

The Social Construction of Nothing

While we operate in this book with an objective sense and definition of nothing, what ultimately matters is the way in which people define things. To put it another way, what often matters most, following a famous work by Peter Berger and Thomas Luckmann, is the "social construction of nothing."[14]

While there is a dispassionate character to the analysis presented in the body of this book—an effort to describe nothing and its relationship to something as objectively as possible—it is recognized from the outset that not only are there problems with such a modern, disinterested approach,[15] but it is people's subjective definitions and constructions of the phenomena of concern here that are of greatest importance. As I have pointed out several times, many of the phenomena that are seen from the point of view of this book as falling toward the nothing end of the continuum are, in fact, viewed by many people as something. As the reader is well aware, the term *nothing* is used here in the analytical sense of centrally conceived and controlled forms largely empty of distinctive content. In this sense, nothing, as well as something, are ideal types that offer no evaluative judgment about the social world, but rather are methodological tools to be used in thinking about and studying the social world. As I pointed out earlier, a major objective here is to develop a series of analytical tools to allow us to do a better job of theorizing about and empirically studying nothing (and something).

While it sometimes will seem as if that is precisely what we are doing, we cannot really discuss these phenomena apart from their relationship to human beings and their definitions of the social world. To put this more generally and theoretically, nothing and something (and everywhere in between) are *social constructions*. In other words, being something or nothing is not inherent in any place, thing, person, or service.[16] All of the latter are transformed into something or nothing by what people think about and do in and/or in relationship to them. It is for this reason, as we will see, that there is often a discrepancy between what is defined in these pages as nothing and the definitions of those involved in, or with, them who are likely to define them as something.

However, while there are no characteristics inherent in any phenomenon that make it necessarily something or nothing, there are clearly some phenomena that are easier to redefine or to transform into something, while others lend themselves more easily to being transformed into, or remaining, nothing. Thus, one could turn a personal line of credit into nothing, but the personal relationship involved makes that difficult. On the other side, one's relationship to one's credit card company could be transformed into something, but the distant, preconceived, controlled, and impersonal nature of that relationship makes that problematic. Thus, still another way of putting the grand narrative of concern in this book is to argue that we have witnessed a transformation from phenomena that lend themselves more easily to becoming something to phenomena that are more easily transformed into nothing.

However, people's definitions are frequently at variance with, and sometimes diametrically opposed to, the objective definitions of nothing and something employed here. This is not only true of defining nothing as something but also the converse definitions of what is conceived here as something as nothing. How else are we to explain the decline, even disappearance, of such forms of something as the meal cooked at home from scratch, the farmers' market, the craft fair, and so on?[17] That is, it appears that they are declining, because people have come to define these forms of something as unimportant. Well, of course there are other explanations. For example, the decline of the home-cooked meal is traceable to the increase of dual-earner families and the resulting fact that no one is home long enough to cook such a meal. However, that is less an alternate explanation and more one way of better understanding why the home-cooked meal has come to be defined as nothing. In any case, there are many interesting issues involved in the dissociation between objective realities and social definitions and constructions.[18]

For example, that which was once considered nothing can come to be seen as something, and, in contrast, that which was once something can come to be viewed as nothing. In terms of the former, an example might be a cafeteria like the Automat (in New York and Philadelphia) that, in its day, might have been seen by many as standing close to the nothing end of the continuum, at least in comparison to small restaurants that it tended to supplant. There was a fair degree of rationalization in the Automat, with the best example being the windowed slots along one wall of the restaurant that held various food items. A customer inserted a few coins, originally nickels, into a slot next to the desired food and was then able to open the door and remove the food. Eliminated was "nonrational" interaction between employee and customer. However, the Automat was far from being totally dehumanized. It also had what defined most cafeterias—a food line (along another wall) with a variety of stations (vegetables, meats, desserts, etc.). A customer moved down the line selecting various items (which were doled out by employees behind the counter) and then moving on to the cashier to pay for the food. Furthermore, customers often became regulars, and many looked forward to regular interaction with people behind the counter, cashiers, and other customers. Overall, it represented, to at least some degree, a step in the direction of McDonaldization and therefore was likely to be found wanting by some who regretted the growth of such cafeterias at the expense of full-service restaurants. Specifically, some were likely to have complained about obtaining their food from compartments rather than directly from a cook or human server. Now, however, perhaps because it has passed into history (there is a display in the Smithsonian dealing with it) and been romanticized, the Automat, at least retrospectively and in comparison to the fast-food restaurant, seems to be anything but nothing and is now described as a "masterpiece."[19]

On the other side, an example of a phenomenon that once was something and is now seen, at least by some, as nothing is the strip mall. When such malls first opened (beginning in 1939), they must have appeared to many to be something. Now, however, that they have become numerous, routine, and routinized, such malls are more likely to be seen by at least some people as nothing. In fact, while shopping malls, especially those that are fully enclosed, continue to be important, older malls, especially uncovered strip malls, are being abandoned in large numbers.[20] Their content (their shops) has literally been lost (they've gone out of business); they have become "derelict landscapes" slowly disintegrating by the side of the road.[21]

Judgments about nothing (and something) are certainly affected by temporal changes. Standards change, as do the systems being judged, and this affects such judgments. The most important change affecting these systems is that they become routine, subject to the same basic blueprints. Thus, while they may have been full of distinctive content when they were newly minted innovations, they come to lose that characteristic as they are re-created endlessly and come to resemble one another to a great degree. At the same time, that which one may not have thought of as loaded with content (e.g., the greasy spoon, discussed below) comes to be redefined as something over time as a function of its decline as well as the rise of alternatives that seem comparatively devoid of content. As older systems decline, or even disappear, nostalgia sets in, and that which in its day may have seemed devoid of content comes to be seen in a completely different light.

This makes another point very clear—judgments about fullness and loss depend upon one's comparison base. Initial visitors to the first supermarkets may have seen them as great wonders, as something, because of all that was combined under one roof, of the cornucopia of goods available in one place. Others may have seen them as abominations, as nothing, in comparison to the content-rich (especially in terms of interpersonal relations) grocery stores, fruit and vegetable stands, butcher shops, and bakeries they were replacing. Today, the prevalence of fast-food restaurants may make the greasy spoon seem like something to at least some diners, but in their heyday many may have seen greasy spoons as largely empty.

However, the proliferation of nothing, including its global spread, raises an important issue about one's comparison base. If nothing becomes so predominant that it drives out, or relegates to the margins, places, things, people, and services, then many people lose a base from which to compare nullities. If virtually all one knows, if all that is available, is shopping malls, Gap clothes, telemarketers, and the "services" of ATMs, then how is one to conclude that these involve a loss? The coming crisis implied here is that people will increasingly come to live their lives surrounded by centrally conceived and controlled settings devoid of distinctive content, consuming things that lack distinctiveness, having interactions with people that are largely indistinguishable from all other such interactions, and receiving similarly indistinguishable services. And it is entirely possible, since more and more of us will be living our lives increasingly immersed in nothingness, that we won't even be aware of this trend and how it is affecting our lives. It could be argued that since the loss of something is, at least in part, in the minds of consumers, they are not aware that such a loss has occurred (at least in comparison to more content-laden alternatives that no longer exist or have been relegated to the margins of society). It may well be that nothingness will cease being seen as involving a loss and come to be seen as full.

The Economics of Nothing (and Something)

This section brings together a variety of thoughts on the economic aspects and implications of nothing (and something). Issues to be discussed include the consumption of nothing, the production and mass production of nothing, the relationship between wealth and nothing, and finally the application of the economic theory of creative destruction to nothing.

The Consumption of Nothing

The implication of much of what has come before is that people are consuming nothing and in ever-greater quantities. Since nothing is increasingly common and available, this translates into an overall increase in the level of consumption. Of course, various forms of something, as well as everything that falls at any point on the something-nothing continuum, are also being consumed. Given growing wealth, especially in developed countries, it is likely that people are also consuming more of something as well. Overall, it is clear that consumption is increasing dramatically.

There was a time when there was little concern for the role of consumption in the economy. The focus was on production and work. An economy was seen as doing well if it approached full production and full employment. However, beginning in the early 20th century and in the United States, greater attention began to be paid to the role of consumption in the economy, and over the years it has come to be seen as of increasing importance. Thus, there is now great interest in measures like the consumer confidence index, since increases or decreases in confidence are likely to lead to great changes in consumption, with profound implications for the economy as a whole. This increasing interest in, and importance of, consumption has been accompanied by a relative decline in the importance accorded to production and work-related measures, again especially in developed countries. This is traceable to the fact that in developed countries like the United States, there has been a dramatic decline in heavy manufacturing, and many of the jobs associated with it have disappeared. Of course, the vast majority of Americans continue to work, but much more now in service industries (such as fast food) that are closely related to consumption. Such work, and the service industries in which they are found, are certainly important to the economy. But in many ways the United States (and other developed nations) has become a consumer society, and it is the economic consequences of such consumption that are of great, and increasing, consequences to the United States and the global economy.

A concern for the economics of consumption largely focuses on those affluent enough to be active consumers, if not hyperconsumers, but it can and should be extended to those who cannot afford to play much of a role in consumption. In affluent countries such as the United States, there are clearly many people who live at, near, or below the poverty line and therefore are, at best, marginal consumers. This is especially true for a large part of Asia and most of Africa, where billions of people are having a hard enough time simply surviving, let alone being active consumers of anything but the barest essentials needed for survival. Thus, a concern for the economics of consumption must include not only the affluent consumers who are increasingly important to the economy but also those who are marginal consumers and relegated to the lower rungs of the system of social stratification.

The Production of Nothing

As is the case above, and throughout this book, the focus is on consumption for a number of reasons, not the least of which is the tendency for many scholars and laypeople to largely ignore it (except in their day-to-day lives) and to focus on issues relating to production (work, factories, unemployment, etc.). There is a wide-scale "productivist bias" that this book seeks to counter by focusing on consumption. As a result, I will have little to say about the production of the goods and services (largely nothing) that lie at the heart of consumer culture, but that does not mean that it is an unimportant issue. When we turn to the production of nothing, we find a very different situation than in the case of the consumption of nothing. That is, while, as we have seen, those who inhabit the least developed portions of the world are largely uninvolved in the world of consumption, can afford to purchase little, if any, of the various forms of nothing, and in any case have little or no access to many of them, it is they who are increasingly likely to *produce* the wide array of consumer culture's goods and services that are so central to the world's more developed countries. Thus, the various forms of nothing are increasingly less likely to be produced in high-wage, developed countries when all of this nothingness can be produced in much the same way, but far more cheaply, in less developed parts of the world.

For example, large numbers of Indonesians are involved in producing Nike shoes.[22] Their wages are a fraction of those paid comparable workers in the United States and not enough to support a family. In addition, workdays can be extraordinarily long (as much as 15 hours per day, six to seven days per week); the factory is likely to be hot, noisy, and smelly; on the glue line there is the danger of inhaling toxic chemicals; it is not unusual for workers to lose parts of their fingers on the shoe-press machine; and sexual abuse and favors are not unknown.

The problems of third world workers in such factories (and in many other settings) are well documented. However, this analysis points to yet another problem that relates to poverty surrounded by unprecedented affluence. As their workday proceeds, third world producers of nothing (say, Nike sneakers) may find themselves surrounded by mountains of it, and in this, they are much like the consumers in wealthy countries. However, *unlike* those consumers, these workers cannot, and likely will never be able to, afford to consume the *non*things (Nike sneakers cost about the same in Indonesia as they do in the United States, while income in Indonesia is a fraction of that in the United States) that are quickly packaged and shipped off to developed nations where there are large numbers of people who can afford them.

Not only are the economic problems of those in less developed countries well known, but so are the ways in which those problems have been exacerbated by globalization.[23] Most generally, the argument is made that instead of bringing untold benefits, globalization has made the situation worse, economically and in many other ways, in the less developed world.[24]

This discussion points to yet another problem—the *double affliction* that confronts those who do such work in those countries. That is, they are both forced to produce much of the developed world's various forms of nothingness *and* they are unable to afford to buy most, if not all, of them, even though they are surrounded by them during their (usually long) workdays and are involved with their production on a daily basis. It must be abundantly obvious that they are producing, at low wages, that which is to be enjoyed by those of much greater wealth in the developed world. To at least some of these workers, this must be frustrating, galling, and the cause of enormous hostility and aggression. Of course, the abject poverty and the many other hardships that accompany all of this are far greater problems, but this poverty, surrounded by an abundance of nothing, can only serve to make everything seem that much worse.

The point is that while I focus on consumption in this book, there are many issues relating to production that are also worth thinking about and pursuing. While we have been discussing the problems of workers in less developed countries in this section, many workers in developed countries face many of the same problems. While they may be able to afford Nike caps, expensive forms of nothing like Gucci bags (unless they are cheap knockoffs) remain out of reach for large numbers of these workers.

The problems of the latter are exacerbated by the fact that they, unlike workers in less developed countries, live in the midst of rampant consumption and the large number of people who can afford a seemingly endless number and variety of goods and services. Thus, they are even more aware of the disconnect between what they are able to afford and what is available in, and an integral part of, consumer culture. Wherever low-income workers in developed countries turn, they see products, advertisements, and people conspicuously buying and using all of these goods and services.

Mass Production and Grobalization

In the context of discussing production we need to deal with the difficult issue of whether it is possible to determine which comes first—nothing or its globalization, or more precisely, its grobalization. The key components of the definition of nothing—central conception and control, lack of distinctive content—tend to lead us to associate nothing with the modern era of mass production. After all, it is the system of mass production that is characterized by centralized conception and control, and it is uniquely able to turn out large numbers of products lacking in distinctive content. While there undoubtedly were isolated examples of nothing prior to the Industrial Revolution, it is hard to find many that fit our basic definition of nothing.

Thus, as a general rule, nothing requires the prior existence of mass production. However, that which emanates from mass-production systems need not necessarily be distributed and sold globally. Mass-produced items may be sold initially locally and then in some cases expand to the national level. In fact, some mass-produced products (beer, for example; milk is another example) may remain restricted to a local market, although some may successfully gain a national market (Budweiser, for example). There are even a few beers (Beck's, Corona, Foster's) that have come to be global but only after they were successes within their home nation. (For more on this, see Chapter 5.) Yet another possibility is a mass-produced product that begins, and succeeds, as that which is to be sold globally.

However, there are great pressures on those who mass-produce nothing to market it grobally. Of course, not all forms can be marketed globally, but that which has such a potentiality is likely to be pushed in that direction. Thus, there is now a very close relationship between mass production and grobalization; the view here is that *both* are crucial to the creation of nothing and are prerequisites to it.[25]

There are many different routes, and even more detours, involved in making the transition from being a local to a grobal product. Some of the most interesting examples lie in the realm of folk art that has come to be mass-produced and sold throughout the world. Take, for example, such historic examples of something as kokopellis from the southwestern United States and matryoshka dolls from Russia. At their points of origin long ago in local cultures, these were clearly handmade products that one would have to put close to the something end of the continuum.

For example, the kokopelli, usually depicted as an arch-backed flute player, can be traced back to at least A.D. 800 and to rock art in the mountains and deserts of the southwestern United States.[26] Such rock art is clearly something, but in recent years, kokopellis have become popular among tourists to the area and have come to be produced in huge numbers in innumerable forms (figurines, lamps, key chains, light switch covers, cookies, Christmas ornaments, etc.) with increasingly less attention to the craftsmanship involved in producing them; indeed, they are increasingly likely to be mass-produced in large factories. That is, they have moved away from the something end of the continuum and toward the nothing end of that continuum. More recently, they have moved out of their points of origin in the Southwest and come to be sold globally. In order to be marketed globally at a low price,[27] much of the distinctive character and craftsmanship involved in producing the kokopelli is eliminated. Furthermore, offending elements are removed in order not to put off potential consumers anywhere in the world. In the case of the kokopelli, the exposed genitals that usually accompanied the arched back and the flute have been removed. The mass production and ultimately grobalization of kokopellis has moved them progressively closer to the nothing end of the continuum.

A similar scenario has occurred in the case of the matryoshka doll (from 5 to as many as 30 dolls of increasingly smaller size nested within one another),[28] although its roots in Russian culture are not nearly as deep (little more than a century) as that of the kokopelli in the culture of the southwestern United States. Originally handmade and hand-painted by skilled craftspeople and made from seasoned birch (or lime), the traditional matryoshka doll was (and is) rich in detail. With the fall of communism and the Soviet Union, Russia has grown as a tourist attraction, and the matryoshka doll has become a popular souvenir. In order to supply the increasing demand of tourists, and even to distribute matryoshka dolls around the world, they are now far more likely to be machine-made, automatically painted, made of poor quality, unseasoned wood, and greatly reduced in detail. In many cases, the matryoshka doll has been reduced to the lowest level of schlock and kitsch in order to enhance sales. For example, the traditional, highly detailed designs depicting precommunist nobles and merchants have been supplemented by caricatures of global celebrities like Bill Clinton, Mikhail Gorbachev, and even Osama bin Laden.[29] Such mass-produced and -distributed matryoshka dolls bear little resemblance to the folk art that is at their root. The mass production and grobalization of these dolls have transformed that which was something into nothing. Many other products have followed that course, and still more will do so in the future.

While I have focused here on *non*things (that were at one time things), much the same argument can be made about places, people, and services. That is, they too have come to be mass-produced and grobalized. This is most obvious in virtually all franchises where settings are much the same throughout the world (using many mass-manufactured components), people are trained and scripted to work in much the same way, and the same "services" are offered in much the same way. They have all been centrally conceived, are centrally controlled, and are lacking in distinctive content. They have tended to replace indigenous shops of all types that were staffed by people who tended to offer individualized services.

Creative Destruction

One of the most influential economic theories, both in and out of academia, is what Joseph Schumpeter has called "creative destruction."[30] By this, he and others mean that economic progress inevitably leads to the destruction of older and outmoded economic forms. However, rather than mourn their passing, we should appreciate the fact that their demise means that space is opened for newer and more advanced forms. In fact, it is the newer forms that are likely to cause the destruction of the older ones. Overall, this is seen by supporters of this perspective as a good thing for the economy, which is, as a result, seen as progressively advancing as newer, more effective and efficient forms supplant older ones.

The theory of creative destruction was intended to apply to production. The replacement of older factories characterized by simple mechanical technologies by ones with advanced automated technologies would be an example of creative destruction in the realm of production. More contemporaneously, the outsourcing of service work from higher-priced American call centers to those in India would also be seen as exemplifying creative destruction as well-paid jobs in the United States are destroyed and lower-paying ones are created in less developed parts of the world.[31]

While the theory was not developed for, and has not been applied to, consumption and nothing, as well as globalization[32] and the consumption of nothing, there is no reason it cannot be used in this way. Indeed, it applies quite well. That is, it could be argued that it is through creative destruction that, for example, consumption settings that lie toward the something end of the continuum are being destroyed and replaced by the various forms of nothing that have concerned us thus far. This can be seen as being creative, because the latter are associated with newer and more advanced technologies, more efficient operations, lower prices due to economies of scale, and so forth.

While there is much merit to the theory of creative construction, even as it applies to consumption settings, it is difficult to ignore the fact that much that is simply destructive, and involves comparatively little that is constructive, is simply glossed over by this argument. This is true even in the realm of production in terms of the loss of older factories (e.g., the current closing of many American automobile plants) and the loss of jobs (e.g., American jobs lost in places like call centers as they are being outsourced to less developed nations). This is at least as true, and probably more so, in the realm of consumption. Many forms of something have suffered absolute declines and may have disappeared or be on the verge of disappearance. Of course, it is to a large extent the great good places that are being destroyed. One example is the greasy spoon,[33] the small café likely staffed by a short-order cook and perhaps a cashier and/or waitress. These were not noted for the quality of the food (the name is derived from the fact that the food was often greasy), but it was cooked to order, and over time the cooks came to know regular customers and their preferences. Friendly, if not intimate, relationships were likely to develop between customers and cooks, waitresses, and perhaps other regular customers. Greasy spoons continue to exist here and there, but in the main they have been supplanted by fast-food restaurants. They are most likely to continue to be found in areas—small towns and rural areas—where the population base is not large enough to sustain many, if any, fast-food restaurants.

A similar fate has befallen the small, local grocery store, which has been driven to the wall, and often out of business, by the supermarket (clearly lying toward the nothing end of the continuum). Likely a mom-and-pop operation, local grocers were apt to know many of their customers quite well. As a result, they were likely to do such things as put together and deliver regular orders and allow customers to run up tabs that were to be settled up on payday. If times were tough, the tab might have been extended for weeks, even months.

Then there is the case, discussed previously, of Wal-Mart and the fact that when it comes to a small town (usually its outskirts), it generally destroys most, if not all, of the downtown small businesses. If this is not destructive enough, there are the cases where some Wal-Marts have found they are not profitable in those locations and simply close their doors. Thus, a small town is left with neither its small shops nor its Wal-Mart. It is possible that in that case, the town itself could be destroyed.

It could be argued that all of these have suffered what they deserved, and in any case their fate was inevitable, from the point of view of "creative destruction."[34] That is, the greasy spoon, the neighborhood grocer, and the small-town shop, among many others, have largely disappeared, but in their place have arisen more "advanced" successors like the fast-food restaurant, the supermarket, and Wal-Mart. While there is no question that extensive destruction of older forms has occurred, and that considerable creativity is involved in the new forms, one must question Schumpeter's one-sidedly positive view of this process. Perhaps some things have been lost, even some measure of creativity, with the passing of these older forms. It may be that the destruction has not always been so creative.

Wealth and Nothing

While consumption and production are certainly economic issues, there is an even broader economic issue of concern here, and that is the relationship between wealth (and its absence—poverty) and nothing (and something), especially in the realm of consumption.

First, it is clear that, in general, there is an inverse relationship between income and the consumption of nothing. That is, those with high income and other sources of money, those who are relatively wealthy, can still afford to acquire various forms of something, whereas those with low income and little money, those who are comparatively poor, are largely restricted to the consumption of nothing.[35] Thus, only the affluent can afford expensive bottles of complex wine or gourmet French meals with truffles. Those with little means are largely restricted to Coca-Cola, Lunchables, microwave meals, and McDonald's fries.

Second, there is an economic floor to this, and those below a certain income level cannot even afford that which is categorized here as nothing. Thus, there are those near or below the poverty line in the United States who often cannot afford a meal at McDonald's or a six-pack of Coca-Cola. More important, there are many more people in the less developed parts of the world who do not have access to, and cannot afford, such forms of nothing. Interestingly, extreme poverty relegates people to something— homemade meals and brews made from whatever is available. However, in this case it is hard to make the argument for something. These forms of something are often meager, and those who are restricted to them would love to have access to that which has been defined as nothing throughout this book and by many people throughout the world.

Third, looking at the society as a whole, some minimum level of affluence and prosperity must be reached before it can afford nothing. That is, in the truly impoverished nations of the world, there are few ATMs, fastfood restaurants, and Victoria's Secrets. There simply is not enough income and wealth for people to be able to afford nothing; people in these societies are, ironically, doomed—at least for the time being—to something. Thus, they are more oriented to bartering, preparing food at home from scratch, and making their own nightgowns. It is not that they would not eagerly trade their something for the forms of nothing described above and throughout this book, but they are unable to do so. It seems clear that as soon as the level of wealth in such a country reaches some minimal level, the various forms of nothing will be welcomed, and, for their part, the producers of these forms of nothing will enter these markets eagerly.

Fourth, even the wealthiest of people often consume nothing.[36] For one thing, as I have pointed out previously, nothing is not restricted to inexpensive *non*places, *non*things, *non*people, and *non*services. Some forms of nothing—a Four Seasons hotel room, a Dolce & Gabbana frock, the salesperson at Gucci, and the service of a waiter at a Morton's steakhouse—are very costly, but they still qualify as nothing—relatively empty forms—as that term is used here. The consumption of these very expensive forms of nothing is obviously restricted to the uppermost reaches of the economic ladder (more on this below).

For example, not long ago I visited a very exclusive resort in Sardinia, Porto Cervo, on the Costa Smeralda. The potential for this area, marked by a beautiful harbor, surrounding hills, and a fine Mediterranean climate, was discovered several decades ago, and it was developed as a resort for the very wealthy. Since many residents arrive by yacht, huge concrete piers were built in the bay. While it may be a beautiful site when the piers are lined on both sides by magnificent yachts—mainly in August—the rest of the year the view is badly marred by these concrete abutments. Thus, most of the time it looks much more like a harbor for commercial shipping than a charming Mediterranean inlet. In other words, a unique and inherently beautiful harbor (something) has been transformed into nothing (yet another harbor for ships) in order to accommodate wealthy tourists and summer residents.

The developer placed tight restrictions on the nature of the housing that could be built in Porto Cervo. The result is that there is considerable uniformity in the housing and the town has the feeling of a sort of very expensive Levittown, albeit one that is built in a beautiful location with magnificent weather. There is little individuality associated with the architecture of the houses in the town and that dominate the hills surrounding the harbor. Thus, the nothingness of the houses looks down upon the nothingness in the harbor.

The town center turns out to be an outdoor shopping mall. However, since it is catering to the well-to-do, it is not characterized by low-end chains—no McDonald's or Wal-Mart is to be found. However, virtually all of the shops are outlets of the high-end chains of Italy (Valentino) and the world (Cartier). There are few local shops (places), and there are no small bakeries, grocers, butchers, and greengrocers. There is a supermarket, but even that is better thought of as a *non*place than a place.

Adding to the sense of nothingness, at least in the off-season—and most of the year is off-season for the wealthy visitors and (part-time) residents of Porto Cervo—is the fact that virtually no one lives in the town most of the time. The wealthy are likely to be there in August and perhaps on one or a few other occasions during the year. Interestingly, virtually no Sardinians live in Porto Cervo—it is simply too expensive for the vast majority of them. Those who work there travel in from the surrounding mountains and villages where the cost of living is a fraction of what it is in Porto Cervo. Thus, most of the year Porto Cervo is a sort of ultimate form of nothingness—a virtual ghost town with similar-looking houses and chain outlets that are both literally and figuratively empty. At those times, Porto Cervo almost seems like an exclusive Potemkin village.[37] Ironically, local Sardinians are "doomed" to live in small villages (places), to eat local fare (things), to be served by people they know very well, and to receive personalized service. Nonetheless—and this, once again, is the perversity of nothing—most local Sardinians would sacrifice their something in an eyeblink if they had a chance to obtain the various forms of nothing, including the ability to live in Porto Cervo.

Fifth, the wealthy are drawn to many of the same low-priced forms of nothing that cater to the mass of the population, even those who would be considered poor or very close to it. Thus, a credit card knows no income barriers, at least at the high end of the spectrum, and the same is true of ATMs. The wealthy, especially wealthy teenagers, are probably just as likely, and maybe even more likely, to be attracted to fast-food restaurants as those from virtually every other income group.

What all of this adds up to, then, is that there is no simple relationship between wealth and the consumption of nothingness. Most paradoxically, the wealthy consume surprisingly large amounts of nothing, and the very poor are sometimes so badly off that they have no choice but to consume something.

Expensive, Global Nothing

If a number of other examples had not already been offered, the thrust of this book might lead the reader to the impression that it is only inexpensive goods and services that are marketed grobally, but this, it should be obvious, would be incorrect. Indeed, one of the more important recent developments in this realm is the increasing global availability of designer products of all kinds. This, of course, is spearheaded by the dramatic expansion of such international brands and chains as Gucci, Valentino, and Dolce & Gabbana. Chains like these are marketing expensive products throughout the world.

Their success, at least from the point of view of the argument being made here, is traceable to the ways in which they have succeeded in applying the principles of nothingness to the high end of the market.

The best example of this is the famous Gucci bag, which is sold in Gucci shops (and elsewhere) throughout the world. That bag was centrally conceived, its production is centrally controlled, and there is nothing to distinguish one Gucci bag of a given type from any other. More generally, there is little to distinguish the essential nature of the Gucci bag from the Benetton sweater, and even the Big Mac, other than price and, perhaps, the quality of its components and workmanship. The Gucci bag is no worse and no better an example of nothing than the Big Mac, and this makes it perfectly clear that nothing can be expensive. Indeed, the wide-scale sale of knockoffs of the Gucci bag, and the difficulties involved in differentiating between real and fake Gucci bags, makes the fact that it is nothing abundantly clear.

Indeed, it could be argued that the high end of the market for expensive products is one of the frontiers currently being assailed and conquered by nothingness. As is clear given the problems being encountered by McDonald's, the low end of the market for nothing—in this case the fast-food market—is saturated, and it is increasingly difficult to derive profits from it. However, the high end of that market, which is occupied by chains and brands like Gucci, is still wide open, with the result that many other competitors will be entering and many more high-priced products will be transformed into nothing.

In Defense of Nothing

In this final section of this chapter I turn one of the main thrusts of the discussion on its head. That is, I have in the main been critical of nothing (and the loss of something), and that theme will continue to define the remainder of the book, especially the concluding chapter. However, there are arguments to be made in favor of nothing and its proliferation. Forms that are largely empty of social content and that are centrally conceived and controlled are *not necessarily problematic*.

There is no question that global proliferation of nothing has brought with it a number of benefits. To argue otherwise would be to believe that people are demanding, purchasing, and flocking to that which is without merit. However, there are many different forms of nothing, and each of them has its own set of benefits. Let us see what might be some of the positive characteristics that most, or all, of these forms have in common.

We would need to start with the perception, and in at least some cases the reality, that nothing is *comparatively inexpensive*.[38] A credit card costs little to acquire and may even be "free." Furthermore, if one pays one's bill in full each month, free credit is also obtainable.[39] Fast-food restaurants these days offer a number of menu items for a dollar, and there are the "value meals" for those who want more than just, say, a sandwich. Those tract houses, even McMansions, in suburban developments offer a lot of rooms, square feet, and amenities for what appears to be a comparatively low price. A week on a cruise ship for one low price—including all the food you can eat—seems like a steal. The list could be extended indefinitely, but the key point is that the various types of nothing seem inexpensive, at least in comparison to the possible alternatives.

A second advantage of nothing is *convenience,* which can take many different forms.[40] Lunchables is an entire lunch neatly prepackaged in its own tray that can be stored in the refrigerator and will not spoil or deteriorate while waiting to be eaten. Disney World offers everything one could want on a vacation—attractions, entertainment, shopping, hotels—at one self-contained location. Much the same could be said of cruise ships and Las Vegas casino-hotels. The credit card is undoubtedly far more convenient than carrying large amounts of cash, especially when one is traveling between countries with different currencies. A similar point can be made about the euro, which makes it far more convenient not only to travel in the nations that use it but also for those nations to do business with one another.

All of the examples of nothingness discussed in this book are characterized by the *efficiency* with which they can be produced and consumed. Mass manufacture and batch processing are intimately associated with all forms of nothingness. That is, the efficient production of products (*non*things) and the efficient handling of consumers (in *non*places, by *non*people, and with *non*services) are characteristic of nothingness. This efficiency is a lure to producers and managers because it promises not only great profits but systems that make for easy handling of products, sites, and people. Efficiency makes it easy for consumers to obtain and use the various forms of nothing.

Perhaps most important, nothingness has made a veritable cornucopia of virtually anything one can imagine available to more people throughout the world than ever before. It could be argued that nothingness has contributed significantly to the *monumental abundance* that is characteristic of the developed world, especially the United States, today. Furthermore, the promise is that this is just the beginning, and the range of that which is available, and the ease with which everything it encompasses can be obtained, will increase exponentially in the coming years.

We could undoubtedly enumerate many more advantages of nothing and in the process extend this list enormously, but this is enough to illustrate the point that there are certainly good reasons for the proliferation of nothing.[41]

Then there is the journalist who makes a strong case *for* nothing in an article titled "Quaint's Nice, But Sprawl Makes Me Weak at the Knees."[42] David Lindley grew up in England, spent most of the past 20 years in the United States, and has become an American citizen. He recently spent a year and a half in England doing research for a book, and he arrived there with "deeply etched images of my native country: thatched cottages, neat rose gardens, narrow country lanes and gruff jolly yokels in the pub, ooh-arr-ing engagingly."[43] At first, his romanticized images of something were reaffirmed: "There I was living on the edge of the Cotswolds. Hills dotted with sheep, secluded hamlets at the end of twisting roads, ancient stone walls, a cock crowing every morning, rabbits and pheasants darting across the lanes and fields. Deer, too, but dainty ones with spindly legs."[44] However, Lindley soon found himself attracted to the English town of Milton Keynes, a centrally planned community with neat houses looking very similar to, if not identical to, one another. In terms of this book's primary definition of nothing, Milton Keynes falls toward the nothing end of the continuum (a *non*place) and is regarded in this way by many in Britain who use it as the butt of many jokes and see it as "the very definition of *soulless modernity* and suburban *aridity*" (italics added).[45] Yet, Lindley liked the fact that

> on either side of the roads smartly trimmed grassy areas ran down to neatly planted trees, which partly conceal the residential areas. At the intersections there were shopping areas, with enormous stores where you could buy all the sneakers and kitchen appliances you might need. There appeared to be plenty of parking. Elsewhere there were industrial areas, of the modern, sanitized kind. . . . In the land of ancient villages and ivy-clad walls, I found myself daydreaming about shopping plazas and suburban sprawl, about strip malls and parking garages.[46]

In other words, the journalist daydreamed about nothing (especially the forms of nothing associated with, and pioneered in, the United States), but he was also put off by the something of old England: "As I was living so close to Oxford, I thought it would be easy to dash into the city for books or exotic foods from the city's covered market, to visit museums or just stroll around and act the tourist. . . . But a couple of times I tried driving into Oxford, only to chug around slowly for half an hour, fail to find a parking place, then give up and go home."[47] As a result, he came to the realization that while the quaintness of old England was okay for vacation, he wanted to live in the modern. England, or at least the area around Oxford, was seen as trapped in the "dead weight of historical tradition," and he found that he preferred the transience of the United States and its strip malls and shopping plazas. He concludes, "I'd rather live in urban America than in any Cotswold village."[48]

Of course, this specific defense of nothing can be extended in many directions. There is much to be said in favor of the proliferation of fast-food restaurants, credit cards, docs-in-a-box, pharmaceuticals, and the like. Thus, while this book has a critical edge, we must not conclude that there are not problems associated with something or that there are not people today, perhaps a majority, who prefer nothing to something and who have good reasons for that preference.

5

The Globalization of Nothing

C ontrary to appearances, and in spite of the great amount of attention
devoted to it throughout this book (and especially in the last three chapters), the central issue here is *not* nothing (or something) per se but rather its
globalization. In order to analyze the globalization of nothing, I introduced
the concept of grobalization as a complement to the idea of glocalization;
the two together are seen as the central processes under the larger heading
of globalization. To reiterate, at least briefly, globalization is seen as a
broad social process that encompasses both glocalization and grobalization.
Glocalization involves the integration of the global and the local, producing
a unique outcome wherever in the world it occurs. Grobalization involves the
imperialistic ambitions of corporations, states, and others and their imposition of their ways of doing things, products, and so forth on the local.
Glocalization is associated with the idea of heterogeneity, while grobalization
tends to produce at least some degree of homogeneity (e.g., the use of not only
credit cards but the same limited number of brands—especially Visa and
MasterCard—of cards) throughout the world.

It will be argued in this chapter that grobalization tends to be associated
with the proliferation of nothing, while glocalization tends to be tied more
to something and therefore stands opposed, at least partially (and along
with the remnants of the local itself), to the spread of nothing. It is the
fact that these two processes coexist under the broad heading of globalization, and because they are, at least to some degree, in conflict in terms of
their implications for the spread of nothingness around the world, that

globalization as a whole does not have a unidirectional effect on the spread of nothingness. That is, in some of its aspects (those involved in grobalization), globalization favors the spread of nothing, but in others (those related to glocalization), it tends toward the dissemination of something. This is also the major reason why the globe has not grown homogeneous, why there continues to be much heterogeneity in the world. More specifically, while we have undoubtedly witnessed a massive proliferation of nothing throughout the world, something continues to exist everywhere. And, something will continue to exist not only because of the coexistence and conflict between the grobalization of nothing and the glocalization of something but for other reasons as well. Perhaps the most important of these reasons is the fact that grobalization, especially the grobalization of nothing, often leads to counterreactions that inevitably involve that which is unique about the local. While this is important, bear in mind that the "local," in this case, is necessarily "tainted" by the grobal because it is brought into existence by it. Therefore, this is not the pristine local we might imagine, but rather it is probably better described as being a glocal phenomenon. These and many other issues are addressed in depth in this chapter.

Figure 5.1 offers the four basic possibilities that emerge when we crosscut the grobalization-glocalization and something-nothing continua (along with representative examples of the places-*non*places, things-*non*things, people-*non*people, and services-*non*services for each of the four possibilities and quadrants). It should be noted that while this yields four *ideal types,* there are no hard-and-fast dividing lines between them. This is reflected in the use of dotted lines in Figure 5.1. By the way, the use of the concept of the ideal type (derived primarily from the work of Max Weber) here makes it clear that the four quadrants developed in this chapter are not meant to be accurate descriptions of social reality as it relates to globalization but rather are methodological tools that allow us to think about that reality. Thus, to take one example—the grobalization of nothing—it should be clear that this is a methodological tool that allows us to better think about globalization anywhere in the world that it occurs (and that is now pretty much everywhere). However, there is nowhere in the world (including in the United States, the center of both grobalization and nothing) where that is all that exists. Thus, in any given locale we must use all four ideal types, all four quadrants, in thinking about, and studying, their relationship to globalization.

It is clear that Quadrants 1 (grobalization of nothing) and 4 (glocalization of something) in Figure 5.1 are of greatest importance, at least for the purposes of this analysis, because their relationship to one another represents a key point of tension and conflict in the world today, especially in the

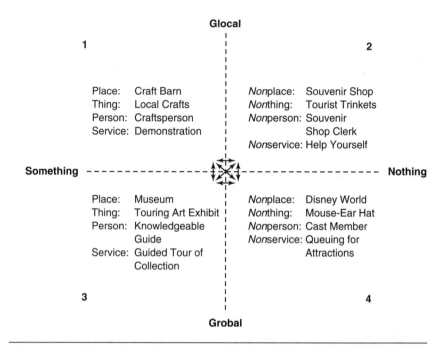

Figure 5.1   The Relationship Between Glocal-Grobal and Something-Nothing
With Exemplary *Non*places, *Non*things, *Non*persons, and
*Non*services

realm of culture in general and consumer culture in particular. Clearly, there is great pressure to grobalize nothing (Quadrant 4), and often all that stands in its way in terms of achieving global hegemony is the glocalization of something (Quadrant 1). I return to this conflict and its implications for our analysis below.

While the other two quadrants (2 and 3) are clearly residual in nature and of secondary significance, it is important to recognize that there is, at least to some degree, a glocalization of nothing (Quadrant 2) and a grobalization of something (Quadrant 3). From the point of view of this argument, they are not as important to the globalization process as the other two quadrants (and ideal types). Furthermore, whatever tensions may exist between them (and the other two types) are of far less significance than those between the grobalization of nothing and the glocalization of something. However, a discussion of the glocalization of nothing and the grobalization of something makes it clear, once again, that grobalization is not an unmitigated source of nothing (it can involve something) and glocalization is not to be seen solely as a source of something (it can involve nothing).

Elective Affinities

Returning to the main argument, the centrally important relationship between (Quadrant 4) grobalization and nothing and (Quadrant 1) glocalization and something leads to the view that there is an *elective affinity* between the two elements of each of these pairs.[1] The idea of elective affinity, derived, like the ideal type, from the historical comparative sociology of Max Weber, is meant to imply that there is not a necessary, lawlike causal relationship between these elements.[2] That is, in the case of neither grobalization and nothing nor glocalization and something does one of these elements "cause" the other to come into existence. Rather, the development and diffusion of one tends to go hand in hand with the other. Other ways of putting this is that grobalization-nothing as well as glocalization-something mutually tend to favor one another; they are inclined to combine with one another.[3] Thus, it is far easier to grobalize nothing than something; the development of grobalization creates a favorable ground for the development and spread of nothing (and nothing is more easily grobalized). Similarly, it is far easier to glocalize something than nothing; the development of glocalization creates a favorable ground for the development and proliferation of something (and something is more easily glocalized).

However, the situation is more complex than this since we can also see support for the argument that grobalization can, at times, involve something (e.g., art exhibits that move among art galleries throughout the world, Italian exports of food like Parmigiano-Reggiano cheese and Culatello ham, touring symphony orchestras and rock bands that perform in venues throughout the world) and that glocalization can sometimes involve nothing (e.g., the production of large numbers of identical local souvenirs and trinkets for tourists from around the world). However, I would *not* argue that there is an elective affinity between grobalization-something and glocalization-nothing. The existence of examples of the grobalization of something and the glocalization of nothing makes it clear why we need to think in terms of elective affinities and not lawlike relationships.

The Grobalization of Nothing

It is grobalization that is the key force in the global spread of nothing. As pointed out above, grobalization and nothing are highly compatible. On the one hand, an increasingly global market insists on large numbers and great varieties of nothing to satisfy the increasing demand for it, at least part of it fabricated (through advertising and marketing) by the forces (corporations, states, and others) that profit from the widespread distribution and sale of nothing. On the other hand, production of so much nothing, and the requirement that it be profitable or successful, leads to increasing pressure to find ever-larger as well as ever-more remote global markets for nothing.

The example of the grobalization of nothing in Figure 5.1 is a trip to one of Disney's Worlds, be it in Anaheim, Orlando, Tokyo, outside Paris, or the most recently opened (2005) park in Hong Kong, China. The existence of these parks at such diverse locales around the world, to say nothing of the many products sold in them and more broadly associated with the many Disney enterprises, makes them a grobal phenomenon. And, of course, all of this is nothing, because it is conceived and controlled by Disney headquarters, and the parks and products are largely lacking in distinctive content. That is, all the Disney parks around the world operate on the same basic principles, are structured in much the same way, have many of the same "lands" and attractions, and sell largely the same souvenirs. In terms of the key concepts being employed here, any of Disney's worlds is a *non*place and all of them are awash with a wide range of *non*things (such as mouse-ear hats), staffed by *non*people (the cast members, in costume or out), who offer *non*services (what is offered is often dictated by rules, regulations, and the scripts followed by employees).

The main reason for the strong elective affinity between grobalization and nothing is basically a far greater demand throughout the world for nothing than something. This is the case because nothing tends (although not always—see below) to be less expensive than something, with the result that more people can afford the former than the latter. Large numbers of people are also far more likely to want the various forms of nothing because their comparative simplicity and lack of distinctiveness make them relatively easy to appreciate. In addition, that which is nothing, largely devoid of distinctive content, is far less likely to bother or offend those in other cultures. Finally, because of the far greater sales potential, much more money can be, and is, devoted to the advertising and marketing of nothing, thereby creating a still greater demand for it than for something.

In contrast, highly distinctive phenomena may be too tied to a specific locale to be extracted from it, and their distinctiveness may make it difficult for them to take root in other locales. Thus, Parmigiano-Reggiano cheese is a product of a specific region of Italy, and while it is available globally, at least on a limited scale, its market potential in locales outside of Italy dominated by other cuisines is limited. For example, it is questionable, to put it mildly, how well such a distinctive cheese would go with a Tex-Mex dish, an Indian curry, or a Chinese stir-fry.[4] In contrast, Coca-Cola, and more generally colas of any brand or even no-name versions, have proven easier to extract from their American roots, fit with virtually every cuisine (it could be, and is, consumed with Tex-Mex, curry, and stir-fry), and have, as a result, been exported successfully throughout the world; in other words, cola, especially Coca-Cola, has been grobalized. In fact, a World War II soldier said he was fighting for "the right to buy Coca Cola again," and an advertising campaign in the 1990s proclaimed, "If you don't know what it [Coca-Cola] is, Welcome to Planet Earth."[5]

In fact, Coca-Cola is a prime example of what we are discussing here, especially since there was, at least historically, a concern for a process—"coca-colonization"—that clearly can be subsumed under the heading of the grobalization of nothing. That is, Coca-Cola is one of the best examples of nothing, and the term *colonization* clearly implies, and is one of the major forms of, grobalization.[6] Coca-colonization was a concern especially in post–World War II France, where many felt that French culture, especially its café and wine culture, was threatened by the arrival of Coca-Cola in the wake of large numbers of American troops.[7] It is also a good example of an issue that I discuss in Chapter 7. That is, Coca-Cola was, and is, a key component of American consumer culture, and wine was (and is) central to French consumer culture. Thus, grobalization, in this case, involved the threat, or at least perceived threat, of one nation's consumer culture to another. And, of course, consumer culture is a key part of any larger culture. While the strong negative reaction by the French to Coca-Cola may seem out of line with the issue involved, that reaction is more understandable when the larger domains of consumer culture and ultimately culture are seen to be involved.

Beer is an interesting case in this context, especially in contrast to cola. As pointed out earlier, beer is certainly a global phenomenon, but no single brand has penetrated much of the global market for it, at least to the extent that Coca-Cola, and to a lesser degree Pepsi-Cola, have become global soft drink brands. The beer brands that are global in reach—Beck's from Germany, Heineken from the Netherlands (described by some as the "only truly global beer brand"[8]), Foster's from Australia,[9] and Corona from Mexico, for example—tend *not* to come from the United States and to be much less important factors in the global beer business than Coke and Pepsi are in the global soft drink business. There are many reasons for this—beer does not travel as well or maintain its quality as long as soft drinks, only the soft drink syrup, or just the formula for the syrup, needs to be exported (there is no beer syrup), and so on. However, a central factor is certainly the fact that beer is a more variable and complex drink than cola, and there are important national and regional differences in beer tastes. In other words, beer, especially the better varieties, is more likely to be near the something end of the continuum, whereas soft drinks fall nearer the nothing end of that continuum. Of course, there are such things as "gourmet" soft drinks,[10] but they tend to be glocal and to represent the glocalization of something. And, there certainly are mass-produced beers, especially dominant in the American market, but most of them are not distributed internationally to any great degree, if at all. However, such beer certainly could use inexpensive ingredients from anywhere in the world and, in this sense, be grobal.

There is also a tendency to modify products of a given time period, to remove much of what makes them distinctive, so that they can be marketed in a different time period. For example, stemming from an era in which there was greater tolerance, and less awareness, of drugs and the problems associated with them, Coca-Cola originally had small amounts of cocaine, but times changed and it quickly became clear that such a drug had no place in a soft drink, and it was removed. Coca-Cola with cocaine would be impossible to sell today, but with the offending drug removed, it is saleable almost everywhere. Similarly, the taco may have deep roots in the history of Mexican culture, but much of what was historically involved in the creation of tacos (especially the way they were made, the extremely hot chilies that gave, and continue to give, traditional tacos their spiciness) has been removed (at least outside indigenous areas where the original taco is still made and consumed) to make it the kind of time-free generic product that chains like Taco Bell can market today around the world.

Given the great demand, it is far easier to mass-produce and -distribute the empty forms of nothing than the substantively rich forms of something. Indeed, many forms of something lend themselves best to limited, if not one-of-a-kind, production. A skilled potter may produce a few dozen pieces of pottery and an artist a painting or two in, perhaps, a week, a month, or even a year (or still longer). While these craft and art works may, over time, move from owner to owner in various parts of the world, this traffic barely registers in the total of global trade and commerce. Of course, there are the rare masterpieces that may bring millions of dollars, but in the main we are talking about primarily small-ticket items. In contrast, thousands, even many millions, and sometimes billions of varieties of nothing are mass-produced and sold throughout the globe. Once one has constructed the basic model of a minimal phenomenon, then all iterations that follow from it are easy to produce, since there is so little substance to the model. Also easing the way toward the proliferation of the model is the fact that only minor variations and deviations over time and across space are permitted.

Furthermore, the economics of the marketplace demand that the massive amount of nothing that is produced be marketed and sold on a grobal basis. For example, the economies of scale mean that the more that is produced and sold, the lower the cost and ultimately, perhaps, the price. This means that, almost inevitably, American producers of nothing (and, as we have seen, they are by far the world leaders in this, although it now seems clear that they are being rivaled, and may soon be surpassed, by, among others, Chinese producers) must, because of increasing competition and lower profit margins, become dissatisfied with the American market, no matter how vast it is, and aggressively pursue a world market for their consumer products. The greater the grobal market, the lower the price that can be charged, and this, in turn, means that even greater numbers of nothing can be sold and farther reaches of the globe in less developed countries can be reached. Another economic factor stems from the stock market, which demands that corporations that produce and sell nothing (indeed all corporations) increase sales and profits from one year to the next. The stocks of those corporations that simply meet the previous year's profitability, or—God forbid—experience a decline, are likely to be punished in the stock market and see their stock prices fall, sometimes precipitously. In order to increase profits continually, the corporation is forced, as Marx understood long ago, to continue to search out new markets, and one way of doing that is constantly to expand globally. In contrast, since something is less likely to be produced by corporations—certainly the large corporations listed on the world's stock markets—there is far less pressure to expand the market for these things. In any case, as we saw above, given the limited number of these things that can be produced by artisans, musicians, skilled chefs, artists, and so on, there are profound limits on any type of expansion.

Also, nothing has an advantage in terms of transportation around the world. These are *non*things that generally can be easily and efficiently packaged and moved, often over vast areas. Lunchables, for example, are compact, prepackaged, and have a long shelf life. Furthermore, because the unit cost of such items is low, it is not of great consequence if they go awry, are lost, or are stolen. In contrast, it is more difficult and expensive to package something— say, a piece of handmade pottery or an antique vase—and losing such things, having them stolen, or being broken is a disaster. As a result, it is far more expensive to insure units of something than nothing, and this difference is another reason for the cost advantage that nothing has over something.

The Glocalization of Something

As pointed out above, there is also an elective affinity between glocalization and something. Something is more likely to emerge out of the unique mix of the local and the global that is the glocal. And, such forms of something are far more likely to appeal to a glocal than a grobal market.

The example of the glocalization of something in Figure 5.1 (Quadrant 1) is local crafts like pottery or weaving. Such craft products are *things*, and they are likely to be displayed and sold in *places* like craft barns. The craftsperson who makes and demonstrates his or her wares is a *person,* and customers are apt to be offered a great deal of *service.* Such glocal products are likely to remain something, although there are certainly innumerable examples of glocal forms of something that have been transformed into glocal, and in some cases grobal, forms of nothing. In fact, as was discussed in the last chapter, there is often a kind of progression here from glocal something to glocal nothing as demand grows and then to grobal nothing (kokopellis and matryoshka dolls) if some entrepreneur believes that there might be a global market for such products. However, some glocal forms of something are able to resist this process, or have been, at least until now, ignored by the forces of grobalization.

Glocal forms of something are likely to remain as such for various reasons. That which is derived from the glocal is, almost by definition, much more complex than that which is grobal and therefore is likely to be produced in more limited numbers. The complexity of the glocal comes from the fact that it involves an idiosyncratic mix of the global and the local, and furthermore there may be subtle differences from one local area to another in the ways in which global and local elements are combined. It is difficult to produce such complex combinations in great numbers; the many different combinations speak to the likelihood of small batch, rather than mass, production (e.g., slight differences in the food served in different parts of Provence in southern France). Furthermore, there is likely to be only a minimal demand for such idiosyncratic products (e.g., only relatively small numbers are likely to be interested in Provençal food). Finally, that which is glocal in character is almost by definition marketed in a limited geographic area—the glocality—and this means that low levels of production might be hard-pressed to satisfy even the (g)local demand, let alone a global market. Thus, the most famous restaurants in Provence are booked long in advance, and the Provençal food served in most French restaurants throughout the world has little resemblance to that served in Provence.

In addition, glocal forms of something tend to be costly, at least in comparison to mass-manufactured competitors. High price tends to keep demand down locally, let alone globally. Glocal forms of something are loaded with distinctive content. Among other things, this means that consumers, especially in other cultures, find them harder to understand and appreciate. Furthermore, their complex character makes it more likely that those in other cultures will find something about them they do not like or even find offensive. Those who create glocal forms of something are not, unlike larger manufacturers of nothing, necessarily pushed by market forces to expand their business and increase profits to satisfy stockholders and the stock market.

While craftspeople are not immune to the desire to earn more money, the pressure to do so is more internal than external, and it is not nearly as great or inexorable. In any case, the desire to earn more money is tempered by the fact that the production of each craft product is time consuming, and there are just so many of them that can be produced in a given time.

Furthermore, craft products are even less likely to lend themselves to mass marketing and advertising than they are to mass manufacture. There are, of course, exceptions to this. For example, there are "artists" such as Thomas Kinkade ("the painter of light") and Wyland (specializing in marine art) who have turned painting into nothing through the mass production and mass distribution of art through branded galleries throughout the United States. Furthermore, to the degree that they have a global audience, they have grobalized their particular forms of nothing.[11]

The Grobalization of Something

While there is a clear elective affinity between grobalization and nothing, that is not to say that something is not being grobalized as well. In fact, some types of something have been grobalized to a considerable degree. This is abundantly clear throughout the world of consumption. However, returning to the idea of elective affinity, the key point here is that there is *not* an elective affinity between grobalization and something. The process of grobalization must, by necessity, involve products and services that, among other things, are in the main not tied to a particular place, especially a place of origin. If they were, they would not have broad global appeal. One of the key factors in being something is such a tie to a particular locale. Thus, in general, successful grobalization, especially on a large scale, requires characteristics that something cannot offer, and if it is transformed to accommodate the demands of grobalization, it moves in the direction of being nothing. In the latter case, it becomes the grobalization of nothing (where, as was explained above, an elective affinity does exist).

Nevertheless, while the grobalization of nothing dominates in the arena of consumption as it is generally defined, we find domains—art, medicine, science, pharmaceuticals,[12] biotechnology,[13] education, and others—in which the grobalization of something is of far greater importance. For example, the worldwide scientific community benefits from the almost instantaneous distribution of important scientific findings, often these days via new journals on the Internet.

In Figure 5.1 I have used as examples of the grobalization of something touring art exhibitions (*thing*) of the works of Vincent van Gogh, the museums throughout the world in which such exhibitions occur for a time (*place*), the knowledgeable guides who show visitors the highlights of the exhibition (*person*), and the detailed information and insights they are able to impart in response to questions from gallery visitors (*service*). To take another example, a touring series of Silk Road concerts brought together Persian artists and music, an American symphony orchestra, and Rimsky-Korsakov's (Russian) *Scheherezade*.[14] More generally, gourmet foods, handmade crafts, and custom-made clothes are now much more available throughout the world and more likely than ever in history to be traded on a transplanetary basis.

However, even with the recent increase, there is far less grobalization of something than there is grobalization of nothing. Why is there comparatively little connection between grobalization and something? Many of the factors discussed previously as helping to account for the prevalence of other permutations and combinations of the grobal-local and nothing-something, especially the grobalization of nothing, are also involved in explaining the relative paucity of phenomena that can be included under the heading of the grobalization of something.

First, there is simply far less demand throughout the world for most forms of something, at least in comparison to the demand for nothing. One reason for this is that the distinctiveness and complexity of something, be it gourmet foods, handmade crafts, or Silk Road concerts, require far more sophisticated tastes than nothing.

Second, the complexity of something, especially the fact that it is likely to have many different elements, means that it is more likely to have at least some characteristics that will bother or even offend large numbers of people in many different cultures. For example, a Russian (or Persian) audience at a Silk Road concert might be bothered by the juxtaposition of Persian music with that of Rimsky-Korsakov.

Third, the various forms of something are usually more expensive, frequently much more expensive, than competing forms of nothing (a fine, complex wine is much more costly than a jug of mass-produced wine). Higher cost means, of course, that far fewer people can afford something. As a result, the global demand for expensive forms of something is minuscule in comparison to that for the inexpensive varieties of nothing.

Fourth, because the prices are high and the demand is comparatively low, far less can be spent on the advertising and marketing of something, and this serves to keep demand low.

Fifth, something is far more difficult to mass-manufacture and, in some cases (Silk Road concerts, van Gogh exhibitions), impossible to produce in this way. The very nature of these complex phenomena serves to limit their numbers and hence their global proliferation. There are just so many world-class rock bands, gymnastic teams, and folk music troupes, and the profit potential of such groups, if that is indeed the objective, is highly limited, to put it mildly. This is not the case with nothing, which, precisely because it is devoid of such characteristics, is far easier to produce in large numbers and to distribute globally.

Sixth, since the demand for something is less price-sensitive than nothing (the relatively small number of people who can afford it are willing, and often able, to pay almost any price), there is less need to mass-manufacture it (assuming it could be produced in this way) in order to lower prices.

Seventh, the costs of shipping something (gourmet foods, the van Gogh paintings) are usually very high, adding to the price and thereby reducing the demand. For example, a Picasso recently sold at auction for over $95 million. The cost of shipping it to its new owner was somewhere between $6,000 and $10,000.[15]

It could also be argued that the lesser degree of the grobalization of something (compared to nothing) helps distinguish something from nothing. Because it is relatively scarce, something retains its status and its distinction from nothing. If something came to be mass-produced and grobalized, it is likely that it would move toward the nothing end of the continuum. This brings us back to the intriguing issue of what comes first, nothing or grobalization and the associated mass production.[16] That is, does a phenomenon start out as nothing? Or, is it transformed into nothing by mass production and grobalization? As I discussed in the previous chapter, the latter is more likely the case; mass production tends to transform everything—including all forms of something—into nothing.

While the grobalization of something is important, it should be noted that it too is subject to the spread of nothing. Take, for example, the touring show of van Gogh art. The art itself will, of course, always be something, but the other aspects of the show can move in the direction of nothingness. Museums are under great pressure to become more and more like theme parks. Like theme parks, their gift shops are likely to sell all sorts of low-priced products associated with a given show. Thus, in the case of a van Gogh exhibit, we are likely to see things like inexpensive posters and prints, gift cards, pens, and mugs, among many other things, decorated with various images derived from van Gogh's work, especially his self-portraits. Instead of individual guides knowledgeable about van Gogh's work, and art in general, we see the proliferation and increasing use of audio guides and rented tape players at such shows and at museums more generally. Instead of individual interaction between guides and visitors, all visitors hear exactly the same things through their headphones.

The Glocalization of Nothing

There is little or nothing in the way of elective affinity between glocalization and nothing. On the one hand, glocalization tends to produce something, or at least that which lies toward the something end of the continuum. The integration of the global and local varies from one locale to another, and what is produced in each location tends to be unique—different from that produced by that interaction in other locations. On the other hand, nothing lends itself far better to the demands of grobalization for generic products than it does to glocalization and its need for products that have at least some measure of uniqueness, especially a unique tie to the locality. In spite of the lack of elective affinity, there *are* instances in which glocalization and nothing come together, especially in the realm of consumer culture.

One of the best examples of the glocalization of nothing is to be found in tourism,[17] especially where the grobal tourist meets the local (if they still exist) manufacturer and retailer in the production and sale of glocal goods and services (this is illustrated in Quadrant 2 of Figure 5.1). There are certainly instances, perhaps even many of them, where tourism stimulates the production of something—well-made, high-quality craft products made for discerning tourists, or meals lovingly prepared by local chefs using traditional recipes and the best of local ingredients. However, far more often, and increasingly as time goes by, grobal tourism leads to the glocalization of nothing. Souvenir shops are likely to be bursting at the seams with trinkets reflecting a bit of the local culture. Such souvenirs are increasingly likely to be mass-manufactured, perhaps using components from other parts of the world, in local factories. If demand grows great enough and the possibilities of profitability high enough, low-priced souvenirs may be manufactured by the thousands or millions elsewhere in the world and then shipped back to the local area to be sold to tourists (who may not notice, or care about, the "Made in China" label embossed on their souvenir replicas of the Eiffel Tower). The clerks in these souvenir shops are likely to act like *non*people, and tourists are highly likely to serve themselves. Similarly, large numbers of meals slapped together by semiskilled chefs to suggest vaguely local cooking are far more likely than gourmet meals that are true to the region or that truly integrate local elements. They are likely to be offered in "touristy" restaurants that are close to the *non*place end of the continuum and to be served by *non*people who offer little in the way of service.

Another major example involves the production of native shows—often involving traditional costumes, dances, and music—for grobal tourists. While these could be something, there is a very strong tendency for them to be transformed into nothing to satisfy grobal tour operators and tourists.

Hence, these shows are examples of the glocalization of nothing, because they become centrally conceived and controlled empty forms. They are often watered down, if not eviscerated, with esoteric or possibly offensive elements removed. The performances are designed to please the throngs of tourists and to put off as few of them as possible. They take place with great frequency, and performers often seem as if they are going through the motions in a desultory fashion. For their part, this is about all the grobal tourists want in their rush to see the performance, to perhaps eat an ersatz local meal, and then to move on rapidly to the next stop on the tour. Thus, in the area of tourism—in souvenirs, local performances, and local meals— we are far more likely to see the glocalization of nothing than of something.

Thus, Figure 5.1, as well as the preceding sections of this chapter, outline what I think is this book's major contribution—a distinctive framework for the analysis of globalization, especially as it relates to consumer culture. The remainder of the book explores the various implications of this model for thinking about globalization, again especially as it relates to consumer culture.

Grobalization: Loose Cultural and Tight Structural Forms

One aspect of grobalization that requires some further discussion at this point is the distinction between the grobalization of loose cultural and tight structural models. In terms of the former first, we have long witnessed the global dispersion of loose and very broad models from one culture to another. It is easy to see that the worldwide spread of such loose cultural models is part of globalization, but there is little that is new about this. Such models have been spread from one part of the world to another for as long as people have had the mobility to move from one culture to another. Thus, for example, many 19th- and early 20th-century immigrants to the United States brought their cultures with them, and many aspects of those cultures have become part of the way many Americans do things. In other words, they have been assimilated into American culture.

However, this has suddenly become a hot topic globally as many nations, including the United States, struggle with the problem of integrating huge numbers of legal and illegal immigrants. Although dealing with this important and pressing issue is well beyond the scope of this book, it is worth pointing out how it is precisely such immigrants who are most likely to bring with them, and to be involved with, loose cultural models. Finding themselves in a strange and often unwelcoming culture, they are likely to seek out the informal and formal settings they knew in the homeland and with which they are comfortable. Such settings are likely to have been created by previous immigrants loosely on the basis of their memory of models that existed at home. They may take the form of an ethnic restaurant serving familiar dishes of one kind or another or a grocery store stocked with foods and brands from the "old country." Furthermore, as the number of new immigrants swell, some of them are likely to become involved in, and create, other structures and institutions built on the basis of these loose cultural models. Thus, in many places in the United States, and elsewhere, we are witnessing the explosive growth of settings based on such models.

By the way, it is worth noting that such structures and institutions are highly likely to fall toward the something end of the continuum, to represent the grobalization of something. On the one hand, grobalization is involved, since models developed elsewhere in the world are being imported into other countries. While there are those in the home country actively exporting these models and all that goes with them, such aggressive exportation is less important here than in the case of the grobalization of nothing. It is more driven by the demand created by those who have immigrated to other nations and cultures. On the other hand, what is being imported is more likely to be something, because the looseness of the cultural model allows local entrepreneurs to create their unique version of whatever entity they are involved in (ethnic restaurant, grocery, clothing shop). That is, every iteration of each of these is likely to be locally conceived, controlled, and rich in distinctive content. Sure, there is some control exerted by the home culture and by producers there of various types of indigenous products, but it is minimal in comparison to the control exerted by those in charge of tight structural forms like a fast-food chain restaurant. Entrepreneurs involved in enterprises derived from loose cultural models have considerable leeway in deciding how to structure and operate their business, and tight structural forms seek to minimize or eliminate such flexibility.

While it is of growing importance, the spread of loose cultural models is *not* my focus when I discuss grobalization, especially the grobalization of nothing. While the grobalization of loose cultural models has a long, even ancient, history, what is relatively new about the present era is the global spread of tight structural models. The best example, of course, is the principles and systems that lie at the base of McDonald's and other fast-food chains. McDonald's is actively exporting its tight structural models to the rest of the world, and it is that which is both relatively recent, grobalizing, and largely responsible for the global proliferation of nothing. Let us look at the distinction between loose cultural and tight structural models in a bit more detail using the example of food.

The cuisines of a number of nations throughout the world (China, Italy, Mexico, etc.) have succeeded in many other nations, and this worldwide proliferation of cuisines was occurring long before globalization became a key issue and buzzword. And, the restaurants that specialize in such cuisines have adapted to local realities (the food served in Chinese restaurants in the United States is very different from that served in such restaurants in China; it has been adapted to the American palate,[18] and adaptations, perhaps slightly different in nature, have occurred in Chinese restaurants in many other nations). However, there is a huge difference between individual entrepreneurs opening Chinese (or Mexican, Italian, Afghan, or any other ethnic) restaurants in many different locales and, for example, the centralized organization that owns Taco Bell (Yum! Brands) opening franchises in those same locales. It is true that both are patterned after larger models, but the former are shaped by loose cultural models that are not centrally conceived and controlled, while the latter are determined by centrally conceived, highly detailed, and very tightly controlled structural models. The result is that all Taco Bell restaurants are more or less identical, whereas there is considerable variation from one Chinese restaurant to another.[19] Nevertheless, no matter how tight the structural model, there is always the need to make case-by-case adaptations to local realities.

That there is global competition between these two models is clear in the case of Chinese restaurants. The success of the loose cultural model in producing successful, independently owned Chinese restaurants throughout the world has effectively served, at least until now, to block efforts to create chains of Chinese restaurants based on tight structural models. Also supporting the loose cultural model in this case is the mass migration of Chinese, creating both a pool of entrepreneurs and a ready clientele (as well as a steady supply of employees) for restaurants (and other businesses) loosely modeled on those they might have been familiar with in their homeland. However, the failure to this point to create a truly successful chain of Chinese restaurants (and there certainly have been such efforts) does not mean that such a chain will not emerge in the future. Loose cultural models are often in danger of being transformed into tight structural models by enterprising entrepreneurs.

The Grobalization of Nothing: Enabling Factors

Why are we now witnessing this explosion in the grobalization of nothing and the extension of it to more and more areas of the world?

Organizational, Technological, and Industrial Developments

First, there is simply an ever-increasing amount of organizational (e.g., the massive expansion of the franchise system) and industrial capacity to produce and broadly disseminate nothing, and this constant increase is fueled by myriad technological and organizational advances. Furthermore, the entities capable of producing nothing are no longer highly centralized in a few advanced industrial nations; that capacity (if not the profits from it) is now spread far more evenly around the globe (industrial production once concentrated in the United States and the West is now dispersed throughout, if not moving increasingly toward, much of the developing world), and it makes the global proliferation of nothing that much easier. Major advances in communication and transportation also make the movement of all forms of nothing easier and less expensive. Thus, for example, the new global shipping businesses—FedEx, DHL, and so on—move huge quantities of goods throughout the United States and ever-greater parts of the world.[20] The development of containers, and huge ships and shipyards that can handle them, has made shipping huge quantities of goods by sea easier and far cheaper than by traditional methods.

Media Influence

Second, the media and its influence throughout the world have grown enormously. The media are themselves not only purveyors of nothing (e.g., the soaps, *CNN Headline News,* sitcoms, reality shows) but the major outlet throughout the world for advertisements extolling the virtues of untold varieties of nothing (including their own offerings). In fact, we are infinitely more likely to see advertisements for nothing (e.g., the wide variety of Kraft cheese products) than something (Culatello ham), and the constant barrage of advertisements for the former adds to their status as nothing. Thus, it is not only easier to produce nothing, but it is also far easier to bring it to the attention of people throughout the world, as well as to bring to their notice all sorts of reasons why they need to purchase the various forms of nothing.

Various technological advances have served to make it easier to grobalize nothing via the media. For example, satellites and cable have made for a great increase in television stations and made it possible for many more people to receive much more programming, along with the commercials that are de rigueur on such programming. Of course, the major technological advance in this realm is the Internet and the emerging fusion of the Internet and television (along with other fusions such as iPods and television). Accompanying most of what can be found on the Internet are advertisements extolling the virtues of a wide variety of nothing, especially that associated with consumer culture.

Global Flows Within Multiple "Scapes"

Third, and more generally, several of the global flows independent of any single nation[21]—one of which is the media (*mediascapes*)—tend to operate better with nothing (e.g., sitcoms, reality shows) than with something (e.g., cultural presentations on PBS[22]) and are excellent conduits for the global proliferation of nothing.

In the world's *financescapes,* to take another example, there is a preference for currencies that are used everywhere, and this gave, and continues to give, the American dollar great advantages over other currencies. Thus, the dollar (like many other things American) has tended to lose its characteristic as something—the currency specific to the United States—and has become a universal medium of exchange (the so-called super dollar) in banking and finance throughout the world. Furthermore, in times of distress, the dollar has tended to become the predominant currency de facto (Russia in the early 1990s) or de jure (Ecuador in recent years).

One of the best examples of the nothing associated with financescapes is the euro, which in 2002 became the currency for most nations in Europe, and it is highly likely that the laggards (current exceptions are Great Britain, Denmark, and Sweden) will jump on the euro bandwagon in the not-too-distant future.[23] Relegated to the dustbin of history were currencies that really were something[24] (the franc, pound, lira, mark, etc.), at least in the sense that they had over time come to have distinctive content associated with them. These currencies were closely tied to a specific nation and had long histories and great traditions. Replacing them was the euro that had none of those things—it was largely devoid of content but brought with it many of the usual advantages of nothing, especially increasing the efficiency with which business can be transacted and tourism undertaken.

Furthermore, gone were the familiar and unique images that adorned the face of traditional European currencies. Instead, the depictions on the euro bills[25] are of no place; they are fictional locales. Because of a fear of offending those in other nations whose locales were not depicted, a decision was made not to use any of the famous real locales in various European nations.

One would have thought there would have been great resistance to the disappearance of these fabled currencies, but the near-total absence of any reaction, let alone resistance, to it reflects the fact that we live in a world increasingly defined by nothing, and any new variant of it is likely to be welcomed, or at least to be accepted with little more than a shrug. Conversely, that which still smacks of something is likely to be abandoned without much ado.

Technoscapes also favor nothing over something.[26] Indeed, it could be argued that technology is nothing but form; the content of any specific technology depends on the use to which it is put. An engine can be used to do innumerable things; what it actually does depends on its particular use. Much the same could be said about the media in general and television in particular. This is, of course, put a bit too strongly—technologies often do tend to favor some types of content and not others. A rifle may be put to many uses, but it does not tend to further the ends of pacifists. The media, especially those that operate in a world of profit and loss, tend to favor material that is likely to be as devoid of content as possible or to offer the most generic of content, which therefore is apt to appeal to the largest audience or at least to alienate the smallest number of people.

However, the other scapes, as well as the more important disjunctures among them, tend to be more ambiguous in their effects, or even to favor something over nothing. Some *ethnoscapes* do tend to foster the global proliferation of nothing. An important example, as discussed above, is the flow of tourists around the world, especially those who travel with preset tours or those who go on their own to such generic destinations as a Disney, or a Disney-like, theme park, a Las Vegas casino-hotel, or a cruise on one of the many massive cruise ships now sailing the world's waters. Then there are the tourists, discussed above, who demand that local performances and foods be watered down to suit their tastes.

Other ethnoscapes are more likely to produce something than nothing. For example, the movement of immigrants and refugees among nations and even continents, sometimes involving very large numbers of people, tends to bring with it the creation of unique enclaves rich in the style of life that they brought with them.[27] This is in line with the point made above about the difference between structural and cultural models. Immigrants are likely to operate on the basis of cultural models and therefore to be less likely to contribute to the proliferation of nothing. They are also more likely, at least initially, to participate in glocalization than grobalization.

As for *ideoscapes,* the global flow of some ideas—especially those associated with a hegemon like the United States and its efforts at obtaining and maintaining global control over ideas—tends to be associated with nothing. That is, to the degree that many nations around the world tend to buy into these ideas (e.g., those associated with the so-called Washington Consensus—market, democracy, materialism, consumerism[28]) is the degree to which there is a decline in unique idea systems that differentiate among societies and regions of the world. However, it is probably the case that, in the main, the worldwide flow of different idea systems, especially the ideologies associated with states, as well as their counter-ideologies, is productive of many diverse idea systems loaded with very different content.

The disjunctures that exist among all of the scapes leave room for much diversity and richness in content. In other words, disjunctures tend to limit the proliferation of nothing. Clearly, if the disjunctures did not exist, if the various scapes formed a seamless system, then there would be an even far greater possibility of the proliferation of nothing. While it is possible to imagine a scenario whereby such a seamless system would be a greater likelihood, that possibility is, at best, a long way off. At the moment, and for the foreseeable future, these disjunctures serve to limit, but certainly do not prevent, the spread of nothing.

Economic Factors

One key economic factor in the explosion of the grobalization of nothing is increased affluence. Especially important in this regard is not the enormous concentration of wealth in a relative few but the great democratization of wealth that allows large and growing numbers of people to afford the proliferating and comparatively inexpensive forms of nothing.

Of course, there are great profits to be made from the creation of ever-greater markets for nothing. Thus, there are great incentives for today's entrepreneurs to continually push the global envelope on nothing in the pursuit of escalating profits. The economies of scale make it de rigueur to sell more and more nothingness anywhere it can be sold. Furthermore, the character of nothing makes each of its units highly profitable and eminently exportable; the more units exported, the higher the profits. As we know, the very nature of nothing—long on form and as devoid as possible of content—makes it generally comparatively inexpensive to produce and transport. Costs are low, because once the form has been created, it can be repeated ad infinitum. Furthermore, content, especially when it is diverse and complex—and content (at least in comparison to form) tends to *be* diverse and complex—is far more costly both to create and to produce. As a result, because it is relatively devoid of content, nothing tends to be comparatively inexpensive and therefore profitable.

Thus, we live in an era in which a variety of its basic characteristics have led to a tremendous expansion in the grobalization of nothing. Furthermore, current trends lead to the view that the future will bring with it an even greater proliferation of nothing throughout the globe.

6

Theorizing Glocalization and Grobalization

The primary objective in this book is to offer a new way of thinking about, of theorizing, the cultural aspects of globalization. While there are implications for other aspects of globalization (e.g., economic, political), my primary focus has been on culture, especially consumer culture (for more on this, see Chapter 7). In the process of rethinking and reconceptualizing globalization, and in order to accomplish the book's objective, I have had to create an equally new way of thinking about that which is being globalized (nothing, something, and the nothing-something continuum), especially in the realm of consumption. The objective in this chapter is to examine the implications of all of this for cultural theories of globalization.

My concern throughout has been with the hegemony of the concept of glocalization (associated with cultural hybridization; see Chapter 1) and the need for a parallel emphasis on the idea of grobalization (that is central to cultural convergence also discussed in Chapter 1). This is addressed in this chapter primarily through a close critique of work that overtly and covertly privileges the idea of glocalization. In the process of critiquing that work, we will see that not only is there a parallel need to theorize grobalization, but in fact what is often discussed under the heading of the former can be seen as really involving the latter.

Theorizing the Globalization of Culture

The theoretical origins of this analysis lie in the growing hegemony of the concept of glocalization and even the emergence of a theory, or a paradigm, that takes that concept as its focus and even as its name.[1] As is clear in this discussion, especially in Chapter 5 and the model developed there, I certainly accept the importance of glocalization. Indeed, it occupies a central place there as one pole in the glocalization-grobalization continuum. However, that is precisely the point—it is *not* all there is to globalization, even in a given locale, *and* it may not be the most important aspect of globalization, at least on a case-by-case basis. It is only one element, albeit a key one, in thinking about globalization. We *always* need to look at the ways in which glocalization and grobalization interpenetrate, and we need to do this without operating with the foregone conclusion that it is glocalization (or grobalization) that tells all, or even most, of the story. Thus, even with my great interest in grobalization and its various subprocesses, I recognize that it is only part of the overall process of globalization.

To put this another way, if we want to elevate glocalization to the level of a theory, or a paradigm (as many seem to want to do), there is at least as much reason to do the same with grobalization. While the latter term has not been used explicitly before, it has certainly been central implicitly to the study of globalization under a variety of other more specific headings—capitalism, colonialism, neocolonialism, Westernization, Americanization, McDonaldization, Disneyization, and much more.

It may well be that glocalization and grobalization are the two leading paradigms in the study of the globalization of culture. If glocalization is seen as a paradigm, then work on hybridization, creolization, and much else, especially the work of a number of anthropologists,[2] can be included within it. In terms of grobalization as a paradigm, in addition to the work in areas mentioned above, we can also include neoliberalism and realist theories of state power relations. In fact, we could, at this point, begin the delineation of these, and perhaps other, paradigms in the study of globalization, but that is a highly complex task that would involve not only dealing with theory but also a range of other issues such as the appropriate research methods for each paradigm.[3] For the purposes at hand here, instead of beginning such a complex undertaking, it would be best to focus on the far more modest preliminary task of seeking to gain a greater understanding of glocalization and grobalization as the two poles of a continuum the entirety of which encompasses much, if not all, of globalization, at least in very general terms.

By the way, it should be noted that there is much else involved in globalization than just grobalization and glocalization. Thus, theorizing the process in anything approaching its entirety would involve much more conceptual, as well as theoretical and paradigmatic, development than is being, or even could be, undertaken here.

Of course, there is a second, parallel continuum and set of theoretical ideas—nothing-something—that is equally important to this work. These ideas are certainly useful in thinking about globalization, but they are perhaps of far greater utility and importance in thinking about the social and cultural world in general and a far wider array of social and cultural processes. Similarly, they are not only useful in theorizing globalization but also have much broader applicability to social and cultural theory in general. We will not follow that more general line of thinking here, although we will return in Chapter 7 to the something-nothing continuum and its relationship to globalization in general, and the glocalization-grobalization continuum in particular, in the context of their relationship to consumer culture.

The origin of the concept of grobalization lies in both my previous work on processes like McDonaldization and Americanization and my critical reaction to the growing hegemony of the idea of glocalization. However, my conceptualization of nothing (and something) has a somewhat different origin lying mainly in the substance of my work in the sociology of consumption, specifically on fast-food restaurants, cathedrals of consumption, and credit cards and my desire to come up with an overarching concept that encompassed them and much else, at least in part. The concept of nothing eventually came to mind as that concept, and as I reviewed what turned out to be a voluminous amount of highly diverse work on it,[4] my own sense and distinctive definition of that concept began to emerge. Thus, while grobalization is a new concept, nothing is a very old idea that is defined in a new way in this book. Once I had a definition of nothing, it became clear that I needed the concept of something, a parallel definition of it, and a something-nothing continuum to parallel and juxtapose with the grobalization-glocalization continuum. While nothing, and the something-nothing continuum, are crucial to this analysis, they will occupy a secondary role in this chapter, where the primary focus is globalization, especially globalization theory. Rather than discussing this in very abstract terms, the focus will be on a critical analysis of culturally oriented work in the sociology of sport and in anthropology (which, of course, is by definition oriented to culture) that tends to privilege glocalization. The objective is to show that while they focus explicitly and implicitly on glocalization, grobalization is, or should be, an integral part of their, indeed any, analysis of the globalization of culture.

Analyzing Sport: Use and Abuse of the Concept of Glocalization

In order to illustrate the critical starting point of this analysis of globalization, as well as the need for a broader analysis of it, I begin with a review of a work that looks specifically at the relationship between sport and globalization. While it is not directly concerned with our focal interest in consumer culture, its focus is primarily cultural. As we will see, it is representative of much work on globalization in that it accords far too much attention to glocalization and, in the process, underplays the significance of grobalization, to say nothing of the relationship between them. I use this critical analysis, and the one that follows, as a basis for outlining, at least briefly and provisionally, what I think a more complete and well-rounded examination of the globalization of sport, and much else, might look like.

David Andrews and Andrew Grainger see sport as both a central element of the global popular (culture) and as an important vehicle for institutionalizing the global condition.[5] For example, as a globalizing force, the Olympic Committee has more members than the United Nations. They argue that at first, sport was clearly local, but by the early 20th century, a global sport system and imaginary had developed. In the second half of the 20th century, that trend accelerated as sport was increasingly colonized by capitalism.

The Andrews and Grainger analysis is heavily informed by the global-local nexus, and they go to great lengths to argue that sport today is best seen as glocal (and not grobal, or as a romanticized local phenomenon). In fact, in a useful elaboration, they distinguish two types of the glocal as well as two subtypes of the second type. The *organic glocal* is globalized, internationalized sport that has been incorporated into the local. The *strategic glocal* involves transnational corporations exploiting the local, either through *interiorized glocal strategizing*—global sport co-opting and exploiting sport's local dimension (and as we will see as in much else in the Andrews and Grainger analysis of glocalization, this sounds very much like a form of grobalization)—or through *exteriorized glocal strategizing* (importation and mobilization of sporting differences into the local market). Let us take a closer look at these two types of the glocal as well as the subtypes under the heading of the second broad type.

Organic Sporting Glocalization

We can begin with a deconstruction of Andrews and Grainger's definition of organic sporting glocalization as the process whereby either globalized or internationalized sport practices (depending on their spatial reach) become incorporated into local (communal, regional, but primarily national) sporting cultures and experienced as authentic or natural (hence organic) signs of cultural collectivity. In a general sense, organic glocalization is associated with local responses to the sporting flows that accompanied broader forces of social transformation (colonization, modernization, urban industrialization, etc.).[6]

There is no question that Andrews and Grainger are describing glocalization, or at least that end of the grobal-glocal continuum, in discussing the incorporation of sport into the local, local responses, and experiencing things as authentic and natural signs of the cultural collectivity. However, what is most striking about this definition is that they are dealing much more with processes that would meet the definition of grobalization and fall far closer to the grobal end of the continuum. These include "globalized or internationalized sport practices," "sporting flows," and most generally the "broader forces of social transformation." Included in the latter are some of the broadest forms of grobalization such as "colonization" and "modernization." Thus, it is clear that Andrews and Grainger are devoting at least as much attention, if not more, to grobalization as they do to glocalization in their discussion of organic sporting glocalization. The point is that this form of globalization, indeed all forms of globalization, cannot be discussed, as Andrews and Grainger demonstrate, without discussing *both* glocalization *and* grobalization.

Strategic Sporting Glocalization

Andrews and Grainger turn next to strategic sporting glocalization, which is

a more recent phenomenon derived from changes in the spatial ambition, organization, and imagination of late capitalism . . . associated with the advent of transnational as the dominating logic of economic expansion and the transnational corporation as the "locus of economic activity.". . . Rather than treating, and hoping to realize, the world market as a single, un-differentiated entity (as in previous stages of development in the global economy), transnational capitalism has become increasingly concerned with commercially exploiting (through negotiated incorporation and commodified reflection) the local differences its international antecedent previously sought to overcome.[7]

This is an even more striking illustration of the fact that glocalization cannot be discussed without discussing grobalization.

Indeed, this entire discussion of strategic sporting globalization deals, in the main, with grobalization. This is clear in the following ways:

1. It is strategic; that is, it relates to the strategies employed by grobalizing forces.

2. It deals with capitalism, especially late capitalism, one of the three central grobalizing processes discussed in this book.

3. More specifically, it deals with the transnational corporation, which is, of course, the most important component of contemporary capitalism as a grobalizing process. Indeed, the very label "*trans*national" communicates a sense of grobalization.

4. Use of terms like "expansion" and "exploiting" clearly imply grobalization.

5. Finally, contemporary transnational capitalism is described as more ambitious than its antecedents in the process of grobalization (exploiting, incorporating, and commodifying local differences).

Interiorized Glocal Strategizing

Andrews and Grainger then turn to the first of two subtypes of strategic sporting glocalization, "interiorized glocal strategizing," which they see as referring to

the manner in which global capital has aggressively co-opted local sport cultures and sensibilities into its expansive regime of flexible accumulation . . . not for global dissemination per se, rather for local market accommodation, and incorporation, as a constituent element of the broader transnationalist project. Thus, the architecture and convictions of the hegemonic corporate sport model [have] become truly globalized.[8]

Note the grobalizing terms and ideas associated with this concept and explicit in the preceding quotation—"strategizing," "aggressively co-opted," "expansive regime," "incorporation . . . [in] the broader transnationalist project," and the "hegemonic corporate sport model." In fact, the authors are forced to acknowledge explicitly that this form of globalization *is* grobalization as it is practiced by such grobal entities as "commercially-driven sport organizations and governing bodies; professional sport leagues and tournaments; sport management companies; media and entertainment corporations; sporting goods manufacturers; and, allied corporate sponsors."[9]

What is it, then, that makes this in any way a glocal phenomenon? The answer is that these grobal forces are strategizing ways of seeking to capitalize on, to exploit, local sporting practices. But even here, Andrews and Grainger point out that the appeals to "indigenous sporting and cultural authenticity" are "contrived" by grobalizing forces. In the end, what is produced is just one more component of a "global economy of sporting locals"—in other words, the forces of grobalization are not only exploiting local sporting practices, but the latter are part of a larger grobal project involving many of these sporting locals. While there is certainly a glocal element to each of these, the main thrust of this discussion focuses, once again, on grobalization rather than glocalization.

Exteriorized Glocal Strategizing

The second subtype of strategic sporting glocalization is "exteriorized glocal strategizing," which

> involve[s] the importation and mobilization of what are commonly perceived to be externally derived expressions of sporting difference into a local market. Here, for those sport consumers looking to express their alterity from the cultural mainstream, the aim is to provide the opportunity to consume the sporting Other. For instance, the exportation of American sport forms even more than the American film and music genres that have become the cultural vernacular of the global popular.[10]

Yet again, the emphasis here is on grobalization as, for example, in ideas like "importation" and "exportation" of American sport forms (and other forms as well). Exporters and importers are seeking to provide local sport consumers with the means to express their differences. This seems to speak to the power of grobalization, not only than sport in sport but also in film, music, and elsewhere. The latter may be even more involved than sport in providing locals with the means to express their differences, even dissatisfaction, with grobalization. This is an extraordinary perspective on the power of grobalization, which is even involved in providing locals with the means to express their hostility to that process. This is, indeed, a powerful process when it is self-assured enough to intrude on, and shape, the very opposition to it.

Monoculture?

Striking in the above quotation is a phrase I have extracted for further deconstruction. In describing the grobalizing ambitions of American sport, film, and music, Andrews and Grainger contend that they are "far from seeking to realize a sporting monoculture." The authors then go on to discuss the various ways in which locals identify with (or against) these things, as well as the various ways these things are received, defined, and consumed. There is no question that all of this is accurate, and, in fact, it lies at the heart of thinking about glocalization. *However, grobalizing forces do not need to seek, or achieve, a monoculture in order to profoundly shape the local.* This kind of exaggerated argumentation is a characteristic way of privileging the glocal and dismissing the grobal. That is, by underscoring the obvious point that we do not, and will never, have a global monoculture in sport or anywhere else, the critics go on to reject the whole idea of grobalization (or, more likely, its specific variants like Americanization) because it has not succeeded in producing such a monoculture. However, while this all-or-nothing argument makes it easy to reject grobalization (or related ideas) and accept glocalization, it ignores the powerful, albeit certainly not all-powerful, process of grobalization.

In their conclusion to this section of their essay, Andrews and Grainger offer a more balanced summation that integrates the glocal and the grobal. That is, they argue that "today's sporting locals can only exist and operate within the structures and logics of the global."[11] If we substitute "glocal" for "local" and "grobal" for "global" in that quotation, as I think we can, we arrive at the kind of more balanced analysis of the relationship between glocalization and grobalization being championed in these pages.

Practices, Spectacles, and Bodies

Andrews and Grainger go on to distinguish between glocal sport practices, spectacles, and bodies. In terms of practices, there is the transposition of imposed, transplanted sporting practices into local contexts where they are transformed by the local. The way in which Indians came to transform British-imposed cricket is treated as an excellent example of this.[12] However, whatever the merits of this argument in the specific case of cricket and India,[13] the following is Andrews and Grainger's opening argument on "glocal" sport practices:

> Once characterized by a patchwork of locally-bound, traditional forms, sport's premodern diversity has collapsed into a relatively small number of *highly regulated, standardized and bureaucratized* sport practices that now dominate and define the sporting landscape. . . . The reasons for this sporting *consolidation* are manifold, yet primarily need to be understood in relation to the sweeping social transformations in western Europe in the period after 1700, that resulted in the establishment of an increasingly industrialized, urbanized, and *Westernized world order.* . . . [C]ontemporary sport is the *regulated* embodiment of the distinctly modern Western (and specifically North Atlantic) values of competition, progress and achievement. [italics added][14]

They then go on to discuss the British role in this process, talking in terms of the "*imperially*" inspired relationship between Britain and the rest of the world, the resulting "global sporting *hegemony*," and how many traditional sports were "*subsumed* within, or largely *expunged* in the face of the *unrelenting march of the modern sport order*" (italics added).[15]

To be noted, of course, is the fact that *all* the terms I have italicized in the preceding quotations, even though they are discussed under the heading of glocalization, could hardly constitute stronger descriptors of the *grobalization* of sporting practices.

Nevertheless, Andrews and Grainger then turn to glocalization, contending that the "patterns of sporting diffusion were certainly not globally uniform."[16] Of course they weren't, and no one would ever argue otherwise! The issue is *always* the relative mix of heterogeneity and homogeneity, of glocalization and grobalization. It is *never* one or the other!

The discussion then turns to cricket in the West Indies and, based on Appadurai's work in India, focuses on the resistance in those settings and how the game was used to create local forms of subjectivity and resistance. They conclude, following Appadurai, that "the empire had struck back." But how had it struck back? By playing the English game of cricket! While I agree there is glocalization going on here, it seems clear that grobalization is also at work in the global dissemination of the English pastime.

Andrews and Grainger next discuss "glocal" sport spectacles and once again begin, paradoxically, by discussing them in terms that clearly deal with grobalization. Their focus here is on the consumers of media content rather than attendees at sporting events, and they emphasize the commodified spectacle produced by the mass media, as part of the "culture industry" (and sport is seen as a part of it as well), designed to be imposed on people and even to "penetrate [their] consciousness." What is disseminated are sport spectacles that are "sporting 'muzak'" that flatten out local sport differences. Again, I could hardly do a better job of describing the process of grobalization as it relates to mediatized sport.

Of course, Andrews and Grainger are unwilling to give this idea its due, and turn immediately to a discussion of how such a (grobalizing) perspective is misleading, inaccurate, and superficial. They seek to demonstrate this in a discussion of the "glocalized" Olympic Games, saying that it "is more a spectacular unity-in-difference [read glocalization] than a serious contribution to global homogenization [read grobalization]."[17] Clearly, this quotation better reflects the view that in discussing the Olympic Games, and much else, we need to be attuned to both glocalization and grobalization.

The example they use is of the games' opening ceremonies and how they are designed to "stage" the local (nation). Thus, the Olympics are seen as reflecting myriad local representations and furthermore are interpreted and lived differently from one locale to another. Again, while this is true, we must also recognize that the local spectacles are created on the basis of the grobalization of the central importance of spectacles as well as a grobal model of how such spectacles are to be staged and intensified by the control exercised by the grobal media for whom the spectacles are staged. As Andrews and Grainger point out, there are global international feeds of Olympic events that can be embellished locally by those nations that can afford to do so. It must not be forgotten in this context that the media are one of the great grobalizing forces in the world today (Andrews and Grainger discuss News Corporation and its efforts to "advance globally uniform processes and technologies"), and they are central to the grobalization of sport. And as Andrews and Grainger admit, only more well-to-do nations can embellish global feeds with local content that reflects local interests. Poorer nations are doomed to grobalization, especially the grobalization of nothing, at least in this context, because all they are likely to receive are the global feeds of sporting events. The media presentations of these events are, of course, centrally conceived and controlled and lacking in distinctive content.

Finally, Andrews and Grainger discuss glocal sport bodies. Here too they focus on what I would think of as grobalization—"corporate sport's scouring of the world for superior athletic talent."[18] That is, they are referring to the big-time sports—professional (and to lesser extent college) basketball in the United States and soccer (usually called football outside the United States)—that are increasingly dominated by wealthy individuals and corporations. (A good example is the recent purchase of the fabled Manchester United football team by American entrepreneur Malcolm Glazer.) They are willing to do—and pay—whatever is necessary to bring great talent from anywhere in the world to their teams. This clearly involves the imperialism of the wealthy teams, as well as the countries in which they reside—almost always the United States or the global North. Quoting a well-known sport sociologist, Andrews and Grainger note: "[T]he core states dominate and control the exploitation of resources and production."[19]

Following their usual pattern, they immediately disown and desert a grobalizing perspective for glocalization, arguing that "it would be wrong to assume unidimensionality" (which, of course, need *not* be assumed to accept the relevance of the idea of grobalization) because "there are various iterations of, and motivations for, the sport migrant experience the *variations* of which depend on the sporting migrants' range of movements, length of stay in any one given space, and level of remuneration."[20] All of this is interpreted through the lens of the various types and subtypes of glocalization while all the while grobalizing terms like "corporeal neocolonialism," "social and economic rape," and transnational corporations incorporating "localities into the imperatives of the global" are employed in the discussion. Most damningly, Andrews and Grainger conclude this section of their essay by discussing an "external and commercially inspired locus of control, which produces little more than *generalized recipes of locality.*"[21] The production of such recipes is unquestionably grobalization. Reasonably, they then go on to say that this may be a "corollary of sporting glocality." Bravo! Here we see a reasonable position in which the glocal is not elevated far beyond its importance and is seen as merely a corollary of something else—and that can be nothing other than the grobal. The essay concludes, predictably, with a discussion of "sport within the glocal age." However, if Andrews and Grainger had not simply *assumed* the dominant glocal paradigm and examined their own argument carefully, to say nothing of the globalization of sport, they would have seen that what they were describing was actually sport in the grobal-glocal age!

Analyzing McDonaldization Anthropologically: More Use and Abuse of Glocalization

I now turn to a much broader example of the exaggerated importance of the phenomenon of glocalization, this time in a body of literature in anthropology. Rather than focusing on grobalization in general, this literature revolves more around a critique of the more specific grobalizing process of McDonaldization. It is traceable to the work of a well-known Harvard anthropologist—James Watson—and some of his students.

McDonald's in East Asia

The key document in this tradition is Watson's edited volume, *Golden Arches East: McDonald's in East Asia.*[22] The heart of this anthology is five essays by five anthropologists, including one by Watson, on McDonald's in five areas in East Asia—Beijing, Hong Kong, Taipei, Seoul, and Japan in general. As an anthropologist, Watson does not appear to know or use the term *glocalization*, nor is it referenced in the Index (the term is more popular among sociologists), but that is clearly what he sees when he looks at East Asia, and much the same is true of the authors of each of the other essays in his volume.

In the Preface, Watson describes the origin of his interest in the impact of McDonald's in East Asia and begins with a 1989 visit to a McDonald's in the New Territories area of Hong Kong. After a number of visits to that

restaurant, he realized the importance of the phenomenon he was observing—
that McDonald's had become central to the lives of many people there. He
recruited the other authors involved in the anthology, and all were aston-
ished to discover "how deeply fast food chains had affected the lives of people we thought we knew well."[23] Clearly, such a statement reflects a deep
understanding of grobalization, but that is not the direction Watson and the
other authors intended to take.

Rather, Watson is animated by what he considers a destructive fad
among anthropologists "to become increasingly detached from the interests
and preoccupations of ordinary people."[24] Thus, he sees the work in this
volume as part of a trend in anthropology to redefine the field as the study
of everyday life. In the case of McDonald's, he seeks to "situate the global
[McDonald's] in the local." He goes on to say that "our aim is to determine
how McDonald's worldwide *system* has been adapted to local circumstances in five distinct societies."[25] Thus, the focus is on the local and how
McDonald's adapts to it. This means, of course, that what is *ignored* are the
ways and degree to which McDonald's imposes itself on the local. While
there is no question that McDonald's adapts, there is also no question that
in various ways it imposes itself on the local. In mentioning McDonald's
worldwide system, Watson clearly recognizes that grobalization exists, but
because of his commitment to redirect anthropology in the direction of the
local and everyday life, he is simply not going to deal with it. To my way
of thinking, in so doing, Watson is excluding from consideration at least
half of what is needed to understand fully globalization.

This orientation leads Watson and the other authors in the methodological direction of "personal interviews and informal conversations with
consumers."[26] While this is a perfectly acceptable methodology, it further
biases the researchers in the direction of the local, since all they are likely
to see and hear about is the local and they are likely to interpret the grobal
as the local. To develop a more balanced view of the grobal-glocal continuum, the researchers would have been well advised to *also* interview managers, as well as executives of McDonald's throughout East Asia and at
central headquarters in the United States. It is they who would have been
able to tell the researchers about the ways in which McDonald's grobalizes
throughout East Asia and the rest of the world.

In his Introduction, Watson early on indicates not only the starting point
but also the conclusion of the volume: "Since the early 1970s, an entire
generation of Japanese and Hong Kong children has grown up with
McDonald's; to these people the Big Mac, fries, and Coke do not represent
something foreign. McDonald's is, quite simply, 'local' cuisine."[27] Key here
is what these phenomena "represent" to East Asians. There is no question

that East Asians can and do redefine these things as local, but just as clearly, the phenomena they are redefining are grobal in character. Again, fully half the equation is omitted from Watson's analysis. Watson concludes, "East Asian consumers have quietly, and in some cases stubbornly, transformed their neighborhood McDonald's into local institutions."[28] Lacking the term *glocal* here, Watson uses the idea of the "local," but since globalization is involved—in this case the spread of McDonald's to East Asia—it is clear that Watson is really describing some combination of the global (or grobal) and the local, or the glocal. It would be more accurate to substitute the term "glocal" for "local" in the preceding quotation.

Watson's bête noire is, of course, grobalization, but lacking such a term or concept, he focuses instead on "cultural imperialism." In order to demean this idea, he argues that this is the view of both (presumably misguided) Chinese officials and "European and American intellectuals." Watson all but says that to adopt such a perspective is wrong-headed and the orientation of ill-informed Chinese officials and fuzzy-thinking intellectuals who have not immersed themselves in the local context. Later in his Introduction Watson explicitly addresses my work and the McDonaldization thesis and implicitly dismisses it almost immediately by linking it to the dreaded "cultural imperialism." To dismiss such ideas in this way is a clear case of anti-intellectualism and involves a very limited conception of globalization.

Watson further biases the argument by associating cultural imperialism with a view of McDonald's as an "evil empire" and as "an irresistible force."[29] Few really see McDonald's as an evil empire, and even in my largely critical analysis, I am careful to point out some of the positive characteristics of McDonald's and McDonaldization. More important, no one portrays McDonald's as an irresistible force. This is another extreme term that is employed to dismiss cultural imperialism, McDonaldization, and, implicitly, grobalization. While these forces are not irresistible, they *are* nonetheless powerful, and we cannot and must not ignore that fact. This view is implicit when Watson argues that "McDonald's does not *always* call the shots" (italics added).[30] Of course it doesn't, but the clear implication is that McDonald's *does* call the shots some of the time. This is another way of saying that it involves *both* glocalization and grobalization.

Later, Watson does much the same thing by arguing that "consumers are not the automatons many analysts would have us believe."[31] Of course no "analysts" are cited here, and the fact is that few, if any, believe any such thing. What many do believe, including me, is that McDonald's goes to great lengths to control its customers. However, there are limits to this. Agents always possess the ability to act in unanticipated and idiosyncratic ways. McDonald's customers are *not* automatons, but their actions *are* nonetheless tightly and highly controlled.

Interestingly, Watson understands the nature of the McDonald's system and the way in which it exports that system to the rest of the world. He discusses the company manual and the ways in which it carefully details how things are to be done—down, for example, to the thickness of the pickle slices—and ultimately how "[n]othing is left to chance."[32] The exportation and employment of the centrally conceived company manual to the far reaches of East Asia is an excellent example of grobalization. Also fitting into the thrust of this argument is Watson's recognition of the fact that the food, the nature of the menu, the character of the work, and the structure of the restaurants are much the same, if not identical, throughout the world. Furthermore, if McDonald's leaves nothing to chance, doesn't this apply, as well, to the actions of consumers in East Asia, at least to some degree?

Toward the close of his introductory essay Watson does come to a conclusion that is not dissimilar to the argument being made in this book:

> The process of localization is a two-way street: It implies changes in the local culture as well as modifications in the company's operating procedures. Key elements of McDonald's industrialized system—queuing, self-provisioning, self-seating—have been accepted by consumers throughout East Asia. Other aspects of the industrial model have been rejected, notably those relating to time and space.[33]

I don't think it distorts this statement much to say, in my terms, that Watson is describing McDonald's in East Asia as existing somewhere between the extremes of glocalization[34] and grobalization.

Even clearer from this point of view is that Watson concludes from his own analysis of McDonald's in Hong Kong that it "is no longer possible to distinguish what is local from what is not."[35] Or, more specifically, "Hong Kong consumers have accepted the basic elements of the fast food formula, but with 'localizing' adaptations."[36] Again, this all could easily be rephrased, in the terms used here, to argue that the local and the grobal increasingly interpenetrate, and therefore what is really being described is that which lies somewhere on the grobal-glocal continuum, albeit closer, at least in Watson's view, to the glocal end of the continuum.

While Watson takes great pains to show the power of the East Asian consumer, he also recognizes how McDonald's, in turn, has transformed that consumer. One of the most striking examples is the role that McDonald's played in transforming Hong Kong children into consumers. Prior to the late 1970s, Hong Kong children rarely ate outside the home, and when they did, they had no choice in terms of what they ate; they ate what they were told to eat. McDonald's catered to the children's market and offered them choice, and it thereby played a central role in the fact that today children are active and choosey consumers in the Hong Kong market. Similarly, the celebration of birthdays in Hong Kong (often at McDonald's) is another recent change in which McDonald's played a central role.

Yet, in the end, Watson feels compelled to return to his "hobby horse" and argues: "[T]he ordinary people of Hong Kong have most assuredly *not* been stripped of their cultural heritage, nor have they become the uncomprehending dupes of transnational corporations."[37] Agreed! But neither have they been unaffected by grobalization in general and McDonaldization in particular. Hong Kong consumers are not dupes, but neither are they all-powerful in the face of McDonald's various impositions on them.

In another analysis in the Watson volume, McDonald's in Japan is seen as "*Americana as constructed* by the Japanese."[38] Again, this kind of terminology can easily be rephrased as a glocal phenomenon involving the integration of the grobal ("Americana") and the local ("Japanese"). While power is accorded to the Japanese consumer, McDonald's did lead to many significant changes in, for example, table manners. Eating sandwiches with bare hands is a problem for the Japanese, and the solution is that sandwiches are often served cut into small pieces and with toothpicks for eating the pieces without using one's bare hands. There are certain "culturally prescribed" foods that must be eaten with bare hands, but in those cases the hands are first cleansed with wet towels. Ohnuki-Tierney observed that this norm was largely unaffected by McDonald's, since most "ate their hamburgers in the paper wrapping in such a way that their hands did not directly touch the food."[39] However, the norm of not eating while standing "has received a direct hit from McDonald's."[40] In other words, in terms of these two dimensions, the Japanese, at least when this analysis was done in the mid-1990s, retain some local traditions (not touching food with bare hands), but in others (not eating while standing) they have tended to surrender to global norms. Another way of putting this is that Japanese behavior in fast-food restaurants can be placed somewhere between the glocal and grobal extremes; it certainly cannot be adequately described as simply "local." Ohnuki-Tierney concludes that the changes that have occurred are "particularly significant"[41] to Japanese society. In other words, things that are very dear to Japanese culture have been changed dramatically, and perhaps forever, by the grobalization associated with McDonald's.

Thus, the most general point here, as in the discussion of sport, is that the anthropological analysis of McDonald's in East Asia leads to the conclusion that while it is couched in other, often antagonistic, terms, what is actually being described is the interplay of the grobal and the glocal in a variety of specific contexts.

In the interpretation being offered here, McDonald's is clearly a grobal force that must adapt to local realities, and in the process it moves toward the glocal end of the grobal-glocal continuum. There are many other examples, beyond those already discussed, of adaptations made by McDonald's throughout the world, especially in this case in East Asia:

- "McDonald's experience in Beijing is a classic case of the 'localization' of transnational systems. . . . When customers linger in McDonald's for hours, relaxing, chatting, reading, enjoying the music, or celebrating birthdays, they are taking the 'fast' out of fast food. . . . It is . . . tempting to predict that, twenty years from now, the 'American' associations that McDonald's carries today will become but dim memories for older generations. A new generation of Beijing customers may treat the Big Mac, fries, and shakes simply as local products."[42]

- In Hong Kong, customers are also more likely to linger, and they do not bus their own debris, employees rarely smile, and napkins are dispensed one at a time. "It is no longer possible to distinguish what is local and what is not. In Hong Kong . . . the transnational *is* the local."[43]

- In Taipei, McDonald's is also a hangout, and regular customers come to know one another quite well. "[M]any consumers treat McDonald's as a home away from home. . . . This establishment has become 'localized' in that it plays a key role in the routines of everyday life for many people who live in the neighborhood."[44]

There are many other examples of this ilk in the Watson volume, and they are all taken, as in the quotations above, to indicate how local McDonald's has become in East Asia. While that is one interpretation, another is that there, as everywhere else, what we are witnessing is the creation of phenomena that have both grobal and glocal characteristics, phenomena that lie somewhere on the grobal-glocal continuum and involve, in some measure, *both* grobal and local elements. Indeed, in every locale there is a unique mix of all of this, with the result that the positions of, let's say, local McDonald's vary in terms of their specific position on the grobal-glocal continuum.

McDonald's in Russia

Melissa Caldwell, a student of Watson's, continues and expands this line of thinking in her analysis of McDonald's in Russia.[45] What she describes is a process by which McDonald's has been "localized" there, although she, unlike Watson, possesses the term *glocal,* which is certainly a better term for what she describes. The integration of a grobal force like McDonald's into the local is clearly glocalization. However, she prefers *localization* because she believes that terms like *glocalization* reify distinctions between the indigenous (local) and the imported (global).

Caldwell describes various aspects of what she thinks of as the localization of McDonald's in Russia. She associates this with the Russian notion of *Nash* (or "ours"). This idea encompasses both the homeland (Russia) and the physical space of one's home. Thus, McDonald's has become Russian, has come to be considered "home," home lives have been brought to McDonald's, and it has been brought into Russian homes. Russians are seen as having become comfortable with McDonald's; it has become familiar, and they have come to trust it. For example, as in various places in East Asia, Russians have come to treat McDonald's as home by, for example, holding important family occasions such as birthday parties there. However, her most important contribution to this line of argumentation is that Russians have gone further and "domesticated" McDonald's—they have made it and what it has to offer both familiar and comfortable. That is, they have brought it not just into their communities but even their homes by preparing and cooking their versions of McDonald's food there. One example is the preparation of milk shakes, largely unknown in Russia before the arrival of McDonald's, at home, as well as in many other venues. Muscovites also are now more likely to cook hamburgers at home, although the preparations sometimes take highly creative forms such as fried cabbage instead of hamburger between two slices of bread. Similarly, fried potatoes have become a staple, and children may well react negatively if potatoes fried at home are not exactly like their counterparts at McDonald's. As elsewhere, especially in the United States, fast food has become the standard, especially for children, against which virtually all other food is measured.

Caldwell clearly is uncomfortable with the idea of McDonaldization and, by implication, grobalization. Furthermore, she is even uncomfortable with the idea of glocalization, arguing that it is not a completely satisfactory idea to describe what she finds in Russia:

> Muscovites do not simply appropriate and refashion foreign elements as happens in processes of glocalization, but rather reorient their attitudes, feelings and affections in order to experience and know the foreign as something mundane and, hence, part of the local landscape. Despite the power of McDonald's to position itself as local, Muscovites are the final arbiters of this distinction.[46]

As we did with many of the arguments on sport, let us deconstruct this quotation:

1. Although there is recognition of grobalization in the form of the "power of McDonald's," it is largely dismissed, unanalyzed, and reduced to the power to "position itself" (even this involves grobalization) as part of the local rather than imposing itself on it.

2. At the same time, the use of the concept of glocalization (while it is acknowledged) does not go nearly far enough, as far as Caldwell is concerned. Foreign elements are *not* simply appropriated and refashioned but *transformed* into something mundane and part of the local landscape.

3. Great power is accorded not only to the local but also to individuals, the agents, who are here seen as the "final arbiters."

These three points serve to underscore an argument made earlier about the affinity between those who prefer glocalization (and in this case, localization) and a postmodern orientation (although Caldwell, like most others who do this work, is certainly not a postmodernist). Thus, like most postmodernists, she rejects totalizing forces like grobalization and McDonaldization and (over)emphasizes the power of both the local and the agent.

So, to Caldwell, "McDonald's is more than a localized or a glocalized entity in Russia. By undergoing a specifically Russian process of localization—Nashification—it has become a locally meaningful, and hence domesticated, entity."[47] But what is it that has been localized, domesticated? In this analysis it is largely the food and to a lesser extent the way customers use and relate to McDonald's restaurants. However, what we need to remember is that it is *this* food and *those* restaurants that have been grobalized. The processes of localization and domestication are taking place within the context of, and could never have occurred without, grobalization. In fact, in our terms, and as with all the other works being described here, what Caldwell is describing is the integration of the grobal and the local and the creation of phenomena that can clearly be positioned somewhere on the grobal-glocal continuum.

Beyond the Food

Furthermore, what Caldwell and most other analysts of McDonaldization and, implicitly, grobalization analyze is primarily the food and the ways in which the settings for food consumption are utilized by consumers. They see local adaptations in the food and the use of the restaurants and use this as the basis for rejecting McDonaldization (as a form of grobalization). However, this ignores the fact that the heart of McDonaldization does not lie in *either* the food or the settings but rather in the *principles* by which the fast-food restaurant, as well as other McDonaldized entities, are run. When one looks at those principles (or, in other terms, systems and structures)—efficiency, calculability, predictability, and control through nonhuman technologies—what one sees is that they have been grobalized, more or less in toto, everywhere McDonald's and other McDonaldized systems have gone.

In fact, a few insightful analysts have recognized the importance of those principles, and the systems that they produce, to the process of McDonaldization. For example, Alan Bryman, who created the idea of Disneyization as a parallel to McDonaldization and as another example of grobalization, makes it clear that it is the basic principles (efficiency, predictability, etc.)—*not* the food or the settings themselves—that lie at the base of McDonaldized (and Disneyized) systems.[48] And he argues that those principles and systems remain essentially the same whatever goods or services are offered and wherever in the world they are proffered. In fact, he goes on to argue that these principles and systems are "potentially more insidious processes because they are far less visible and immediately obvious in their emergence than the appearance of golden arches or of magic kingdoms on nations' doorsteps."[49]

Uri Ram offers a more complicated account of McDonaldization that takes into account both products (and services) and principles (and structures).[50] He differentiates between one-way (structural) and two-way (symbolic) models of globalization. The latter involve more of a grobal-local mix—that is, they are more glocal, whereas the former is more purely grobal in nature. The one-way model involves structures, and this idea is very close to the interrelated ideas of systems and principles that lie at the heart of McDonaldization. Furthermore, a one-way model implies the kind of processes suggested by the idea of grobalization. Thus, for example, McDonaldization involves the one-way grobalization of structures, systems, and principles. The two-way model involves products (and their associated symbols), including, say, the Big Mac. Such products are more likely to be glocal, to adapt to local realities, and to involve both global and local symbols. Furthermore, as symbols they can coexist with other very local symbols. Thus, in the Israeli case examined by Ram, the Big Mac coexists with the falafel, thereby creating a unique two-way, glocal combination of highly symbolic foods. However, even here Ram is forced to equivocate, arguing that such symbolic differences have done little more than to survive. In other words, the implication is that they too are likely to succumb to the one-way process of grobalization. That is, falafel will become so McDonaldized (grobalized) that it will become indistinguishable from the Big Mac. However, until that happens, Ram sees a continuation for the foreseeable future of the combination of structural uniformity and symbolic diversity. He calls this "glocommodification," but in my terms it involves a combination of the grobal and the glocal. In other words, what exists in Israel in this case at the present time can be located somewhere between the extremes of grobalization and glocalization. However, the clear trend, as far as Ram is concerned, is further movement toward the grobal end of the continuum.

It may well be that anthropologists, given the nature of their discipline, are locked into the concept of the local. After all, what defines the field is the ethnographic study of locals, of specific locales and their defining characteristics. Thus, anthropologists have difficulty moving from the local to the glocal, and of course they have even greater problems adopting a notion of grobalization. While anthropologists may have good disciplinary reasons for their inability to see these processes (at least in these terms), there is no excuse for those in other fields, especially sociology, to don the same blinders. While it may be acceptable, even desirable, for those in a given discipline to have a specific focus, it is incumbent on them to at least acknowledge and recognize the broader contexts in which their focus exists.

Take the most recent developments in the relationship between McDonald's and the Chinese market. In terms of the food, McDonald's continues to adapt to local tastes (although it also continues to sell its usual fare) by selling such foods as rice burgers (beef or chicken patties between two compressed rice cakes) and triangle wraps (a tortilla-type wrapper that might include beef or chicken, vegetables, and rice).[51] However, the big change undertaken by McDonald's was the introduction in 2005 of the drive-through (called De Lai Su—Get It Fast) to its restaurants. This structure is so foreign to the Chinese that McDonald's had to print flyers instructing people on how to use them and deploy employees in parking lots to direct customers to the drive-through lanes. The whole idea of takeout food is foreign to most Chinese, who, until now, have preferred leisurely meals in restaurants when they go out for a meal. But China is moving strongly in the direction of a car culture, and McDonald's is betting that more people will echo the sentiments of a Shanghai electronics company manager who regularly uses the drive-through at lunchtime and who says (sounding *very* American): "I don't have time to sit in the restaurant. . . . The pace of life here is very fast."[52]

Thinking About the Fate of the Local

A crucial issue in the preceding sections, and more generally in globalization theory, is the impact of globalization on the local. Melissa Caldwell and Eriberto P. Lozada, Jr. have addressed this topic in an essay titled "The Fate of the Local."[53] They are explicitly and implicitly addressing a range of theories associated with the idea of grobalization and the implications of that process for the local. They argue that among the implications of that paradigm are that grobalization imposes itself on the local, it destroys heterogeneity and leads to homogeneity, and as a result it greatly alters, if not destroys, the local.

They acknowledge the fact that grobalization does greatly impact on, change the fabric of, the local, but its impact is, in their view, ameliorated by a number of factors. The local is populated by agents who are not passive in the face of grobalization; they are not cultural "dupes." They do not simply accept grobalized cultural practices but rather are selective and adopt some while rejecting others. In addition, grobal commodities are not simply imposed on them, but locals actively want, and seek out, at least some of them. Then, the impact of grobalization is not equal; those with more social and economic resources will be better able to resist than others. The net result of all of this is that it is difficult to generalize about the fate of the local in light of grobalization, and that fate will be different from one setting to another.

They also argue that much of the concern about the fate of the local in the era of globalization is animated by mythical ideas about the local. Among those myths are the ideas that the local is an area untouched by civilization's modern conveniences; that the cultural practices of the local are unique, static, exotic, and primitive; that they are small in scale; and that they are locales where "everyone knows your name." Much of the concern about the local and its demise is animated by these ideas, and if the local is idealized, romanticized, and mythical, then there is far less reason to be concerned about threats to something that never really existed.

Perhaps their most potent argument is that the local is not what most globalization theorists think it to be. That is, they see it as a thing, but Caldwell and Lozada see it as a process of social change. The local is constantly being created and re-created by a wide range of larger and smaller social processes and social changes. Furthermore, it is an ongoing accomplishment of those who comprise the local, and that accomplishment is fragile and therefore subject to constant change and disruption. Relatedly, it is the "location-work" of locals that creates the local, and that location-work is ongoing and continual. In sum, the local is a dynamic, interactive, and continually renegotiated process.

This leads to the view that the local is not a thing being buffeted by grobalization but is itself a process that has been, and is, always affected by innumerable such processes.[54] There is nothing new about what is happening to the local today, and the implication is that the local, at least viewed as such a process, will continue to survive, if not flourish. As they put it, "[L]ocality is not lost in the tide of globalization."[55]

There is no question that Caldwell and Lozada offer some unique and useful ways of looking at the local. However, they do seem to exaggerate the power of the local and of those who live in such settings. At the same time, they underestimate the power of the grobal forces impinging on them. While it is true that the local has always been affected by larger forces, there is something new and more powerful about grobalization today.

What about the local from the point of view of the argument being made in this book? Clearly, the whole idea of the glocal assumes a local that is being integrated with the grobal. However, is there a local that exists independent of the grobal? Theoretically, it is certainly possible to conceive of a local existing independent of the grobal (and glocal). Prior to the recent and dramatic expansion of the grobal, the local was empirically predominant and easy to identify. However, the fact is that it is now increasingly difficult to identify the purely local. The vast majority of that which at one time could have been thought of as local is strongly influenced by the grobal. This means, among other things, that local products are likely now to be intertwined with imports from other parts of the world and themselves exported to other places to be integrated with that which is indigenous to them. In any case, the point is that the local, at least in the sense of anything that is *purely* local, is fast disappearing from the world scene.

This has many implications. For example, the disappearance of the truly local has dire implications for global cultural diversity. Where are the most important differences in the world to come from, if everything that we think of as local is, in fact, glocal? One answer, of course, is from distinctive glocal creations in different locales throughout the world, but those innovations will be, from the outset, informed and affected by the grobal. This will inherently limit their capacity to be true cultural innovations. More promising would be the interaction of two or more glocal phenomena producing unique entities that are not reducible to the glocalities that lie at their source. It may be that with the death of the local, the best hope for cultural innovation lies in the interaction among glocalities. It seems clear that distinctive glocal mixes will continue to provide diversity, but it also seems likely that it will not approach the amount and degree of diversity that existed throughout the world when it was possible to find something approaching the genuinely local.

Thus, the argument being made here (and in Chapter 1) is extreme as far as the local is concerned. That is, I am contending that we are witnessing the *death of the local,* at least as we have known it. This is a view that would upset many globalization theorists, especially those discussed herewith. And this argument holds even taking into consideration the interesting and useful arguments made by Caldwell and Lozada about the nature of the local. The bottom line is that it is increasingly difficult to find anything local in the world that has not been affected by grobalization. It can either be utilizing grobal elements (e.g., raw materials from other parts of the world), or it can be reacting against grobalization and seeking to sustain or re-create the local. However, in either of those cases, and in virtually any other one can conceive, it is increasingly difficult to find anything local unaffected by the grobal. It is that which leads to the view that we are witnessing the death of the local.

The idea of the death of the local is seemingly contradicted by a recent article by Darrel K. Rigsby and Vijay Vishwanath in the *Harvard Business Review* titled "Localization: The Revolution in Consumer Markets."[56] While the authors do not directly address globalization, they argue that in the United States, especially, many large companies are moving away from standardization and in the direction of localization. However, this does not mean that they are selling products tailored to the local market (something), but rather that they are tailoring the mix of their general products (nothing) to local markets. Thus, for example, while Wal-Mart sells three types of chilies in all its stores, it allocates almost 60 other types according to local tastes. In the terms of this book, Wal-Mart is distributing different mixes of various types of nothing, depending on the nature of local markets. This is the essence of what is meant by localization in this context. It is certainly *not* the idea that Wal-Mart is selling something (in this case, locally conceived and controlled chili that is produced by local cooks and is rich in distinctive content) in its various locales. To take another, even more extreme, example, Wal-Mart discovered that while ant and roach killer sold well in the South, the word *roach* put off northern customers. Rather than create a unique product for the northern market, Wal-Mart simply relabeled the same product "ant killer" and saw its sales increase dramatically.

That what is being discussed in terms of localization involves nothing is clear in the use of the idea of "templates" (and "modules") in this context. That is, Wal-Mart uses a variety of templates to decide what set of things should be found in a particular type of locale (e.g., Wal-Marts near office parks should have prominent islands with easy-to-obtain ready-made meals). As pointed out in Chapter 4, such templates are basic patterns that are conceived and used centrally to create each new form. Since the same pattern is used over and over, each iteration of the form is more or less exactly the same as every other. Thus, even in a case of what is called "extreme localization," Tesco in the United Kingdom uses five templates for selling its foods—traditional grocery store, one-stop hypermarket, a smaller supermarket, a tiny convenience store, and a Web site. Again, the use of a limited number of templates has no relationship to what is discussed in this book as that which is local and something. Thus, what is seen by Rigsby and Vishwanath as a revolution in localization is better seen as still more evidence of the death of the local.

Contributions to Cultural Theories of Globalization

Given this critique, what can we say in summation about the contributions of this book to cultural theories of globalization? I think they can be summarized in a series of succinct statements:

1. Globalization is a very broad process that encompasses a number of major subprocesses.

2. One way of looking at globalization is to see it as encompassing a wide range of processes that form a continuum ranging from the well-known "glocalization" on one end to the newly coined "grobalization" on the other.

3. The idea of a continuum makes it clear that most of what we think of as globalization falls somewhere between these two poles.

4. Another way of saying this is that both glocalization and grobalization are "ideal types" with few, if any, actual global processes being one or the other.

5. Thus, in looking at global processes or phenomena, we must assess their relative degree of glocal and grobal elements.

6. The local is largely downplayed in this formulation largely because it has been, or is being, decimated by the grobal. That which remains of it is integrated into, and adulterated by, the grobal.

I should add that while I do not go into the issues here, I believe that these ideas and orientations are also of relevance to other theories of globalization, including those dealing with economic and political issues. Clearly, the ideas of globalization and glocalization, as well as something and nothing, can easily be extended to these domains and theories.

7

The Globalization of
Consumer Culture—and
Global Opposition to It

As is clear throughout the preceding chapters, my focal interest in these pages is in the globalization, especially grobalization, of nothing, within the realm of consumption, itself proliferating throughout the globe at a breathtaking rate. For example, supermarkets, chain stores of all sorts, shopping malls, and airports (sites that make possible the taking, the "consumption," of flights, and in which, by the way, one increasingly finds shopping malls dominated by chain stores), among many other phenomena (e.g., credit cards, Gap jeans, Gucci bags, ATMs, clerks at chain stores and their scripted ways of interacting with customers), can all be thought of as nothing in the way that concept is used here, as obviously centrally involved in contemporary consumption and as being globalized extensively. Consumption is clearly playing a growing role in the lives of people in developed countries and, to the extent that they can afford it, in less developed countries as well (although they are more likely to be producers of nothing than its consumers). To the degree that consumption is increasingly dominated by nothing, people's lives are similarly involved with nothing and to an increasing degree.

However, it is not just consumption itself—the products people consume, the settings in which they consume them, the workers who serve consumers, and the services they offer—that is of interest here but also the existence and global proliferation of a more general consumer culture. The first task in this chapter is to define what I mean by "consumer culture." We will see that this culture encompasses not only some very familiar domains (shopping, for example), but has been extended in some rather surprising directions (e.g., education). Second, we turn to a discussion of the three major grobal processes—Americanization, McDonaldization, and capitalism, which have been of great concern in earlier discussions—as driving forces in the global expansion of consumer culture. Third, I introduce a new process—branding—that is not only important in producing consumer culture but also in the grobalization of nothing in the realm of consumption. That is, it is because products are increasingly moving toward the nothing end of the continuum that branding has become of such increasing global importance in seeking to differentiate the largely undifferentiatable types of nothing—for example, colas such as generics, Coca-Cola, Pepsi-Cola, and now Mecca-Cola (see Brands and the Something-Nothing Continuum section). Furthermore, the brands themselves are increasingly grobal phenomena. Fourth, I extend the discussion beyond the obvious consumer products to see just how broad consumer culture has become. Finally, we turn to the global backlash against the grobalization of consumer culture and, in this context, discuss the attacks of September 11, 2001, which can be seen, at least in part, as a response to such grobalization.

Before getting to this discussion, it should be made clear that there is obviously far more to globalization in general, and grobalization in particular, than consumer culture or even culture more generally. To make this book in general, and this chapter in particular, more manageable, the focus is on consumption, but clearly that is just the tip of the iceberg as far as globalization is concerned. In fact, early in Chapter 1, I enumerated some of the many domains that have undergone globalization and been studied by a wide range of scholars. This chapter seeks to communicate a better understanding of the globalization of consumer culture. Similar chapters could be written about the globalization of politics, criminal justice, education, and much else. Thus, this chapter should be seen as simply an example of what can be seen when the ideas developed in this book are applied to the social and cultural world.

Elements of Consumer Culture

To this point in the book, I have discussed various aspects of consumption[1]— especially the four nullities: *non*places, *non*things, *non*people, and *non*services—largely in isolation from one another. What has connected them until now is the fact that they are all involved in globalization and all are examples of nothing. However, they are connected in another important way. That is, they are key elements of, and important contributors to, consumer culture.

Before getting to a definition of consumer culture, I need to make two points. First, this discussion clearly implies that overall consumer culture itself tends toward the nothing end of our continuum. Second, that culture is, in pretty much its entirety, being grobalized.

Values

As with all other forms of culture, the idea of consumer culture has a broad, even all-embracing quality. Most generally, consumer culture means that a large number of people, perhaps most or all of a society, have come to *value* consumption. That is, consumption is not just about acquiring the basics that people need in order to survive. Rather, people collectively come to see consuming, as well as the goods and services obtained, as important and valuable in their own right. Douglas Goodman is very clear on this: "It is the focus on consumption as a central value that makes ours a consumer culture."[2] This is in stark contrast to the view that consumption is bound up with larger values such as choice, individualism, and the market.[3] While that is true, much more is being said with the idea of consumer culture, since it does not simply reflect our values, but "it has become a cultural value."[4] Thus, to talk about the globalization, or grobalization, of consumer culture is to discuss the worldwide proliferation of the propensity to value consumption. Thus, it is not just goods, or services, or settings that have been grobalized, but the idea that consumption is of value in its own right.

The globalization of consumer culture is not only important in itself, but also because it fosters all sorts of consumption not only of nothing but also of something (and everything in between). However, of greatest interest to us here is the fostering of the consumption of nothing, of *non*things in *non*places populated by *non*people who offer us *non*services.

People throughout the world who come to value consumption, who come to be part of consumer culture, are, to put it simply, more likely to be impelled to consume. While they may not yet have adequate means to consume very much, because of their involvement in such a culture they are likely to seek out ways of acquiring the means needed to consume more and more. While some may come to acquire the desire and the means to consume something, for most those desires and means will likely come to focus on the consumption of nothing, and in increasing quantities.

One sees the more tangible existence of consumer culture in others who share the same or similar ideas and values. This is especially the case when one is surrounded by other consumers throughout the world at the mall, at Disney World, in a casino-hotel, and so on. However, the tangible existence of consumer culture is far more pervasive than that. Billions of people see it many times a day in the ubiquitous advertisements for all manner of goods and services on the radio, television, computer screen, billboards, and even at the movie theater where moviegoers now pay, at least in part, to see commercials that are run prior to the beginning of the feature movie. And we are not just talking about the traditional commercials for other movies (previews or "coming attractions"), but advertisements for many of the same products, and in many cases the very same ads, people see on television.

But there is a way that the tangible aspects of consumer culture are even more pervasive and ubiquitous than that. That is, we are constantly engaged in acquiring goods and utilizing services, and, more important, surrounded by people who are displaying their latest acquisitions, often with very visible logos. Consumer culture is on display on the ride into, and home from, work—the various cars that surround us (often in traffic jams caused by the love affair in many parts of the world with the consumption of automobiles, especially the new models) and the signs and billboards that pop in and out of view—at work (acquisitions being sported by fellow workers); at lunch (other kinds of acquisitions being displayed by a wide array of others); and so on.

However, it is not just other individuals who value consumption; the collectivity as a whole comes to value consumption. I will soon turn to the centrality of the United States in the idea and reality of consumer culture, but to anticipate that discussion, it is worth pointing out that it could be argued that consumption is valued by American society in general. In the United States, consumption is of collective importance. The vast majority of Americans seem to value consumption, and it is of great importance to the collectivity that large numbers of people consume as much and as often as possible. The collectivity needs Americans to do this not only because it is necessary that what the culture values be reaffirmed regularly, but also because active consumption generates needed jobs and incomes for others. And it is with those jobs and the resulting incomes that others can themselves be active participants in consumer culture and, in the process, reaffirm that culture themselves. More generally, we are constantly reminded by business and political leaders of the importance of doing our patriotic duty by consuming. I return to the latter theme below in my discussion of September 11 and its aftermath.

Of course, the United States is not the only collectivity that values consumption. With globalization, the collectivities in many other nations have come to value it. Furthermore, the global North in general not only values consumption, but also most have the means to afford a wide range of consumables. It is likely also that large portions of the global South are coming to have a similar set of values, although the ability of most of the people who live there to afford very much is highly limited or, in some cases, nonexistent. Nonetheless, consumer culture has penetrated deeply into the global South, and this is likely to create high levels of frustration among many of those who live there who may have internalized its values but lack the means to achieve them. Of course, the same sort of thing could be said of the poor in the North who are in much the same situation.

Practice

So, in consumer culture, people value consumption and they are likely to be surrounded by its many manifestations virtually everywhere they turn. Beyond that, they act it out often; they *practice* consumer culture. Such practice is important in all forms and types of culture. Culture becomes little more than a set of ideas, especially values, unless it is acted out, and regularly, by the members of the collectivity. For example, in primitive cultures, people act out their cultures through, among many ways, engaging in various rituals. In a consumer culture, people act out and reaffirm that culture by engaging in the process of consumption and in displaying, sometimes conspicuously, that which has been consumed. It could be argued that in consumer culture, there is a wide range of acts that involve acting out consumer culture. Examples might include a daily visit to the fast-food restaurant, the Saturday afternoon trip to the mall (and perhaps the multiplex in or near the mall), and yearly vacation trips to Disney World, to a Las Vegas casino-hotel, on a modern cruise ship, or to innumerable other major cathedrals for the consumption of tourism. Indeed, many of these take on the quality of rituals that must be enacted and reenacted as often as possible. Thus, it could easily be argued that those weekly trips to the mall, the yearly trips to Vegas, and the once-in-a-lifetime hajj to Disney World for each of one's children have such a ritualized quality.

These practices, like the values associated with consumer culture, have been globalized. Thus, increasingly many people around the world engage in similar practices associated with consumer culture. For example, whether one is an American (or a Canadian) going to Disney World in Orlando, a Japanese going to Disney World in Tokyo, a Chinese going to Disney World Hong Kong, or a citizen of virtually any European nation going to Disney World outside Paris, one engages in very similar, and on occasion identical, practices, such as driving to the park, parking in the contiguous lot, paying for admission passes, entering via Main Street, queuing for attractions, and buying food and Mickey Mouse hats.

Objects and Artifacts

This is related to the point that culture in general, and consumer culture in particular, manifests itself in a wide range of *objects* and *artifacts* (the very familiar and ubiquitous Mickey Mouse hat mentioned above would be a prime example).[5] They are not only an expression of culture but become critical components of it. For one thing, the huge, and ever-increasing, number of goods (and services) available for purchase is clearly an expression of a consumer culture that not only values consumption but the consumption of virtually everything and anything one can imagine. The various settings (cathedrals of consumption) in which we consume can also be seen as objects that express the value we place on consumption. Then there is the credit card, which is both an object that expresses today's consumer culture but also one that allows us to consume virtually all the other objects (and services) that constitute it.

Enforcement

Another important part of any culture, including consumer culture, is the ability of, indeed need for, others to reward those who are dedicated consumers and to sanction those who do not conform to the demands of the culture. Culture, especially that which is valued, needs to be *enforced*. This is obvious and powerful in some cases, such as the use of law enforcement agencies to be sure that people act in law-abiding ways. However, it is far more difficult in the case of an aspect of culture like consumption where there are no laws (at least as yet!) compelling people to participate in consumer culture. Thus, control in this domain is far more subtle, stemming from things like advertisements or the cues and comments from those around us. However, even though such control is usually quite low key, it is still a form of control. Furthermore, even though it is more subtle than the use of the police officer's billy club in the case of law enforcement, it is no less important. Consumer culture, indeed modern society as we now know it, would collapse if large numbers of people did not consume, or did not consume enough. Indeed, some observers have described such people as "dangerous consumers."[6] That is, they pose a danger not only to consumer culture but also to the larger society by not consuming enough or by consuming the wrong things (say, used and discarded clothing). A consumer culture, especially one characterized, as ours is, by hyperconsumption, can ill afford very many dangerous consumers. The result is that people who, for example, wear used clothing or even clothing that is merely out of fashion are likely to be looked at askance by their peers, and such looks are often enough to persuade most people to alter their buying habits and upgrade their wardrobes. More generally, most of those enmeshed in a consumer culture feel great pressure from others to consume not only that which is new and in fashion but to consume lots of everything that falls into those categories.

Meaning

Perhaps above all, consumer culture involves a search for *meaning* in one's life through consumption.[7] At one time, and to a lesser degree today, people derived great meaning from work, family, community, religion, but all of those seem less important today as sources of meaning (and practice).[8] Instead, meaning is increasingly likely to come from shopping[9] or touring,[10] both of which are likely to involve visits to one or more of the cathedrals of consumption. In fact, it seems clear that some of our most important *rituals* involve those trips to the mall and to a place like Las Vegas.

A good example of the search for meaning through consumption, and of the growth of consumer culture more generally, is the degree to which various holidays have become commercialized. The best example of this is, of course, Christmas (although Chanukah and Kwanzaa have also undergone the same process). Then there are all the holidays—Valentine's Day, Halloween, Mother's Day, Father's Day, Easter, St. Patrick's Day, New Year's Day, and so on—that involve seemingly obligatory purchases of one kind or other (chocolate rabbits, scary costumes, noisemakers), especially greeting cards. To many critics, the original meanings of many of these holidays, and the traditional rituals associated with them, have been perverted and even lost in an avalanche of consumption. In many other cases, the holidays are wholly, or in part, fabrications of commercial interests, especially the greeting card companies and their interest in creating ever-new ways of spurring on sales of their cards. The issue becomes: What sort of meaning do people derive from holidays that have become, to a large degree, commercialized?

The aforementioned should give the reader at least a sense of what is meant by consumer culture in this context. The fact is that it, as well as the idea of culture more generally, is highly complex, and entire volumes could be written about it alone. However, this should suffice to allow us to make the point that at the most general level, it is consumer culture that has been, and is being, grobalized.

One of the best examples of this grobalization of consumer culture relates to the preceding discussion of the commercialization of various holidays. It is quite amazing to see many commercialized holidays that are partly or wholly American fabrications (e.g., Valentine's Day) being celebrated in an increasing number of countries throughout the world. More generally, it can be argued that consumer culture in its entirety—its values, practices, modes of enforcement, objects and artifacts, rituals, and meaning—has been grobalized.

Driving Forces Behind the Globalization of Consumer Culture

What are the forces behind the grobalization of consumer culture? While many forces could be identified, I focus here on our three "usual suspects"— capitalism, Americanization, and McDonaldization.

Capitalism and Consumer Culture

Capitalism is ordinarily associated with production in general and manufacturing in particular. From a Marxian perspective, capitalism is defined by the private ownership by the capitalists of the "means of production"[11] (e.g., the factories). Also central is the work occurring in those means of production, especially that performed by the proletariat. With such factories and work of declining importance in advanced capitalist societies, the focus has shifted to other kinds of settings and work, especially those associated with services of all types and the knowledge society. However, even with this shift, the focus remains on production (of services and knowledge) and (service and knowledge) work. Within the context of this view of capitalism, globalization can be seen as the global spread of these production and work systems as well as the interrelationships among them.

However, there has been an increasing realization over the years that capitalism not only requires the globalization of production and work but also the global spread of consumer culture. A neo-Marxist thinker, Lesley Sklair, deals with this under the heading of the globalization of what he calls the "culture ideology of consumption."[12] A number of things are clear in this concept. First, in slightly different terms, Sklair is obviously talking about the consumer culture of concern here. Second, by adding the idea of "ideology," Sklair is implying various things, including the fact that consumer culture involves a system of ideas (e.g., values), that there is at least an element of distortion involved in that set of ideas, and that it is expansionistic seeking to involve an increasing number of people, potentially across the globe.[13]

The most important point, however, in this line of thinking is the idea that capitalism can no longer rely solely on production but also must concentrate on creating ever-larger numbers of people in more and more parts of the world willing, even eager, to consume the products being produced. Thus, capitalism is increasingly as much about producing consumers and consumer culture as it is about creating products and services. Consumption has come to be deemed too important to be left to the whims of consumers. The latter need to be led to consume various things, ideally in great quantities. A major factor involved in leading consumers to do this is the creation, nurturance, and global dissemination of consumer culture and all of its elements.

Americanization and Consumer Culture

This is all clearly closely tied to Americanization, because capitalism itself has obviously reached its peak in the United States, which is the global center of capitalism. At one time, it was America's production systems that lay at the center of global capitalism, but that is no longer the case as more and more production has moved, in part as a result of advances (in shipping, communication, etc.) in globalization, to many other places in the world, especially less developed countries. However, the United States remains a potent force in global production because, in Sklair's terms, it remains the center of many *transnational corporations* (e.g., Microsoft, Nike) and it contains many members of the world's *transnational capitalist class,* including many of the wealthiest, most powerful, and most influential members of that class (e.g., Bill Gates).[14] Nonetheless, the fact remains that other places in the world (China, India) have replaced the United States as the center of various types of production and the work associated with it.

Like modern capitalism, modern consumer culture did not develop originally in the United States but has been traced to 18th-century England and 19th-century France and perhaps even to 15th- or 16th-century England. However, it is clear that the United States has become the global center of consumption and consumer culture, but more important, of the creation and global dissemination of that culture. Initially, that consumer culture emerged during the heyday of American manufacturing, but in recent years it has expanded enormously, even though it now is more likely to benefit manufacturers in many other parts of the world. However, the United States benefits as well, especially in the service-sector jobs created by consumer culture. It also benefits from the exportation of its cathedrals of consumption and other mechanisms associated with consumption (most notably credit cards) that have been heavily exported and that bring great profits to American corporations. Among other things, this means that America has sought to have much of the rest of the world value consumption in general, as well as the consumption of more specific goods and services, as much as it does. Once others value these things, they will come to engage in the various practices and rituals (and related modes of enforcement) associated with such a culture and that are necessary to sustain it. The goal is to create others throughout the world who find consumption, especially shopping (and the associated objects and artifacts), as meaningful as do Americans. And, to a large degree this has been successful as one sees centers of consumer culture—the indoor and high-rise shopping malls that line Orchard Road in Singapore are a good example—that, if anything, exceed those found in the United States. There is now a burgeoning literature on consumer culture in Japan,[15] China,[16] Russia,[17] India,[18] and other parts of the world.

The United States has achieved this position by being the point of origin, and still the global center, of many of the agencies responsible for consumer culture. For example, modern advertising and marketing were to a large degree American inventions, and the United States continues to occupy a hegemonic position in those domains.[19] Needless to say, it is advertising and marketing campaigns, many of them now global in nature, that have played a huge role in generating and sustaining consumer culture. Then there are the mass media, especially television and the Internet these days, and the fact that they too were American inventions that now play a central role in consumer culture. Marketing and advertising campaigns generally focus on these media outlets. Furthermore, much of the content (e.g., the programs on television) serves to support, and is representative of, advanced consumer culture, especially as it is manifested in the United States. This is true of another medium—motion pictures—that has long been dominated by the United States and, indeed, is a domain in which the U.S. dominance has been increasing and is likely to increase further in the future. The images one sees in such movies—say, the James Bond series (ironically based on a fictional British secret agent)—reflect the latest in consumption items such as gorgeous homes, up-to-date fashions, and expensive automobiles. Indeed, in recent years, manufacturers have signed deals with the motion picture companies in order to have their cars (and innumerable other products)—via what is called product placement—featured in important movies.

A particularly good example of the link between consumer culture, Americanization, and grobalization is the spread of the "new means of consumption,"[20] most of which were created in the United States and are now proliferating throughout the world.[21] The new means of consumption are, in the main, settings (a supermarket is one example, although one that is not very new) that allow us to consume or that serve to increase the amount that we consume. There has been an almost dizzying creation and proliferation of settings that allow, encourage, and even compel us to consume innumerable goods and services. These settings have come into existence, or taken revolutionary new forms, in the United States since the close of World War II. Building upon, but going beyond, earlier settings, they have dramatically transformed the nature of consumption. Furthermore, they have become an integral part of consumer culture as well as the settings in which much of that culture expresses itself and plays itself out.

The following are the major new means of consumption, with notable examples and the year in which they began operations:

- Casino-hotels (Flamingo, 1946)
- Theme parks (Disneyland, 1955)
- Franchises (McDonald's, 1955)[22]
- Shopping malls (the first indoor mall, Edina, Minnesota, 1956)
- Superstores (Toys"R"Us, 1957)
- Discounters (Target, 1962)
- Cruise ships (Sunward, 1966)
- Eatertainment (Hard Rock Cafe, 1971)
- Megamalls (West Edmonton Mall, 1981; Mall of America, 1992)
- Home shopping television (Home Shopping Network, 1985)
- Cybershopping (Amazon.com, 1995; eBay, 1995)

With the exception of megamalls and the Edmonton Mall (created in Canada but now supplanted in importance by Minnesota's Mall of America) and eatertainment and the Hard Rock Cafe (which was created in London, albeit to bring "American" food to England), all of these are American innovations that, in recent years, have been aggressively exported to the rest of the world—that is, they have become grobal phenomena.

What is it about these new means of consumption that make them distinctly American (in Germany, the McDonaldized Starbucks have been described as "Anywhere USA"[23]), excellent examples of Americanization, when they are exported to other countries? First, and most obviously, they are about consumption, and the United States has been, and still is, by a wide margin the world leader in consumption and in innovations in that realm.[24] When anyone in the world thinks of consumption, a cornucopia of goods and services, and a rate of consumption so frenetic that one can only think of "hyperconsumption," one thinks of the United States.

Second, most of the new means of consumption relate in one way or another to the high rate of mobility associated with American culture. The vast majority of them have to do with the massive addiction of Americans to their automobiles, extensive and frequent automobile travel, and the consequent development of a road and highway system unparalleled in the world. Others relate to other types of mobility by plane (Las Vegas casino-hotels, Disney theme parks), by boat (cruise ships), and over the Internet (cybershops, cybermalls).

Third, the sustenance of these means of consumption requires the level of affluence that is so widely available in the United States. While other nations may have higher average levels of income, no nation has nearly as many people affluent enough to afford to visit, and to consume in, these sites on such a regular basis. So many Americans are so affluent that they can afford to eat more meals out in franchises,[25] eatertainment sites, and the like than people in any other nation. Only they can afford to descend in droves on meccas of consumption such as Las Vegas, Orlando, and Minneapolis.

Fourth, many of the new means of consumption reflect the American mania for that which is huge and enormous. The idea is that the United States is a huge country, and that necessitates that as much as possible be done in a big way. Many of the cathedrals of consumption reflect this peculiar mania for size—the megamalls, superstores, theme parks, cruise ships, and casino-hotels all seek to outdo each other in terms of size. Size is also reflected in the sheer quantity of products available in these settings. Malls and megamalls are chock full of well-stocked stores (often franchises); superstores have virtually everything one could think of in a particular line of products (sporting goods, athletic shoes, linens, etc.); Disney theme parks, especially Disney World, are characterized by a number of worlds, tens of thousands of hotel rooms, many restaurants, and much kitsch for sale; and of course Las Vegas is over the top in terms of everything it has to offer, and it increasingly seems to offer everything. Then there is, of course, the tendency for fast-food restaurants of all types to be in the business of "supersizing" everything they possibly can.

McDonaldization and Consumer Culture

This process is, of course, closely related to the preceding two processes. The fast-food restaurant and chain was, like many of the other phenomena discussed above, an American invention that has been globalized. And it is, of course, a capitalistic enterprise. Of main importance here is the fact that it plays a central role in consumer culture. There are many things that could be pointed to in this context, but one must certainly be the ubiquity of the fast-food chains and their mundane character. That is, it seems that everywhere one turns, there is a familiar fast-food restaurant and it is offering the kind of things that people need (or think they do) on a regular, if not daily, basis. Thus, many people in advanced societies eat a large proportion of their meals in fast-food restaurants instead of at home. Consuming in a fast-food restaurant has become a fundamental part of consumer culture. Furthermore, while many other forms of culture such as purchasing homes, cars, or consumer electronics occur very infrequently and irregularly, eating in a fast-food restaurant is for many a weekly, if not a daily, occurrence. It is the regularity and ubiquity of it that gives eating in fast-food restaurants, and participating in other McDonaldized activities, their centrality in consumer culture. It also transformed something that was in the past consumed in one's home, often with many homegrown ingredients, into a central part of the larger consumer culture.

Of course, fast-food restaurants and other McDonaldized systems are tied into consumer culture in many other ways. For example, advertisements for them are ubiquitous throughout the mass media, and one often sees them prominently displayed in the movies. Then there is the wide array of tie-ins to other aspects of consumer culture, most notably advertising campaigns that link giveaways or sales at fast-food restaurants with movies, especially blockbusters targeted to a large degree at children.

McDonaldized systems are not just bastions of consumer culture; they are also important grobalizing phenomena. As a result, as they grobalize, they help bring with them the consumer culture of which they are an integral part.

Overall, then, consumer culture is at the heart of globalization/grobalization today. It is both a product of, and disseminated by, a variety of processes, especially the highly interrelated processes of capitalism, Americanization, and McDonaldization.

The Role of Branding

Many brand names have been touched on throughout the course of this book and in the preceding discussion of consumer culture. Indeed, brands are central to consumer culture, *and* they are themselves not only being grobalized, but they are playing a central role in the grobalization of consumer culture. Brand names such as Disney, McDonald's, and Hallmark are, increasingly, global phenomena. The companies that they represent, as well as the marketing and advertising firms hired to develop and refine them, are key forces in the grobalization of brands, as are the media to which they are so important and which could not exist without them. Indeed, the global media—CNN, BBC, Al-Jazeera—have themselves become global brands.

Up to this point, however, our concern has been with the phenomena being branded—things, places, people, and services—rather than with the branding process.[26] That process is closely related to the others discussed above—the grobalization of consumer culture, capitalism, Americanization, and McDonaldization—but it is of such growing importance that it needs to be dealt with separately in terms of its role in consumer culture and its grobalization, as well as its relationship to nothing. In terms of the preceding processes, branding is

- central to the success of *consumer culture*;
- of crucial importance to many contemporary *capitalistic* businesses (even the brands in pharmaceuticals such as Viagra), especially the biggest and most successful of them (e.g., Wal-Mart);
- strongly rooted in the *United States* and its premier marketing and advertising firms;
- central to *McDonald's,* which is a prime example of the importance of this process, including on a global basis, in order to succeed in today's economy.

Branding and Consumer Culture

A brand may be defined "as a name, logo, or symbol intended to distinguish a particular seller's offerings from those of competitors."[27] The great success of branding can be seen in the degree to which not only most Americans but many throughout the world, developed and less developed, are intimately familiar with brand names such as Coca-Cola, McDonald's, and Nike, as well as the logos associated with them such as the Coca-Cola signature, the Nike swoosh, and, of course, McDonald's golden arches.

Branding can be seen as the process by which great time, effort, expertise, and money are invested in creating and publicizing names, logos, and symbols with the goal of having them recognized, perhaps even instantaneously, wherever the product in question is sold. Of course, the majority of such efforts fail, but great rewards await those corporations, marketers, and advertising agencies that succeed. For one thing, the creation of a successful brand leads, and is closely related, to increased sales and profits. For example, when McDonald's arrived, belatedly, in Russia in the early 1990s, its brand name was already well known, and for a long time after the first restaurant opened, people waited patiently in block-long lines to enter the restaurant and sample the food. Of course, this illustrates not only that brands are important to sales and profits in one's own country but in many cases also globally. For another thing, a successful brand becomes a prominent part of consumer culture and, in some cases, culture more generally. In terms of the latter, a brand like Coca-Cola was able to become synonymous, at least for a time, with American culture. That is, if Americans and many in other nations caught sight of a bottle of Coca-Cola (especially its original, very distinctive bottle) or even just its logo, it could automatically lead people to conjure up images of America and its culture. Conversely, if people thought of America, Coca-Cola would be pretty close to the top of the list of symbols that came to mind as being closely associated with, if not indistinguishable from, it.

More important for our purposes, a successful brand is a key component of consumer culture, perhaps its most visible representation:

1. A successful brand is in the end an *idea* that has come to be not only part of that culture but is internalized in, and become meaningful to, large numbers of people who participate in consumer culture. Thus, when many people feel thirsty, they automatically think of a "Coke." Indeed, for many, the word and the symbol are nearly synonymous with a soft drink. In fact, the most successful brands achieve that status and thus, at least for a time, bury the competition. Although it is not as important as it once was, the brand name Levis was synonymous with jeans. In addition, there was a time when Bayer was synonymous with aspirin and probably still is for some members of the older generation. Today, McDonald's has become synonymous with fast food, Starbucks with coffee and coffee shops.

2. As part of that consumer culture, we come to *value* the brand itself; somehow or other, Coca-Cola, Starbucks, and Wal-Mart become important to us.

3. Whenever we can, we are likely to engage in the *practice* of consuming one of those brands rather than any of its competitors.

4. Of course, brands are not just ideas, but they are embodied in various material *objects,* and it is usually those we actually purchase and consume (although it has been argued often that we are also, and perhaps more important, consuming the sign that is the brand[28]).

5. Finally, we are likely to be sanctioned, at least mildly, by others if we are consuming a less well-known brand, or worse, a generic product. Thus, in the case of the United States, if we are not drinking a Budweiser ("Bud") beer, we are likely to be looked at askance by those around us who are.

Thus, there are great rewards involved in creating a successful brand and having one's brand become an integral part of consumer culture. Indeed, it could be argued that what defines today's consumer culture is the preeminence and ubiquity of brands, the efforts to maintain and expand the successful ones, as well as the continual effort to launch new brands.

Branding can be seen as an effort to have a product's name, logo, or symbol become a key component of consumer culture. Of course, that is not an end in itself from the corporate point of view, but rather that attaining such a position translates into increased sales and profits. As was pointed out previously, the United States is the epicenter of *both* consumer culture and branding, but because they are closely linked to the demands of capitalism, both have become grobalized. The United States, especially its capitalistic businesses, has been very successful in exporting its consumer culture to many parts of the world. Furthermore, and much more obviously, its most successful brands have been grobalized, and in some cases they are not just recognized but have become a common vocabulary throughout great stretches of the world. It could be argued that the ultimate objective of the branding process is to have one's brand recognized around the world and to have that recognition translate into increased sales. In other words, at least the penultimate objective of the branding process is the grobalization of the brand.

Brands and the Something-Nothing Continuum

If the most successful brands are defined by grobalization, are we describing the grobalization of nothing or something when we discuss branding? Given the definitions of something and nothing, it is not easy to think of brands as something (even though they mean a great deal to many people, but of course many products that lie toward the nothing end of the continuum are also highly meaningful to many) in that they are *not* locally conceived and controlled. That is, brands are usually conceived and controlled by advertising agencies hired to manage a given account. However, brands *are* forms with distinctive content; the (ideational, emotional[29]) content associated with one brand is different from that associated with other, especially competing, brands. Thus, brands are centrally conceived and controlled, but they are also endowed with distinctive content. As a result, they *cannot* be thought of as nothing, or something for that matter, at least from the perspective of the definitions employed here. Thus, thinking of brands as either something or nothing is a difficult matter, and it would require considerable time and effort to try to unravel the complexities involved in this issue. I will leave such analysis for another occasion, but I do want to deal with another aspect of the relationship between brands and something and nothing in this section. That is, I want to argue that it is the increasing proliferation of nothing, nationally and globally, that makes branding increasingly important.

The importance of brands and branding is especially clear in the case of the mass-produced *non*things. If one manufacturer's mass production creates *non*things, and the mass-production processes of other manufacturers fabricate almost identical *non*things, then producers are faced with the task of seeking to differentiate their *non*things from those of their competitors or to create difference where little or none exists. A brand, especially one that is successfully marketed and imprinted in the minds of consumers, often serves to differentiate that which has little or no difference from its competitors. For example, there is little to distinguish Nike's running shoes from many other brand-name or even no-name shoes. Thus, great amounts of money and attention are devoted to promoting the brand and the icon—the swoosh—that has become inextricable from it. Indeed, Nike is almost a pure example of this because the corporation itself (and its advertising agencies) produces little other than the brand and the infrastructure to support and perpetuate it.

While we are accustomed to thinking of brands as applying to things (and especially *non*things), there has been a dramatic trend toward trying to brand not only things but also *non*places (e.g., Niketown), *non*people (the characters, played by cast members, that populate Disney World—Mickey Mouse, Snow White, etc.), and *non*services (AOL's "You've got mail").

Of course, perhaps *the* best example of the branding of nothing, and on a global basis, is bottled water.[30] Bottled water is centrally conceived and controlled, and it is perhaps the ultimate in a *non*thing lacking in distinctive content. There is little, if anything, to distinguish one (global) brand of bottled water (Perrier) from another (Evian), to say nothing of that available from our faucets. As a result, there is a very aggressive effort by these brands to create difference where absolutely no difference exists.

While all of this might not be so clear to consumers—indeed there are active efforts to conceal it from them—it is clear to experts in the field. One such expert argues, "Marketing is a battle of perceptions, *not products.* . . . *There is no objective reality* [italics added]. There are no facts. There are no best products. All that exists in the world of marketing are perceptions in the minds of customers or prospects. The perception is the reality. Everything else is an illusion."[31] In fact, in this world of illusion, that which is nothing has a great advantage over something. That is, since there is no distinctive substance to constrain it, the perceptions surrounding a given brand are free to be led, and to roam, anywhere and everywhere. In contrast, a brand that represents something is much more constrained by the distinctive content it represents.

Furthermore, there is relatively little need for branding when we are considering *things* (as well as *places, people,* and *services*). Not only is the mass production of things generally a contradiction in terms,[32] but a thing is defined by the fact that it is locally conceived, controlled, and produced, and little mass production takes place in and for local areas. A thing is further defined by its possession of truly distinctive content, and therefore there is little or no need for branding to differentiate that which is already well differentiated. That is, the more there is something on offer, the less the need for a brand. To a large degree, something sells itself. In one sense, there is little or no need to brand something. In another sense, something more or less automatically brands itself (a Picasso, or a Michael Jordan[33] or LeBron James dunk, for example). This is not to say that there are not active efforts at times to brand something. The examples that come to mind are tourism and the cases where great efforts are made to "brand" a locale that draws tourists from around the globe (e.g., Acapulco or Negril, Jamaica). However, it should be said that many such locales have moved in the direction of nothing, with, for example, row after row of large hotels owned by huge chains coming to dominate the landscape. Then there are local chambers of commerce or governmental agencies that centrally conceive and control such locales, turning them into largely mirror images of similar resorts elsewhere in the world.

Thus, the central points to be made here are that (a) a major reason for the existence of brands is to deal with the problem of nothingness in the world of consumption and (b) branding has grown exponentially because of the tremendous expansion, including globally, of such nothingness. Great expenditures and efforts are made to make that which brands represent seem like something. This need is inversely proportional to the degree of nothingness of that which the brand represents. In addition to the obvious example of bottled water, what could be more prosaic, more lacking in distinctive content, than a cola; innumerable companies can and do make colas, and there is little to differentiate one from another. Similarly, Nike's shoes are famously manufactured by independent contractors in Southeast Asia (and other places) that, on the same assembly lines and perhaps on the same day, may produce very similar running shoes under other brand, and no-brand, names. With little to distinguish the product, there is little choice (other than the price competition that most companies despise because it cuts into profits[34]) for the aspiring manufacturer than to create the illusion or image of difference through the creation and active promotion of a brand. Thus, Coca-Cola (and Pepsi-Cola), as well as Nike, are among the companies that spend the largest amounts on the "care and feeding" (to say nothing of the advertising) of their brands.

A very interesting example of this was the arrival in late 2002 of Mecca-Cola in France and its spread to over 50 countries (including Israel!) by 2006.[35] The content of the product is not the issue, since Mecca-Cola "is aimed at Muslims who like the taste of the classic American drink but do not want to contribute to American economic success."[36] The motivation of the founder of Mecca-Cola is both economic (to make money) and political. In terms of the latter, 10% of the profits go to Palestinian causes (and another 10% to other charities), and the soft drink's Web site offers pictures of Palestinians battling Israeli soldiers on the West Bank. More important, for the purposes of this discussion, this involves the creation of a brand that not only seeks to distinguish itself from Coca-Cola but also to make it clear that it is of the same genre. Thus, the packaging, including white lettering on a red background, is very similar to that of Coca-Cola. However, of greatest importance is the fact that ultimately the content—cola—is indistinguishable from that of Coca-Cola or many other brand and nonbrand colas. It is the brand, and its politicized call to Muslims to support one another and not the United States, that is being sold in this case.

The commonness of branding, and its proliferation, is related to the proliferation not only of *non*things but also of the other nullities. That is, those who offer *non*places, *non*people, or *non*services, either on their own or in conjunction with *non*things, are confronted with the problem of creating brands that distinguish that which is not distinctive. Thus, for example, H&R Block (and other chains offering income tax services) offers uniform services to taxpayers; indeed, most of those services are derived from computerized computations and decisions that taxpayers themselves could do and make if they had access to those programs. Indeed, computerized programs are available to taxpayers that do much the same thing as those employed by companies like H&R Block. Furthermore, H&R Block offers services that are indistinguishable from those offered by many other companies and independent tax consultants. Indeed, if there is anything distinctive about what that company has to offer, it is that its services are apt to be offered by less skilled personnel who are less likely to give great personal attention to each client. Given all that, H&R Block clearly has a great need to promote its brand of service aggressively in order to compensate for the nothingness that is the essence of the tax services it has to offer.

Thus, another old-fashioned grand narrative is being offered here. The tremendous expansion of *non*things, -places, -people, and -services has led to an ever-expanding need, including and increasingly on a global basis, to distinguish between competitors within each of them. Since they are all nullities, there is by definition little or nothing distinctive about any of them. Thus, it is not their inherent qualities that serve to distinguish among them. There is, therefore, a need to create the illusion of distinction, and one of the most important ways that is accomplished is through branding. As a result, the proliferation of nullities of all types has led to a tremendous expansion in the number, types, and importance of both national and global brands.

Beyond the Usual "Consumer" Suspects

The preceding discussion of consumer culture and its grobalization has focused on very familiar consumables, but another aspect of consumer culture, its growth and its global expansion, is the degree to which products, services, and settings that we do not usually associate with consumer culture have become integral to it.

Two examples are education and medicine. It was not long ago that while it was clear that people were consuming medical services and medicines, as well as educational services and the knowledge they possessed, few would have seen them as part of a consumer culture. Somehow they were different and apart from the more mundane kinds of consumption. Today, however, students and patients increasingly think of themselves as consumers and adopt a consumerist attitude toward education and medicine. They, for example, shop around for the best, the lowest priced, education and medical care. Physicians, teachers, and professors are seen as paid providers of services and are to be treated accordingly and without much of the deference accorded such professionals in the past.[37] Furthermore, the settings in which such consumption occurs—universities and hospitals—have come to be seen increasingly as cathedrals of consumption and, indeed, often seek to model themselves on the most successful of these cathedrals (e.g., theme parks). In these and other ways (e.g., the existence of fast-food restaurants in universities and hospitals), education and medicine have become integral parts of consumer culture.

Higher Education and Health Care

In the realm of higher education, the textbook is a consumable that falls toward the *nothing* end of the thing-*nothing* continuum.[38] The textbook is largely an American invention, a consumer product produced by capitalistic, profit-making corporations (that, like many other capitalistic domains, have come to be dominated by a small number of conglomerates, some global in scope), *and* it can be seen as a book oriented to rationalizing, McDonaldizing, the communication of information. That is, instead of having to read many books, or excerpts from them, the student is given a textbook that offers the authors' summaries of those works. It further McDonaldizes reading by eliminating overly complex texts and ideas, and it offers a single accessible voice rather than that of diverse authors, many of whose voices may not be easily comprehended by students. After all, those authors originally wrote for an audience of peers, not students, and frequently the works were written quite some time ago when the norms that applied to writing were very different. The textbook business has become big business, and there is great emphasis placed on getting professors to assign a given textbook and to getting students to purchase them. Furthermore, there is a rather interesting tug-of-war that takes place in the competition for the textbook market. Publishers have an overriding interest in having students buy *new* copies of their books; they make no additional profits from the sale of used books. However, there are resellers, especially a few large ones, that buy back student textbooks and then sell them as used copies at a lower price than the new ones. This drives publishers to revise textbooks very rapidly, every two years in the case of big-sellers in introductory courses in many fields, in order to make used copies of past editions obsolete. The point is that the textbook is not only a good example of nothing but also an example of the way higher education has become part of consumer culture.

Furthermore, the textbook has come to be grobalized. In many nations where the American use of the textbook was ridiculed or frowned upon not too long ago, one now finds American textbooks in use, and indigenous textbooks are growing in popularity. In some cases, successful American texts are revised by local academics to reflect better the nature of a field in a given country. Especially important is the replacement of examples from the American social world by local examples. There are even "grobal" textbooks—books that have specifically been written in such a way that they can be used in many different nations.[39]

Turning to health care, it could be argued that the changing market for pharmaceuticals is a good example of the process whereby that which was not in the past part of the consumer culture has become increasingly integral to it. It was not long ago that pharmaceuticals were marketed directly and only to physicians, who then would prescribe selected ones to patients who then went out and purchased them. While advertising and marketing to physicians continues to be important, it has been supplemented, and in many cases surpassed, by direct marketing to the ultimate consumer, the patient. This is most visible in the greatly increasing number of advertisements in newspapers, magazines, and on television for sophisticated and expensive pharmaceuticals designed to treat a wide variety of illnesses, some of them quite esoteric. Among the most active and aggressive these days are ads for erectile dysfunction ("ED") with great competition between Viagra, Cialis, and Levitra. (Not long ago, it was ads for pharmaceuticals that were aimed at arthritis [e.g., Celebrex, Vioxx] that were most prevalent, but they have largely disappeared because of findings of negative health effects associated with those drugs.) Ads for these pharmaceuticals are now aimed mainly at the end consumer, the patient. Interestingly, patients cannot purchase these drugs on their own but must go to their physicians and request a prescription for them. Once at the mercy of their physicians in terms of such prescriptions, patients are now increasingly informed consumers (at least to the extent that advertisements actually provide useful information) of pharmaceuticals and are in a better position to play a more active role in their own treatment. And, like the textbooks discussed above, there has emerged a grobal market for these medical components of consumer culture.

These examples also make it clear, once again, that the proliferation of nothing, and its grobalization, are often welcome and positive developments. While textbooks, and their grobal proliferation, can be looked at in a negative light (the fact that students are reading *non*books rather than the original books on which the texts are based and that are rich in distinctive content), that is not the case with the global spread of pharmaceuticals as well as a variety of standard medical procedures. The latter are nothing in the sense that they are centrally conceived and controlled forms largely devoid of distinctive content (e.g., there is now a standard procedure for performing something as complex as open heart surgery), but in most cases they are to be welcomed. Lives are clearly being saved and prolonged as a result of the widespread use of these drugs and medical procedures.

In contrast, a textbook can be looked at as *both* an empty form and as a *non*thing that is, in the main, not to be welcomed because it plunges students into the void of an educational system dominated by textbooks. The focus on texts means that fewer original works, with their unique and distinctive content, are required (another loss!). In fact, it is because of this content that they are dealt with in textbooks. But instead of reading these originals, students read greatly simplified summaries of them in textbooks.

I have previously criticized textbooks for the cookie-cutter format imposed on textbook writers by publishers. That is, to be published, textbooks, especially those for the large introductory courses, must follow the general pattern laid down by the successful texts in the field. It is centralized conception and control exercised by publishers that are major factors in making textbooks nothing. In the end, they lead to texts in which there is little to distinguish one from another. In contrast, of course, the original books, the ones on which texts are built, are loaded with distinctive content—there is no cookie cutter for truly original scholarly works. In addition, such scholarly books are much more the product of individual authors, in stark contrast to the textbooks that, as we have seen, are likely to be conceived and controlled by publishers. Of course, there is great variation in the degree and extent to which this cookie-cutter approach can be applied, both in and out of the educational system. For example, introductory textbooks and Big Macs lend themselves very well to it, while in open heart surgery, there is a standard approach, but because of the complexities and contingencies involved, there is great variation from one operation to the next.

Other Domains

However, we need not stop with education and health care—many other domains can be seen as involving consumption and therefore subject to the proliferation of consumer culture (as well as nothing and its grobalization).

- For example, the public, especially criminals, can be viewed as consumers of police services. The grobalization of nothing here would involve, among many other things, the development of standard police practices that are disseminated throughout the world.[40]
- In the same domain, convicted criminals can be seen as the consumers of prison services. The development of standard structures within the penal system (e.g., panopticon-like structures that permit total visibility of inmate behavior, the rise of "supermax" prisons) creates the likelihood that such structures, if they are deemed successful, will be picked up by prison systems in many geographic locales throughout the world.[41]
- The church certainly has its "customers" (those who attend, or whom the church would like to see attend), and churches develop techniques for attracting and keeping a flock that, if successful, are copied by churches around the world.[42]
- Even in politics it is possible to view the public as consumers of the political system. It is clear that democratic principles have proven to be the most stable and reliable way of dealing with the public, with the result that those principles have proliferated throughout the world.[43] Furthermore, politicians have become just another commodity to be marketed by slick advertising campaigns. These advertisements take on a standard form, and there is little variation from one candidate or campaign to another. Furthermore, such advertising campaigns (another American invention) have been grobalized, with many other nations now employing many of the same techniques.

These examples make it clear that the basic theses of this book are not as delimited as it first appears. If so many domains can be seen as falling under the heading of consumer culture, then clearly nothing and its grobalization are affecting not only many countries but a wide range of structures and institutions in those societies as well.

Global Attacks on the Symbols of American Consumer Culture

The expansion of both consumer culture and branding are not only closely linked to grobalization in general but more specifically to one of its subprocesses—Americanization. In that context, it is interesting and important to examine the recent acceleration of deadly attacks on American interests in general and more specifically on symbols of American consumer culture and their associated brands throughout the world, especially fast-food restaurants, and particularly McDonald's restaurants. McDonald's has become a major symbol of Americanization and a favorite target around the world, with innumerable examples of protests against (Jose Bové's efforts in France are the best-known example[44]), and even bombings of, its restaurants. In recent years there have been bombings in a McDonald's in Indonesia, killing three people, and attacks on McDonald's in Pakistan, among many other places. This, of course, points out that the assaults are also aimed at McDonaldization. It shows, as well, how closely linked that process is to Americanization, especially in this case, because attacks on America often take the form of assaults on one of its most important symbols and brands— McDonald's. And, of course, capitalism is deeply implicated in this because McDonald's is a capitalist firm and America is seen as the center of the capitalist world. Indeed, many around the world are enraged by the incursions of all of these interrelated processes into, and effects on, their lives.

In terms of the specific arguments being made in this book, these attacks reflect a growing awareness that consumer culture, branding, capitalism, Americanization, and McDonaldization, and more generally the process of grobalization under which they can be subsumed, are threats to indigenous cultures. It is clear to an increasing number of people around the world that ever-increasing and accelerating expansionism lies at the heart of grobalization and that resistance is necessary if they wish their cultures to survive.

Making this argument should not be construed as a defense of the kinds of deadly actions mentioned above. Clearly, other ways need to be found to oppose these processes. Such responses are far worse than the problems they seek to deal with. Nonetheless, they do make it clear that the processes discussed here have great power and they are being met with strong, albeit sometimes misguided and even downright malevolent, responses.

For many around the world, McDonald's is both capitalistic and a key symbol of the United States and Americanization.[45] For example, on the opening of McDonald's in Moscow, one journalist called it the "ultimate icon of Americana," and on the opening of a Pizza Hut in that city, a student labeled it a "piece of America."[46] Furthermore, while many attacks on McDonald's are on the chain itself, as well as the process it represents, others, especially the most violent and deadly, are motivated by the idea that McDonald's is a worldwide surrogate for the United States and assaults on it are attacks on the United States and its interests. To those who oppose capitalism and Americanization, and want to do something about them, a McDonald's restaurant represents a far more ubiquitous and easily assailable target than, say, American embassies or General Motors factories. Thus, when Jose Bové wanted to protest increases of American tariffs on French products, he chose McDonald's as his target (there are many of them, they are easily accessible, and they do not have the heavily armed Marines one finds in and around American embassies and the guards around large factories throughout the world).

In addition to its association with capitalism and the United States, and its vulnerability to attack, McDonald's is an attractive target because forays against it get enormous attention throughout the world from the mass media. The reason is McDonald's enormous success and visibility worldwide, as well as the fact that it is a prime example of grobalization. It is an icon to many people around the world in both a positive and a negative sense.[47] Thus, there is great interest in news of attacks on it.

In spite of the close association in this discussion of all of the major processes discussed in this book, it continues to be important to adhere to the distinctions between grobalization, consumer culture, capitalism, Americanization, and McDonaldization, at least for analytical purposes. While there are important overlaps among them, the fact is that there are global processes that can more easily be included under one or more of these headings than the other(s). The spread of foreign fast-food chains into the United States can be included under the heading of McDonaldization and capitalism, but not Americanization. The political and military influence of the United States throughout the world is an example of Americanization, but not of McDonaldization and only partially of capitalism. The opening of a General Motors factory in Mexico is mainly linked to the dynamics of capitalism, has less to do with Americanization, and is hard to relate to McDonaldization. And consumer culture involves only part of capitalism, Americanization, and globalization.

This discussion leads to another issue: Does the acceleration of attacks on consumer culture, capitalism, Americanization, McDonaldization, and grobalization represent the beginning of the decline of these processes? This is a complex question involving multiple, overlapping processes and predictions about the future. Let me offer four thumbnail answers to close this discussion.

First, as pointed out above, rather than slowing down, capitalism is expanding at an unprecedented level in the wake of the decline of the only global alternative to it—communism/socialism. The current wave of attacks on it is unlikely to have any impact on its continued expansion because, for no other reason, there exists no viable global economic alternative to it. Since consumer culture is increasingly important to capitalism, it too is likely to expand.

Second, anti-Americanism is so strong and is growing so fast in many parts of the world that it is possible to conceive of some slowdown in the incursions of Americanism throughout the world. However, there are powerful economic (capitalism!) and political forces behind Americanization, with the result that such a slowdown, if it occurs, is likely to be mild and short lived. Furthermore, existing side by side with anti-Americanism is widespread and powerful pro-Americanism. Thus, a recent Pew Survey found that anti-Americanism was on the rise and that a majority of those surveyed in many countries opposed the spread of American ideas, but they also liked American culture, such as its movies, music, and television.[48]

The situation in France is a good example of this.[49] On the one hand, France has long been noted for its opposition to the United States in general and to various specific instances of Americanization. To take an example discussed earlier in this book, after World War II there was a major uproar over the arrival of Coca-Cola in France. Indeed, there was fear that this would lead to the coca-colonization of that country.[50] In the 1950s, there was a great public storm over the seeming dominance of American capitalistic businesses and the threat they posed to French, and more generally European, business. And, in the 1990s, the arrival of Disney World led to great hand-wringing and the fear that this would lead to a "cultural Chernobyl" in France. Of course, the French have led opposition to the United States and Americanization on many other fronts, most notably the 2003 war against Iraq. However, there is at the same time much acceptance of, and even love for, things American, especially the products of its consumer culture. So, for example, in spite of public concern for the decline of French cinema because of the grobalization of the American movie business, the most popular movie in the history of France is *Titanic*.

Third, a slowdown, even reversal, of the global fortunes of McDonald's is much more likely than a similar development in the realm of Americanization. This is a corporation that not only has difficulties in its global operations (a large number of McDonald's in Great Britain were shut down in early 2006), but it is in even more serious difficulties in the highly saturated American market for fast food. However, a slowdown in the proliferation of McDonald's, or even its disappearance, does not spell the decline or demise of McDonaldization. While the paradigm may change (Starbucks, with over 11,000 outlets and growing rapidly, is a strong possibility), the underlying process of rationalization, encompassing the basic principles (efficiency, etc.) discussed in Chapter 1, is likely not only to continue but to accelerate.

Finally, grobalization is the major worldwide development of the age, and it is almost impossible to envision a scenario whereby it would slow down, let alone be stopped.[51] Much the same could be said more specifically about the grobalization of consumer culture. There is too much power behind the forces pushing grobalization, the forces opposing it (at least at the moment and for the foreseeable future) are far too weak, and there are far too many real and imagined gains associated with it.[52] In any case, for most nations of the world, there is little choice. Efforts to opt out, even if they were successful (and that's not likely), would push the nations that do so into the backwaters of the global system. A more likely option for most is to become, themselves, active players in the grobal system rather than being passive recipients of that which is created and produced elsewhere, especially in the United States.[53]

The Globalization of Nothing and September 11, 2001

On the surface, it seems difficult to argue that the grobal spread of nothing in general, and consumer culture (and brands) in particular, had any relationship to the events of September 11. How can nothing in general, and products as seemingly inane as Big Macs, have anything to do with events that have clearly meant something of such monumental importance to perpetrators and victims alike? Part of the answer, of course, is that nothing means a great deal to many people, as does the grobalization—including capitalism, McDonaldization, Americanization, well-known brands, and consumer culture—of nothing. I am not arguing that there is some sort of direct link between September 11 and the grobalization of nothing, especially as it relates to consumer culture. However, it is my view that the latter provided at least some of the fuel, if not for that attack, then at least for the kind of atmosphere that exists in many parts of the world that is conducive to the development of the kinds of feelings behind assaults on American interests, including embassies, military installations, and that most favorite of all targets—McDonald's!

In saying this, I am once again *not* excusing the attacks, dignifying them, or according them any sort of rational basis. I am simply saying that we need to understand the contexts in which September 11 occurred, and one of those contexts is the grobalization of nothing.

The attacks of September 11 were aimed at key American symbols—the World Trade Center, the Pentagon, and perhaps the White House. Among other things, these structures symbolized America's grobal reach economically (including its consumer culture and brands), militarily, and politically. In attacking such cultural icons, the attackers were clearly trying to make a statement, in fact many statements—that the United States was vulnerable, that such attacks could have long-term disastrous consequences for a complex society, *and* that there is bitterness in the world about the United States' grobal ambitions and what they are doing to local institutions that remain dear to at least some people in almost every culture.

While our focus here is on consumption, and therefore the economy, as well as culture, it is important to underscore the point that the concept of grobalization is robust enough to encompass both politics and the military. With the demise of the Soviet Union, the United States reigns supreme in the world, and it is difficult to think of any serious competitors in these realms.[54] The fact is that grobalization is a good term to describe the United States' efforts to exert its power both politically and militarily throughout the world. Recent examples include the 1991 war with Iraq, the ousting of the Taliban in Afghanistan in 2001–2002, and the 2003 war that led to the ouster of Saddam Hussein and his regime.

In these cases, it is clear that Americanization is part of grobalization, since such a high proportion of political and military grobalization stems from the United States. And it is clear that capitalistic interests are involved in, for example, the large quantity of oil that exists in Iraq (and elsewhere in the Middle East), as well as the military hardware that was used, and needed to be replaced, because of the war. McDonaldization can also be associated with these processes and, at least to some degree, be distinguished from capitalism and Americanization. For example, much of the advanced, highly rationalized weaponry that was developed in the United States is being used to support military and political grobalization. Examples that come to mind are drone aircraft, cruise missiles, and smart bombs. These are certainly not only *non*human technologies but in many cases are designed to all but completely eliminate the human combatant. They are also clearly efficient. Because of the heightened accuracy, fewer of them need to be employed than more conventional alternatives. They are highly predictable, since their advanced technology means that they are highly likely to end up almost exactly where they are sent. They are precisely calibrated, and elaborate and detailed calculations are involved in giving them such precision.[55] Of course, like all other manifestations of McDonaldization, they are subject to the irrationality of rationality. For example, wars are more likely to be undertaken, and these weapons deployed, because there is a far smaller risk of human casualties, at least on the American side.

Returning to our focal concern with consumer culture, the exportation of largely empty consumption-oriented forms to other nations is likely to be deeply offensive to some, especially when they serve to threaten, reduce the importance of, or replace (g)local forms rich in substance. To many, the threat to, and the replacement of, (g)local phenomena rich in substance by those that are largely devoid of substance is likely to represent a great loss and a great insult—after all, nothing has usurped a position formerly held by something. Thus, the grobalization of consumer culture is likely to lead to great resentment among some (and it is likely to be openly embraced by others).

As discussed previously, Americanization (and those forms of capitalism and McDonaldization hard to distinguish from it) is likely to be resented for exactly the opposite reason as well. That is, some are likely to react negatively to the growth of forms heavily saturated with Americanism within the context of their own cultures and societies. Of course, there is a large element of subjectivity in these judgments, and some in other countries may see a form as empty while others may see it as the epitome of American cultural imperialism, and still others may see it as both. There is also another possibility here—empty forms can come to be seen as the product of the United States, an inherent characteristic of American culture that is being aggressively exported throughout the world. Thus, empty forms—nothing—may be resented not only in themselves (for their emptiness) but also because they seem so American.

Whatever the form, and however it is perceived, nothing is likely to take on enormous symbolic importance when it is exported to other cultures. Another paradoxical aspect of this line of analysis is the argument that nothing is often of enormous symbolic importance, especially in nations and cultures to which it is exported. Whether the Visa credit card is seen as nothing, a manifestation of capitalism, a form of McDonaldization, a form of Americanization, or some combination of all of them (grobalization), it is an important symbol in many nations around the world. While many welcome, use, and accept the card, many others are likely to be offended by it, especially when it is taken together with the many similar forms that are likely to accompany it. How do those who are offended respond? There are many ways—refusing to use or accept the card, for example—but more symbolic responses are possible, especially when the threat is viewed in symbolic terms. Thus, cutting up a Visa card, perhaps in public, might be one such symbolic response. Smashing the window of a locally owned shop that displays the Visa logo would be another, more dramatic, response. However, such responses are unlikely to have much impact on the banks that support Visa (although assaults on those banks would) or on one's own society, let alone on consumer culture or the society—the United States—that is the creator and main exporter of these cards and all that they mean and symbolize.

Thus, those who want to have a greater impact are likely to strike at more visible and important symbols, and they are likely to choose targets to which damage is likely to bring great public attention. It is in this context that we can think about such things as the looting, bombing, and destruction of McDonald's restaurants, attacks on American embassies, assaults on American ships, and, of course, the crimes committed on September 11. The World Trade Center was a powerful symbol of grobalization in the economic realm (including consumer culture), and its collapse seemed to its perpetrators and supporters as a dramatic symbolic blow against economic grobalization. If the World Trade Center symbolized grobalization in the economic realm, then the Pentagon is a powerful symbol of military grobalization. The collapse of one of its walls had an impact in the military realm similar to that of the collapse of the Twin Towers on the economic sector. And just think of the impact that a direct hit on the White House might have had on the political system and America's propensity toward political grobalization.

Just as the impact of grobalization is far more than symbolic—people's lives are altered in innumerable ways—much the same thing can be said about the assaults against the symbols of grobalization on September 11. Grobalization is viewed by many as having a deleterious effect on the economies of many nations.[56] For example, when the Argentinian economy collapsed not too many years ago, many in that country blamed the collapse on what is here being called grobalization.[57] Similarly, the attacks of September 11, especially the implosion of the World Trade Center towers, had stunningly negative consequences on the American economy in general (and especially that of New York City) and more specifically on American industries like the airlines and tourism. For a time, consumption all but came to a halt in New York City and other locales, and had that continued and spread, it would have posed a threat to that culture, as well as to the economy as a whole, not only in the United States but also globally.

The argument being made here is that the grobal spread of nothing in general, and specifically within the realm of consumer culture, provides at least a context for gaining a better understanding of one of the most meaningful (and heinous) events of our time.

8

Loss Amidst Monumental Abundance—and Global Strategies for Coping With It

Throughout this book I have emphasized the utility of the unique, even idiosyncratic, definition of nothing employed here as a tool in analyzing the process of globalization. While I confessed a critical intent early on in utilizing such a value-laden term as *nothing*, critique has been subordinated to analysis to this point in the book. However, it is now time to focus on the critical elements of this analysis, as well as actions that might be taken to deal with, or at least ameliorate, the problems identified.

Because it tends to expand inexorably into nooks and crannies throughout the globe occupied by something, nothing in general—and more specifically in the realm of consumer culture—in most cases,[1] leaves less and less room for the something. With the explosion of *non*places, *non*things, *non*people, and *non*services, there is generally progressively less room for places, things, people, and services. We live in a world increasingly denuded of something in its various forms.

Take, for example, the case of the impact of Ikea. "The low prices draw people away from small neighborhood shops, the nodes of community exchange; the volume of business attracts other mass retailers, creating big-box strip malls."[2] More generally, *The Harvard Design School Guide to Shopping* describes the implosion of shopping into museums, churches, schools, libraries, and hospitals, and it concludes: "In the end, there will be little else for us to do but shop."[3] We end up with a world, especially in the realm of consumption, in which that which has, from time immemorial, been something is either disappearing or being transformed, in whole or in part, into nothing.

This impoverishment of the world is, paradoxically, coming at the same time that the (developed) world is awash in an unprecedented number and variety of *non*places, *non*things, *non*people, and *non*services. This produces an odd kind of privation, *loss amidst monumental abundance*, but this is an apt description of a major problem of the age in the developed world, at least from the point of view of this analysis of the globalization of nothing, especially as it relates to consumption. This means that even though we find ourselves surrounded by a plethora, a cornucopia, of increasingly afford-able (at least for most in the developed world) *non*places, -things, -people, and -services, we are simultaneously being deprived of the distinctive con-tent that has always characterized places, things, people, and services.[4] We could be said to be dying of thirst even though we are increasingly sur-rounded by drinkable water.

Theory and the Paradoxes of Consumer Culture

This rather unique diagnosis of societal ills reflects the fact that we are living in a dramatically new and different era. Thus, the judgments of the classic social theorists of a bygone era either no longer seem so accurate and relevant or, at least, do not appear to get to the heart of contemporary realities and problems. For example, while, as we saw in Chapter 1, Karl Marx's ideas on capitalism are perhaps more relevant than ever in an era of globalization, his notions of alienation and exploitation are too work related to have much rel-evance to the contemporary developed world where consumption is increas-ingly central (although it is probably more relevant than ever to the less developed world where much of the kind of production-oriented work ana-lyzed by Marx is increasingly done). Émile Durkheim's ideas on anomie (a sense of normlessness, of not knowing what we are expected to do) seem quaint in a world in which it is not only quite obvious that we are expected to consume but also crystal clear how, what, and how much we are supposed to consume. There is certainly a "tragedy of culture" in this deprivation amidst unprecedented affluence, but it is not one, or at least not mainly one, that has anything to do with, as Georg Simmel argued, a growing gap between objective (cultural products) and subjective (the ability to create those products) culture. Finally, Max Weber may have been closest to the mark with his ideas on the "iron cage of rationalization," that we are increasingly surrounded and constrained by rational structures (like bureaucracies and now chains of fast-food restaurants). However, Weber's theories had little direct relevance to consumption, and even when they are extended in that direction, they do little to help us understand loss amid unprecedented affluence.

Nor are the theories of leading contemporary thinkers of great utility in thinking about society in those terms. This is largely because they, like their predecessors, focused on issues of production and work and generally ignored the growing centrality of consumption. Thus, for example, Anthony Giddens's thinking on the "juggernaut of modernity" and the "runaway world" associated with globalization, while quite insightful, has little to offer on consumption. The same can be said of Jürgen Habermas's "colonization of the lifeworld," which, like the juggernaut and runaway world ideas, is pitched at too general a level to be of much help in understanding the kind of problem of interest here. Ulrich Beck is too preoccupied in his thinking on the "risk society" with issues like the danger to the environment to concern himself with the more mundane world of consumption. Jean Baudrillard is very useful to us, given his concern with consumer society, but he is too much of a postmodernist to subscribe to the kind of grand narrative of something to nothing developed here, or for that matter to any grand narrative.[5]

Interestingly, all of these contemporary theoretical ideas can be reinterpreted to apply to the issue of loss amidst monumental abundance. Thus, we could say that the cause of this loss is, in broad terms, the juggernaut of modernity and the runaway world of globalization. It is the colonization of the lifeworld, and its somethingness, by nothing that lies at the root of the kind of loss of interest here. That is, the lifeworld is the heart of somethingness, but it is being robbed of it by the colonization by a system that is more likely to be nothing. In Beck's terms, the great risk is the loss of something in the face of the proliferation of nothing. And, in Baudrillardian terms, the loss is very much within the realm of consumption and it involves an increase in simulations or inauthenticity. However, while the main theses of this book can be restated in terms of these theories, it is not clear that doing so is of much utility in advancing this analysis. Nor is it clear that these theories are of much greater utility than the classics in helping us to better understand the issues of concern here.

Thus, it seems clear that we need new theories of this very new and different world, and we need new diagnoses of the defining problem(s) of this new age. Globalization theory is undoubtedly one of the most promising of the new theories, and it, along with another set of very useful theories of consumption, has led to this work on the relationship between grobalization/glocalization and something/nothing. They have helped clarify the idea of loss amidst monumental abundance as, at the minimum, a leading candidate for a description of the dominant, perhaps defining, problem of the age, at least in the developed world.

Of course, the less developed world is less well-described by this problem. Nonetheless, even there people are implicated in it both because (a) they are increasingly the global producers of the monumental abundance of consumer culture and (b) while they may not be suffering from loss, they are certainly well aware of the fact that they are not getting anywhere near their share of that abundance (of nothing). The paradox is that they want more of nothing, more of precisely that which is leading to the loss that characterizes the developed world. To the degree that they succeed in getting it, they too are doomed to this loss (of something).

Loss Amidst Monumental Abundance

The major critique of nothing being offered here—the idea of loss amidst monumental abundance—is beautifully illustrated in the movie *One Hour Photo*, discussed in Chapter 3. First, the superstore depicted in the movie, Savmart, is absolutely crammed full of stuff; it is a metaphor for the unprecedented affluence—*the monumental abundance*—of the United States (and much of the developed world) today. Second, Sy, the photo lab employee, and several of his customers seem to be deprived even as they find themselves enmeshed in this affluence. Third, in spite of its stocked shelves, Savmart seems barren, and this is made abundantly clear in the dream sequence where Sy finds himself surrounded by shelves that have been emptied of all their stuff (*non*things). A sense of *loss* pervades Sy's life, the store, and the movie, but it is not made clear exactly what has been lost. From the point of view of the themes of this book, what has been lost in those contexts, and in the developed world more generally, are the locally conceived and controlled forms with distinctive substance associated with places, things, people, and services.

A Few Examples

While all of the main concerns in this book lend themselves well to a diagnosis of loss amidst monumental abundance, I focus in this section on two phenomena dealt with often throughout this book—fast-food restaurants and credit cards—as well as a new one—online betting on horse races.

Fast-Food Restaurants

The fast-food restaurant lends itself easily to being considered in terms of monumental abundance, which is represented, among other ways, by those bloated chains of fast-food restaurants, their *Big* Macs and *Monster* Burgers, to say nothing of the growing number of overweight and obese customers that are increasingly linked to them. Furthermore, the ideas of emptiness and loss are also easily applied to fast-food restaurants. It is hard, to put it mildly, for most customers to find anything of distinctive substance in these empty structures, much less the drive-through lanes through which the fast-food restaurant prefers to shunt as many customers as possible. In a sense, the drive-through lane implies not only that nothing of any distinctive substance is going to be derived from the restaurant experience, but it is preferred that the customer not even dare enter the restaurant itself in the (nearly hopeless) pursuit of such substance. The consumption of the same food over and over, produced in a kind of assembly-line process, is hardly likely to give the food itself much in the way of distinctive substance. Because they are so impersonal, routine, and even scripted, relations with the counter people or those who staff the drive-through window are unlikely to have much in the way of substance. Finally, it is virtually impossible to find distinctive substance in the service, which is all but nonexistent. Implied in all of this is a loss, especially of all that is associated with "great good *places*" where *things* are offered by *people* who also provide *service*.

Credit Cards

Many problems have been associated with easy access to credit cards. For some users, credit cards open up a magical world of a cornucopia full of life's delights, but for others it becomes a nightmarish void where it is impossible to extricate themselves from debt in a world characterized by a continuous round of often empty and unfulfilling consumption of largely unneeded and unnecessary goods and services. Many who are deeply enmeshed in the credit card world complain about its emptiness and their inability to find meaning in it (of course, many others revel in it). Clearly, it is hard to find much in the way of distinctive substance in an unsolicited letter (or phone call) making a largely impersonal offer of a credit card and loan associated with it.

Not long ago, a journalist pointed out the emptiness of the credit card world in general, in part through the metaphor of a description of the barrenness of the center of the credit card business in the United States (and therefore the world)—Wilmington, Delaware ("Plastic City"):

I walked all the way around MBNA's four, beigey-blah, interconnected green-awninged buildings, where I saw *nothing,* and nobody: I looped around the Chase building, too, and then walked seven blocks down toward the Christina River, to ponder First USA's buildings. This is a lot of concrete and *empty* plazas and walkways. . . . The *emptiness* here left me wishing I could write a song about credit card problems. [italics added][6]

This article is not only a critique of the credit card (and its associated culture and home base) but also the emptiness and loss associated with the consumer goods that its author (like the hero in the movie *Fight Club,* discussed below) acquired with it over the years:

> I would like to be able to tell you that in all those thousands of dollars there was a three-week trip to Italy when I was 24, during which I fell madly in love.
>   Unfortunately, I have to be honest: There was never an Italy.
>   There was Banana Republic, there was Barnes and Noble, there were new Midas brakes for the car. There was the removal of my wisdom teeth at 24, paid for in part on my Citibank MasterCard, because insurance only covered half. There were motel rooms, and even a few hotel rooms, but they tended to be in places like Yuma, Az., and Lexington, Ky., and Shreveport, La., because I have always seemed to be just driving through. . . .
>   There was something Gucci, but there was so much more Gap. . . . For every nice meal charged to my plastic, there are, I am sad to report, many more charges to what appear to be Chinese takeout joints.
>   There were glasses of wine that I bought in hotel lobby bars while I waited.
>   Sometimes I was waiting for someone in particular, and sometimes I was waiting for *nothing* at all. [italics added][7]

This critique of the emptiness associated with the credit card, as well as the consumer culture and the hyperconsumption it plays such a great role in supporting, can be extended to all of the forms of nothingness associated with contemporary consumption and discussed in this book. Indeed, a number of specific examples of them—Banana Republic, Barnes & Noble, Midas, (all) motel and (most) hotel rooms, Gucci,[8] Gap, Chinese takeout joints, (most) hotel lobby bars—are enumerated in the previous quotation. Implied is the absence of a variety of things that would be considered something in terms of this analysis—trips to Italy, love, nice meals, and so on.

Online Betting

The preceding argument applies to all consumption on the Internet. That is, the major way to pay for goods and services purchased on the Internet is by credit card. It is not only easier to spend money—when it is an abstract and only vaguely perceived number that will show up at some later date on one's credit card bill—than cash, but that ease is amplified when one is consuming on the abstract, impersonal, and immaterial Internet. The combination of the credit card and the Internet make consumption so easy and seemingly so remote that the numbers add up quickly, and the goods and services consumed, as well as the amounts owed, can quickly get out of hand. The marriage of the credit card and consumption on the Internet makes it easy for an economic void to develop that large numbers of people have tumbled into and from which many have had great difficulty extricating themselves.

For example, TVG broadcasts horse races from throughout the United States (and sometimes internationally) over many cable TV systems. Broadcasting live horse races would not interest many people were it not for the fact that there is an associated Web site—TVG.com.[9] The latter is interactive, allowing bettors to wager on horse races without going to the racetrack (it is possible to watch the races online or over the TVG cable television network). This clearly has many advantages as far as horse players are concerned—convenience, efficiency, the ability to bet on many different races at a number of racetracks, and so on. While the gambler who went to a traditional racetrack usually had about nine races on which to wager, the online gambler has the monumental abundance of hundreds of races a day on which to gamble.[10]

Just as TVG offers a monumental abundance of races and betting opportunities, it also involves a loss, a loss of the something, associated with no longer actually being at the racetrack. While we must be wary of romanticizing racetracks (or anything else), they do have many characteristics of a great good place. Racetracks usually have a number of regulars who form a community and look forward to interacting with one another, renewing old acquaintances, telling stories associated with the track and its lore, sharing tips on horses, and so on. Furthermore, there is the experience of actually being at the track, watching the horses run, and rooting for one's favorites. On the relatively rare occasions that one actually wins, there is not only the joy of collecting the winnings in cash but bragging about it immediately afterward with friends at the track. All of this, and more, is lost when bettors stay at home, bet on TVG.com, and watch the races on television. Of course, in spite of the loss, many opt to do this (racetrack attendance is way down) because of its many advantages in comparison to actually venturing to the track.

By the way, this leads to another kind of void—largely empty racetracks! While there are other reasons for the decline in racetrack attendance, online (and offtrack) betting is certainly a major contributor. In any case, the rather strange and eerie sight of races being run at tracks with relatively few people in the stands and in attendance is increasingly becoming the norm. More and more, races are being run not for the people in attendance but for those who bet online, as well as those wagering at offtrack betting parlors and in the horse rooms at casinos in Las Vegas and elsewhere.

There is another very material kind of loss associated with TVG. Betting on horse racing is made so efficient and so easy that horse players can descend into an endless round of wagering and losing (because of the way odds are set on horse races—with, for example, a percentage of all that is wagered being retained for expenses like state taxes and for TVG profits—everyone in the long run must lose). To put it another way, it is far easier for people to get lost in an endless round of consumption (betting is a form of consumption) on the Internet. Furthermore, while betting at a racetrack might be possible for, say, five hours a day, races on the Internet and the related TV channels are available for at least twice that amount of time. In the future, we are likely to see the increased availability of races from other parts of the world making betting on, and watching, races possible around the clock. This greatly expands the void of betting (and losing) into which people can descend. Overall, it is far easier now to bet than it was in the not-too-distant past when people actually had to trek to the racetrack[11] to wager and watch the races on which they bet.

The immateriality of online wagering makes it more likely to be, and to seem like, a void, and that void is increased in the likely event that people lose large sums of money, perhaps larger than they can afford, thereby plunging into an abyss of indebtedness. For example, all-star professional hockey player Jaromir Jagr accrued $500,000 in losses betting on sports events on Caribsports.com.[12] After all, if, as has been shown, it is generally far easier to spend electronic money than it is cold, hard cash,[13] then it is easier to charge bets on the Internet than it is to wager cash at the track. There is an even broader and deeper void associated with the Internet, only a portion of which is associated with consumption sites. While we can easily imagine people losing themselves in Caribsports.com or TVG.com, it is much more likely that people will get lost in a far wider range of Internet activities that might include keeping up with one's e-mail, playing an MMORPG (massive multi-player online role-playing game), reading a newspaper online, spending time in a chat room, and, of course, making purchases on eBay.com or Amazon.com. While the idea of a void leads to a fear of losing oneself in the abyss of the Internet, another fear is of the rending of the self[14] into many different and perhaps conflicting parts as one jumps around among the different selves expressed in chat rooms, MMORPGs, MUDs (multiuser dimensions), and in e-mail relationships with many different people. This serves to make it clear that consumption may be only a part of a broader set of problems involving the Internet, consumer culture,[15] and the void.

Loss and the Perception of Loss

We can distinguish between the objective loss being discussed here (e.g., of actually being—and wagering—at a racetrack) and people's feelings about those phenomena that involve such a loss. The point here is that something is lost when we go from personal loans to credit card loans, from great good places to fast-food restaurants, from racetracks to TVG, and so on. Most generally, in the historic movement toward that which is centrally conceived and controlled and lacking in distinctive content, there is a tendency to lose that which is locally conceived and controlled and is brimming with distinctive content. Thus, this is an objective, material loss that people can define subjectively in many different ways. That is, people's subjective definition need not be, and indeed often is not, in accord with their objective circumstances. How do we explain the disparity between the above argument about loss and the fact that most people, especially in America—but also globally—fail to perceive a loss and, furthermore, seem generally quite happy with all of the forms of nothing described above and involving such a loss?

There are many possible answers to this question, such as the fact that there is often, if not always, a gap between perception and reality. Another is that there are active efforts by the forces that gain from this gap to conceal it and to play up the advantages of the current system. Another possibility is that many people, and that number is increasing, have no experience with that which is being described here as something. Without such experience, without such a comparison base, it is very difficult, if not impossible, to see the loss involved in many contemporary forms of nothing. Thus, those who rarely if ever have personally negotiated a loan, eaten in a great good place, or gone to the racetrack will find it difficult, if not impossible, to see the loss associated with credit card loans, fast-food restaurants, and TVG.

This problem is exacerbated by the fact that while there is an overall increase in some cases (see the next section), many forms of something are rapidly declining in number or are fast disappearing. It is difficult to use something as a comparison base if it is hard to find or has disappeared completely.

Furthermore, those born in recent years may know only the various forms of nothing and would have little reason to know about these forms of something, let alone to take the time and energy to try to root them out.

Thus, for these and other reasons, most people, at least those with moderate means, are not only largely unaware of the loss being discussed here but also generally quite content with the abundance of nothingness available to them.

The Parallel Increase in Something

Before getting to steps that might be taken to overcome the loss of concern here, it is worth reiterating a development that tends to ameliorate the trend toward nothingness. That is, in spite of the spread of nothing, many forms of something have not experienced a decline in any absolute sense.[16] In fact, in many cases, forms of something have *increased*; they have simply not increased at anything like the pace of the increase in nothing. For example, while the number of fast-food restaurants has grown astronomically since the founding of the McDonald's chain in 1955,[17] the number of independent gourmet and ethnic restaurants has also increased, although not nearly at the pace of fast-food restaurants. This helps to account for the fact that a city like, to take an example I know well, Washington, D.C., has, over the past half century, witnessed a massive increase in fast-food restaurants *at the same time* that there has been a substantial expansion of gourmet and ethnic restaurants.[18] In fact, it could be argued that there is a dialectic here and the absolute increase in nothing sometimes serves to spur at least some increase in something. That is, as people are increasingly surrounded by nothing, they are driven to search out, or create, something.

This countertrend would seem even more likely outside the United States, where people are more intimately familiar with something. Thus, the spread of nothing is more likely to be of concern and therefore more likely not only to lead to efforts to retain traditional forms of something but to found new ones as well.

However, it should be noted that nothing is generally far more affordable and popular than something. Therefore, nothing and something tend to constitute two separate worlds. Those immersed in the domain of nothingness have a hard time gaining access to that characterized by something. The reverse is far less true, so that those with means who dominate the world of something can easily move into the domain of nothingness, and often do. This is another of the ways in which the well-to-do are differentiated from those who are not well-off by their far greater mobility.

In spite of the increase in various forms of something, it is important to remember that it is dwarfed by the increase in nothing.

Grobalization and Loss

The argument made in Chapter 5, and throughout this book, about the grobalization of nothing fits perfectly with this argument about loss. That is, grobalization has brought with it a proliferation of nothing around the world, and while it carries with it many advantages (to say nothing of those associated with the grobalization of something), especially the grobalization of monumental abundance, it has also led to a loss as local (and glocal) forms of something are progressively threatened and replaced by grobalized (and glocalized) forms of nothing.[19]

Indeed, the reality and the sense of loss are far greater in much of the rest of the world than they are in the United States. As the center and source of much nothingness, especially as it is associated with consumer culture, the United States has also progressed furthest in the direction of nothingness and away from somethingness. Thus, Americans are long accustomed to nothingness and have fewer and fewer forms of somethingness with which to compare and evaluate it. Each new form of, or advance in, nothingness creates barely a ripple in American society.

However, the situation is different in much of the rest of the world. Myriad forms of something remain well entrenched and actively supported. The various forms of nothing, often at least initially imports from the United States, are quickly and easily perceived as nothing, since alternative forms of something, and the standards they provide, are alive and well. Certainly large numbers of people in these countries flock to nothing in its various forms, but many others are critical of it and on guard against it. The various forms of something thriving in these countries give supporters places, things, people, and services to rally around in the face of the onslaught of nothing. Thus, it is not surprising that the Slow Food movement (discussed in detail in the last section), oriented, among other things, to the defense of "slow food" against the incursion of fast food, began in Italy (in fact, the origin of this movement was a battle to prevent that paradigm of nothingness— McDonald's—from opening a restaurant at the foot of the Spanish Steps in Rome) and has its greatest support throughout Europe.

Strategies for Overcoming
the Sense of Loss

We can get a sense of the kind of argument to be made throughout the remainder of this chapter by beginning with a discussion of the plot of the movie *Fight Club* (1999) (which, as in the previous discussion of the center of the credit card industry in Wilmington, Delaware, appears to take place in that city). That movie's protagonist is not only employed by a financial corporation such as one of those mentioned above, but he is deep into consumer culture and a hyperconsumerist lifestyle heavily financed by credit card use and debt. Among other things, he is shown on the telephone ordering inexpensive, mass-produced furniture from the global chain Ikea, also discussed above. Both that firm's stores (examples of *non*places) and its products (*non*-things) are, as has been mentioned several times before, prime examples of what is considered in these pages to be nothing. Purchase of these *non*things in that *non*place is made possible in the movie, and for most people on a reg-ular basis, by the credit card. Living a boring and empty existence dominated by *non*places and *non*things, dramatic changes take place when the movie's "hero" is introduced to the Fight Club, a place where he is able to find at least part of what has been lost in a modern, consumerist society. This is

> where men beat each other senseless as a response to the *numbness* they feel living in an *empty*, consumeristic culture.
>
> By the movie's end, the narrator learns that his Fight Club is a hallucination; and as a metaphor and tragic finale, he blows the skyscrapers of this pseudo-Wilmington to smithereens. It's not a bad movie for anyone who ever had credit card debt and entertained notions of an Armageddon that would set people free.[20]

The club devoted to fighting and depicted in this movie may be many things, but it is *not* empty (or centrally conceived or controlled)! What tran-spires in the Fight Club is something—it is conceived and controlled by the fighters themselves, and each of the fights is quite distinctive in its content.

While beating people senseless is obviously an extreme way of dealing with the loss (even if it is illusory), the nothingness, of concern here, it does high-light the idea that there are things that can be done to deal with this problem.

Given the fact that loss amidst monumental abundance has been identi-fied as the key problem associated with the grobalization of nothing in gen-eral, and as it relates to consumer culture in particular, the issue that will concern us for the remainder of this chapter is the nature of the efforts that can be, and have been, taken to deal with it.[21]

The Construction of Subjective Meaning

Of course, taking actions to alter the nature of nothingness usually depends on developing an alternative subjective construction of the reality of nothingness. Again, the point is that since so little of substance is associ-ated with nothing (at least in comparison to something), creating alterna-tive constructions of that reality is relatively easy. Thus, for example, one must begin to think about a pair of jeans as nothing (although not neces-sarily totally consciously or in exactly these terms) and as a product that one could modify in order to move it toward the something end of the con-tinuum. Similarly, one must realize the fast-food restaurant lacks distinctive content and seek to give it some by using it in unique and personal ways.

Since those who are behind the various forms of nothing are obsessed with expansion nationally and internationally (grobalization), they often care little what sort of social constructions or reconstructions (especially mental and even in some cases physical) people undertake as long as they buy the product or service. Thus, the manufacturer of jeans doesn't care much how customers define or redefine them, or what they do with them, after they have been purchased. If the buyer wants to define jeans as a source of cutoffs or a blank slate for a wide range of artwork of various kinds, that is just fine with the manufacturer. This is less true of the owner of a fast-food restaurant, because certain definitions and, more important, actions might serve to reduce business (rowdy teenagers defining the restaurant as a place in which to monopolize tables for long periods of time and then acting on that new definition), but even there, if an unanticipated redefinition leads to increased business (more teenage customers), it may well be welcomed.

Thus, redefining nothing is a fairly universal phenomenon, but how, specifically, does it play itself out globally? For a variety of reasons, I would argue that such redefinitions are far more likely outside the country of origin of a particular form of nothing than in it.

First, the existence of, to stay with our examples, a pair of jeans or a fast-food restaurant outside the United States (the origin of both) is likely to lead to all sorts of redefinitions simply because they now exist in a different culture and meaning system. Thus, those in another country who put on a pair of jeans or visit a fast-food restaurant bring much of their own culture and its meanings to those activities. As a result, they are likely to reinterpret and redefine both within those contexts. Thus, in a relatively poor country, a meal at McDonald's might be defined as a rare special treat, an elegant night out, or a date with a special significant other. Similarly, a pair of jeans might be defined as dress pants or something to be worn only on special occasions.

Second, in order to succeed in other societies, the companies themselves might advertise, market, or otherwise present themselves differently than in their home country in order to better appeal to the local population. Thus, they might consciously and purposely lead people to alternative definitions. For example, McDonald's presents a very communal image to those in various East Asian countries in order to lead them to be more likely to define that restaurant chain as a place where they can relax for hours or do their homework after school. Clearly, this is very different from the way McDonald's presents itself in the United States, in which the emphasis is on efficiency and therefore on getting people in and out as quickly as possible.

Then there is the history of the relationship between the country of origin and other countries to which nothing is exported. A history of friendly relations might lead to one definition by locals, but a tense history would lead to another definition. Thus, the post–World War II history of largely amicable relations between the United States and Japan has led many in the latter to have a positive definition of McDonald's and has led to its great success in that country. On the other hand, there has long been tension, or at least ambivalence, between the United States and South Korea (in spite of their military alliances), and this has led to more negative definitions of McDonald's in Korea.

While redefining nothing is quite universal, the reverse is true in the case of something. For example, a gourmet restaurant is what it is because of its extraordinarily rich content. It is unthinkable that diners would seek to redefine and reconstruct it so that it was something other than what it was. Thus, one would not dream up a plan to demand a quick hamburger and fries (perhaps to go) at one of Provence's renowned French restaurants or request plastic utensils with which to eat one's meal.

Individual Action

Turning to things individuals can do (such as participating in a fight club), the point is that there is much that can be done to modify the largely empty phenomena of concern here so that they are closer to being something, to being locally controlled (little can be done about central conception) and fuller of distinctive content. Paradoxically, because they are so empty, the various forms of nothing make it much easier to take an array of actions to change them so that they can be more laden with content and, therefore, more meaningful.[22] In doing so, people are exerting more local control.

Take jeans, for example. Here is a form of apparel that is very simple in conception and contains very few design elements. Although there are exceptions (very expensive designer jeans), and even design changes in jeans (e.g., the craze for jeans that look as if they have whitened with age), in the main jeans are of a uniform design, are made of denim, and are the familiar blue in color. The standard pair of jeans is a pretty empty form; one pair is much like all the others. Because jeans are so empty, people can do all sorts of things to them in order to give them content or accord them more content (and meaning). In fact, their emptiness invites such modification. Examples include cutting them off in midleg, allowing them to fray at the bottom, creating holes in all sorts of places (some quite revealing), plastering them with all sorts of appliqués, and washing them in a wide range of ways to give them certain characteristics. Of course, even the most unadorned and unadulterated pair of jeans can become meaningful to its owner over time as it grows more comfortable, frays in various places, and is marked by stains that bring back fond memories. Most important, simply wearing a pair of jeans over a long period of time can make it something as it comes to be associated with past events and activities.[23] Even though various forms of nothingness are largely devoid of distinctive content, people develop a personal history with them. It is the actions associated with that personal history, rather than the content (or lack thereof), that moves nothingness more toward the something end of the continuum. In these and many other ways, that largely empty pair of jeans purchased in the store is transformed into apparel that can be extraordinarily meaningful to those who own and wear them.

While jeans as a form of nothing can be easily modified in these and other ways, this is less true of clothing that is rich in content or that is something. For example, custom-made slacks, or those made by a fashion designer out of expensive cloth and with elaborate design elements, are more likely to be something (especially rich in distinctive content), with the result that there is little need to do anything to them. In any case, there is already much content in such slacks. Adding design elements (e.g., appliqués) becomes more difficult because, among other things, they might conflict with those that are already part of the slacks. In contrast, because they are so empty of content, jeans seem capable of absorbing virtually any alterations. Removing some elements from designer slacks might be a form of action that gives them more meaning (although this is highly unlikely as well), but adding things to something already rich in content is simply more difficult than if it was lacking in content.

As a result of grobalization, jeans have become popular throughout the world. On the one hand, it is likely that people everywhere would take the kinds of actions described above to move jeans more toward the something end of the continuum. On the other hand, while jeans may not only be nothing, but also defined as nothing by Americans, to those elsewhere they may be defined as something, and therefore there will be less felt need, at least initially, to take action to modify them. This relates to the centrality of social definitions, an issue I deal with below.

Turning from a pair of jeans (a *non*thing) to the fast-food restaurant (a *non*place), the basic argument is, of course, that one of the sources of its national and international success is its relative emptiness as far as distinctive substance is concerned—simple structures, utilitarian tables and chairs, limited menus, few options for those menu items that do exist, and so on. In fact, as I pointed out earlier, the increasing popularity of the drive-through window, even outside the United States, means that virtually all substance associated with the structure of the restaurant has been removed, at least as far as those customers who use those windows are concerned, since they never enter the structure at all.

However, in spite of (or maybe because of) the emptiness, and even the negativity, diners throughout the world continue to come to fast-food restaurants in droves. One reason they do so is that the settings are so empty that they can, at least potentially, make of them what they want (even if that is opposed to what the owners and managers want as well as to what consumers do most of the time). Thus, in the United States, pensioners are known to use fast-food restaurants as meeting places for coffee in the morning, and some restaurants have allowed their restaurants to be taken over by bingo games during nonpeak hours. In spite of the best efforts of management, teenagers, among others, do use the fast-food restaurant as a hangout.

Globally, fast-food restaurants have come to be used in all sorts of unexpected ways. Thus, in Japan, teenagers with only small apartments in which to do their homework stop off at a fast-food restaurant after school and use it as a place to meet friends and do their homework. They spend hours there, a nightmare from the perspective of an American fast-food restaurant manager, since they are likely to occupy space for long periods of time and spend comparatively little money.

Become a Craft Consumer

The concept of the "craft consumer" casts considerable light on what people can do to deal with loss amidst monumental abundance. Craft consumers are those who "consume principally out of a desire to engage in creative acts of self-expression."[24] These are consumers who single out parts, or a segment, of the available mountain of nothingness and alter them, sometimes so dramatically that they become virtually unrecognizable. Those who do this can be thought of as purchasing various forms of nothing but with the idea of transforming them, perhaps by combining them in unique ways, into something. Such a desire for creative self-expression is part of a long-standing cultural tradition that defines important aspects of modern selfhood. People engage in activities in which they do not "merely exercise control over the consumption process but also bring skill, knowledge, judgment, love, and passion to their consuming in much the same way that it has always been assumed that traditional craftsmen and craftswomen approach their work."[25] Craft consumers both design and make the products that they consume, sometimes out of raw materials. However, not all elements are necessarily made by consumers who may simply put together various mass-produced finished products in unique ways. Thus, it is clear that the craft consumer is adept at transforming nothing, or several elements each of which in itself is nothing, into something. The focus is on what consumers do with what they buy *after* they have purchased it.

There are three processes involved in the transformation of mass-produced products that do *not* qualify as craft consumption even though they do represent the transformation of nothing into something, at least to some degree. One is *personalization,* in which a product is "marked" by the owner (retailers or manufacturers can also do this) to indicate that it is the singular possession of a given person.[26] Examples include a personalized license plate, initials on a briefcase, or the sewing of name tags into children's clothing. The second is *customization,* whereby store-bought items like skirts and trousers are altered (e.g., shortening pant legs or hemming a skirt) by the consumer in order to fit better. Finally, there is *subversive customization,* in which products are used in ways other than those envisioned by the manu-facturers. Wearing baseball caps the wrong way around or the various modi-fications of jeans mentioned above would be good examples of this process. New electronic technologies allow consumers to customize entertainment habits, but they also create the opportunity for subversive customization. For example, TiVo allows people to avoid commercials. MP3 players (espe-cially the very popular iPod) and file-sharing programs (such as the infamous Napster) encourage the creation of personal music mixes and the free exchange of digital music files. This not only threatens the commercial via-bility of large homogenous record companies, but it also clears space for the distribution of indigenously created forms of music.

While the latter do *not* qualify as craft consumption (but are important in dealing with loss amidst great abundance), what does qualify is the cre-ation of "ensemble-style products" involving the unique combination of finished products used as raw materials. Such do-it-yourself (DIY) activity can include home modification, gardening, and cooking. The seeming grow-ing popularity of such craft consumption is seen in the increasing ubiquity of TV shows, magazines, and books devoted to food and cooking, house-hold makeovers, and gardening. We can also include collecting under this heading—the creation of a unique set of manufactured objects—as craft consumption. That is, putting a variety of forms of nothing together into unique sets (something) can be seen as craft consumption.

There is an even more extreme form of craft consumption that involves not only the creation of a unique finished product using generic compo-nents but the creation of at least some of those components as well. One example might be the gardener who creates and then cultivates his or her own varieties of flowers. Another is the DIY homeowner who creates at least some components of his or her home improvement project out of raw materials on a lathe in the basement or in a garage.

There are many ways to interpret the significance of craft consumers, but in this context they can be seen as attempting to deal with loss amidst monumental abundance by seeking to create something out of bits and pieces of that abundance. Since what has been lost is something, the activities of the craft consumers and what they create can be seen as efforts at coping with the loss of concern mentioned throughout this chapter.

Keep the Local Alive

It may be that what the kinds of cognitive switches and actions discussed above need to focus on first is a *defense* of the ever-shrinking remnants of something at the local level. The sense of loss would be eliminated if, in fact, the something associated with the local was retained. This would do nothing to stem the tide in the direction of the increase in the monumental abundance of nothing, but it would at least provide alternatives to those who want them.

The argument for keeping the local alive (Caldwell and Lozada would say it already is; it never died) is based on the conviction that much of what is something has, at least historically, flowed from the local. It is also based on the view that the local is under assault by the grobal and in the fact that it is likely to be either destroyed, minimized, or glocalized. In any case, the local, in anything approaching its pure sense, is rapidly disappearing. Its defense is premised on the idea that it is far easier to protect that which is already in existence or in process, even if it has already begun to decline, than it is to re-create phenomena that have disappeared. When phenomena have disappeared, interest will wane or disappear, among other things, and those (the artisans, or even artists) who created local phenomena may well pass from the scene or move on to some other undertaking. Consumers' memories of these phenomena will fade and begin to disappear. Whole generations will be born with no direct knowledge of local phenomena once considered something.

Building on that which is being protected and defended, it becomes possible to expand the production of forms of something already in existence and to produce new forms of something. What is needed is the defense *and* further creation of places, things, people, and services. That is, those concerned with loss amidst monumental abundance would want to prevent a further erosion of, *and* encourage the creation of new, places, things, people, and services that (a) are unique and one of a kind, (b) have local geographic ties, (c) are specific to the times, (d) involve human relations, and (e) are enchanted. Secondarily, this means support for those places, things, people, and services that have an aura of permanency, are locales, offer people a source of identity, and are authentic.

If current trends continue, something will be increasingly reduced and pushed into more remote and narrower corners of the world. Grobalization will threaten something more and more, and that which is something will be increasingly glocalized and thereby moved toward the nothing end of the continuum (at least in comparison to the truly local).

It is important not to overromanticize the local—it is the source of much that is not so desirable and perhaps even destructive and reprehensible. It is not that one would want to return to a world dominated by the local; grobalization and glocalization have given people throughout the world much that has advanced their lives and that seems to have made many of them happier. What is needed is a world in which people continue to have the *option* of choosing the local—a world in which the local has not been destroyed as a viable alternative by grobalization and glocalization.

What of the argument of economists and others in the social sciences who adopt a rational choice perspective?[27] That is, what of the argument that people the world over are freely choosing nothing—*non*places, *non*things, *non*people, and *non*services—and therefore there is no need to defend the local—the natural home of places, things, people, and services—because it is clear that increasingly few want that which is local? The view here is that the struggle between the local on one side and the grobal and glocal on the other is a highly uneven one—one that is being won by the twin forces of globalization. Virtually all of the power—economic, marketing, advertising, and so on—lies with the forces that support globalization. In the so-called free market, the grobal and the glocal are rapidly destroying the local. The result is that there must be active efforts to support and sustain the local. The goal is not to push the world back centuries to an epoch in which the local was virtually all there was for the vast majority of people on the planet. Rather, the goal is the retention of at least some aspects of the local so that people can make a truly rational choice between it, the grobal, and the glocal.

But this is not merely a matter of permitting greater choice; it is also a matter of sustaining a crucial source of innovation in the world.[28] Without ideas and innovations bubbling up from below, from the local, the world will be much more stagnant and greatly impoverished. This is certainly not true of innovations in areas like medicine and science that are highly dependent on grobalization (although there are problems here as well, such as the stifling of new and alternative medicines from many local areas around the globe or the destruction of local plant life that might be the source of future pharmaceuticals), but it is true in the domain of culture conceived in its broadest terms and, more specifically, consumer culture. We need grobal innovations in medicine, science, and the like in order to survive (although many of them—in military technology, for example—threaten us as well) and to live the kinds of lives we wish to live, but we also need culture and cultural innovations in order to be truly human beings. Continued cultural innovation depends, at least in part, on the sustenance of the local in the face of grobal processes that are, at this moment, well on their way to overwhelming it.

Promote Something

Keeping the local alive is a specific version of a more general set of actions and programs designed to promote something (rather than nothing). Those entities that are associated with something in this book—personal loans, great good places, racetracks, and so on—tend to be associated with the past. Indeed, this is closely tied to this book's grand narrative of a historical transition from something to nothing.

However, all of these forms of something and many others (e.g., home cooking, authentic ethnic restaurants) continue to exist in the United States and to a far greater extent in most other parts of the world. More important, there are many ongoing and very active efforts to sustain, if not resuscitate, places, things, people, and services. A good example is the Slow Food movement. This is a lively and growing movement that is devoted to protecting endangered foods and to sustaining and reviving traditional small farms and their farming techniques, small and excellent facilities for food production, high-quality restaurants, traditional and high-quality foods, and those who know how to prepare and serve such foods.[29] While there is a strong element of maintaining the past in the Slow Food movement, it is very much oriented to the present (it explicitly does *not* want to become a museum for dead or dying foods) and the future.

A critique of the loss associated with the growth of nothing and the decline of something must not remain rooted in the past but must be oriented to the present and especially the future. That is, it is not just a matter of reviving past, or sustaining extant, forms of something, but also, and perhaps more important, building on them as well as creating entirely new forms of something. Surely all of the magnificent advances of recent decades need not be restricted to aiding the increasing predominance of nothing. For example, advances in science and technology can be used to create new types of gourmet foods and meals, new great good places, and people with skills that extend far beyond those of their predecessors and that enable them to offer undreamed-of services. It could be argued that the golden age of something is not to be found in the past but awaits us in the not-too-distant future.

Collective Responses: Brand Communities

While collectivities may be involved in the various activities discussed above—groups that band together to keep the local alive or to promote something as well as clubs that bring craft consumers together—in this section and the next I deal directly with such more collective responses.

In recent years we have seen the emergence of groups, sometimes global in scope, in which people's involvement serves as the basis for the transformation of nothing into something and in this way coping with the loss of concern here.[30] While the emphasis is often the fact that consumer society destroys traditional forms of community, it is also clear that it gives rise to various types of communities, including "brand communities."[31] Even though these communities aggregate around consumer objects and practices (the Apple Macintosh or the Saab automobile), they also possess characteristics that define traditional communities, including "consciousness of kind, rituals and traditions, and moral responsibility."[32] As such, even as the Apple computer or the Saab automobile are mass-produced exemplars of nothing, the meanings of these objects are transformed once they are taken up by a community of dedicated users.

The activities of brand communities serve to transform symbolically (and sometimes materially) consumer objects so that they acquire a significance and social status that is not reducible to marketing strategies or properties inherent in the design of a product. Saab users, for example, develop communal myths and stories about their cars. Many members of the Saab brand community share personal stories about how their Saabs saved their lives. As the telling of these stories proliferate, they serve to integrate the community and to transform the meaning of the automobile so that it is seen not simply as another car but as a life-saving vehicle. Furthermore, members of these communities use brand logos (such as the Macintosh "bomb") in unique and innovative ways. Consumers do not merely engage in social psychological machinations that create illusory meanings for commodities lacking in substance. They also engage in rituals, narratives, and social networks in brand communities that serve as a base for modifying brands and their meanings.

The brand is often modified by the community, who use it to express social meaning beyond the brand's centrally conceived and controlled marketing plan. It becomes part of the unique and distinctive culture of the community because it is used in ways that are unique to the community.

Brand communities can also be involved in the physical transformation of nothing into something. Brand communities and their supporting social networks operate as grounds out of which commodities are physically elaborated and modified. For example, the Apple Newton was an early version of the now popular personal digital assistants (PDAs). Due to its many flaws, this Apple product was discontinued in 1998 but continued to live on in the Apple community. Web sites and e-mail lists provided technical support for Newton users even after the Newton was no longer being produced. For example, far beyond its original use, the Newton community has created software that transforms the Newton into an MP3 player, keeping up with demands of the community that were not initially built into the product.[33]

Today, brand communities are mediated almost entirely through the Internet, and this serves to make them a more global phenomenon. These communities (e.g., the Apple Newton community) create virtual social space on bulletin boards, e-mail lists, Web logs (blogs), and wikis (shared, real-time-edited Web content) or are nested within news filters that support the brand, such as slashdot.org. Often these communities bleed into other, related interests; through shared interests with other members, or through news filters or online chat, they find other communities. All this takes place in a social space created and stored online, often for profit—almost all Web site hosting costs money, and many of these social spaces are supported by advertisements. The absolute nothingness of a mass-produced computer, of empty Web space that does not exist geographically, and of mass-marketed software is converted into something—communities that often become a central part of people's social worlds.

The brand community, among many others, can be seen, or reinterpreted, as being involved, sometimes globally, in an effort to deal with loss amidst monumental abundance. However, there are organizations that are clearly and unequivocally both global and involved in such an effort. In the final section of this chapter I deal with in greater detail an increasingly important global organization and movement—Slow Food—that is actively engaged in dealing with loss by *both* promoting something and in keeping the local alive.

Global Responses:
Slow Food and Other INGOs

Slow Food can be seen as one of the growing number of international nongovernmental organizations (INGOs) that are playing an increasing role in globalization. These are global organizations that, unlike IGOs (international governmental organizations such as the World Bank and the International Monetary Fund), are independent of any state, of even global forms of government (e.g., the U.N.). Many of them are also independent of multinational corporations, and some are even opposed, at least in part, to them. Specifically, in terms of our interests here, some are opposed to the global consumer culture being spawned and sustained by those corporations.

Slow Food is one such INGO, but there are others that share at least some of its interests. For example, Greenpeace and the World Wildlife Fund are interested, in part, in the problems created by the grobalization of consumer culture as they relate to the environment. More generally, many of the organizations associated with the World Social Forum would have many interests in common with Slow Food, as well as Greenpeace and the World Wildlife Fund. Such organizations represent some hope against the spread of the grobalization of nothing and the resulting loss amidst monumental abundance.

However, this suggests that the formation of an INGO much more targeted directly at the problems being discussed here would have a greater likelihood of success. Such an IGO would have as its goals support for the grobalization and glocalization of something, opposition to the increasing pervasiveness of the grobalization and glocalization of nothing, limitations on the growth of the monumental abundance of nothing, and ultimately the prevention of the losses associated with the latter as they increasingly replace something throughout the world. Of course, these objectives would need to be couched in much less academic, and much more conventional and down-to-earth, terms in order to have any hope of success.

In addition to such general IGOs, we can conceive of the need for four specific types of IGOs oriented to sustaining and defending the major forms of something: (1) places, (2) things, (3) people, and (4) services. Of course, beyond that, innumerable, much more specific, IGOs would need to be created to sustain and defend specific places, things, people, and services. Following the basic dimensions laid down in Chapter 2, all of these IGOs would be devoted to the maintenance and defense of that which is unique, has local geographic ties, is specific to the times, involves human relations, and is enchanted. Indeed, the Slow Food movement is devoted to just such things and therefore stands as a successful grobal model for those interested in protecting and furthering something in a world increasingly characterized by the grobal spread of nothing, or those oriented to the prevention of the loss of something in a world increasingly characterized by the monumental abundance of nothing. However, rather than dealing with what might be, let us focus here on what already exists, specifically Slow Food.

Slow Food has sought, quite successfully, to become a force throughout the world and now has in excess of 80,000 members in over 45 countries.[34] However, unlike virtually all others of its ilk, it is a grobal organization interested in sustaining that which is locally conceived and controlled and is rich in distinctive content (in other words, it is interested in both the maintenance of the local and the grobalization of something). In terms of the problem of loss amidst monumental abundance, Slow Food is not opposed to monumental abundance, even of nothing. However, it is in favor of dealing with the problem of loss by being sure that there is also a place in the world for something for those who want access to it. Thus, those who feel such a sense of loss would at least have some place to turn to reduce, or eliminate, that feeling and that reality.

The Slow Food movement does the following:

- Supports traditional ways of growing and raising food that is exceptional in quality and taste
- Favors the eating of such food as opposed to the alternatives produced by grobal corporations
- Seeks to continue local traditions not only in how food is produced but in what is eaten and how it is prepared
- Favors food preparation that is traditional and as close to handmade as possible
- Favors raw ingredients that are as specific to the place in which the food is made as possible
- Fights against environmental degradations that threaten local methods of producing food
- Supports the local shopkeeper and restaurateur (it favors "local inns and cafes"[35]) in their efforts to survive in the face of the onslaught of powerful grobal competitors
- Creates local "convivia" that meet and engage in actions to further the above causes
- Has created an "Ark of Taste," which lists hundreds of foods that are endangered and in need of protection. "Ark foods must live in the modern world—must withstand the threats posed by bland, synthetic, mass-produced and menacingly cheap food."[36]
- Seeks to involve restaurants, communities, cities, national governments, and intergovernmental agencies in the support of slow food
- Offers annual Slow Food awards, especially to those "who preserve biodiversity as it relates to food—people who may in the process save whole villages and ecosystems"[37]
- Offers special prizes and support to third world efforts, and it seeks to help organize local efforts there to help conserve "prizewinners' plants, animals, and foods"[38]

In these and many other ways, Slow Food is fighting to sustain the continued existence of something within the realm of food.

In 2004 Slow Food sponsored the first Terra Madre meetings in Turin, Italy (the second took place there in 2006). Nearly 5,000 delegates attended the 2004 meetings, representing 1,200 food communities from 130 countries. The key here is the idea of a "food community," which "consists of all those working in the food sector—from production of ingredients to promotion of end products—whose products are of excellent quality and produced sustainably. A food community is connected to a specific geographical area from a historical, social, economic and cultural point of view."[39] There are two types of food communities. The first is *territory based*. In this case, while there may be diverse products, they are all derived from a given geographic area or native ethnic group. The second is *product based* and may include all farmers, breeders, processors, distributors, and others involved in producing a given product in a defined geographic area. Limited quantities are produced, and what is produced tastes good; does no harm to the environment, animals, or humans; and involves fair compensation and no discrimination or exploitation.[40] While Slow Food has always been concerned with production, it seemed to focus more on consumption than production. With Terra Madre, Slow Food signaled that it was concerned with *both* consumption and production, especially the production and consumption of something.

There is also a Slow Cities movement that focuses on helping cities remain places rather than succumbing to the trend toward them becoming *non*places. Somethingness in all realms and of all types needs organizations—especially IGOs, like Slow Food (and Slow Cities), and efforts such as these—if we are not to be inundated by a sea of nothingness. There is no reason why similar global organizations cannot be formed with the objective of sustaining something and warding off the onslaught of nothing, in various realms.

While the maintenance and defense of something are both important, it must be remembered, once again, that the Slow Food movement does *not* want to be seen as creating a "museum." That is, it is not interested in simply maintaining the past and present; it is also concerned with creating the future. This means that it is important for it, and all organizations like it, to be actively involved in encouraging the creation of *new* forms of something. This may involve new combinations of that which already exists or the creation of entirely new places, things, people, and services. The latter is no easy task, but it must not be lost sight of in the maintenance of extant forms of something.

I have used Slow Food here as an example of what can be done at the level of an INGO about the problem of loss amidst monumental abundance. However, we must be careful not to exaggerate its significance—Slow Food has its limitations and weaknesses. Nevertheless, it is a rudimentary example of the fact that there are things that can be done about this problem and, more generally, this book's focal concern with the global loss of something and the increasing proliferation of nothing around the world.

Notes

Chapter 1

1. Albrow, M. (1997). *The global age.* Stanford, CA: Stanford University Press.

2. As will be seen, the meaning of this concept is not unambiguous. An effort will be made to sort this out in the ensuing discussion.

3. Probably the largest-selling and most visible of the popular works are by Friedman, T., especially *The Lexus and the olive tree* (1999). New York: Farrar, Strauss & Giroux, and *The world is flat* (2005). New York: Farrar, Strauss & Giroux. For an overview of academic work on this topic, see Scholte, J. A. (2005). *Globalization: A critical introduction* (2nd ed.). Basingstoke, UK; Ritzer, G. (Ed.). (in press). *The Blackwell companion to globalization.* Oxford, UK: Blackwell. Among the social theorists who have addressed the issue of globalization are Bauman, Z. (1998). *Globalization: The human consequences.* New York: Columbia University Press; Beck, U. (2005). *Power in the global age.* Cambridge, UK: Polity Press; Beck, U. (2000). *What is globalization?* Cambridge, UK: Polity Press; Giddens, A. (2000). *Runaway world: How globalization is reshaping our lives.* New York: Routledge; Kellner, D. (2002). Theorizing globalization. *Sociological Theory, 20,* 285–305; Urry, J. (2003). *Global complexity.* London: Polity Press. I will deal with some of the other important contributions to this literature in the next several pages.

4. Robinson, W. I. (in press). Theories of globalization. In G. Ritzer (Ed.), *The Blackwell companion to globalization.* Oxford, UK: Blackwell.

5. While they dealt with global issues, none of them (save, perhaps, for world-system theory) are generally considered globalization theories.

6. Rostow, W. W. (1960). *The stages of economic growth: A non-communist manifesto.* Cambridge, UK: Cambridge University Press; Tiryakian, E. A. (1992). Pathways to metatheory: Rethinking the presuppositions of macrosociology. In G. Ritzer (Ed.), *Metatheorizing* (pp. 69–87). Beverly Hills, CA: Sage. The opposition to modernization theory plays a particularly central role in the work of Appadurai. See Appadurai, A. (1996). *Modernity at large: Cultural dimensions of globalization.* Minneapolis: University of Minnesota Press.

7. Although in the eyes of some, modernization theory is alive and well. See, for example, Korzeniewicz, P., & Moran, T. (in press). *World inequality in the twenty-first century: Patterns and tendencies,* as well as Firebaugh, G., & Goesling, B. (in press). Globalization and global inequalities: Recent trends. In G. Ritzer (Ed.), *The Blackwell companion to globalization.* Oxford, UK: Blackwell.

8. This line of work was inaugurated by the publication of Wallerstein, I. (1974). *The modern world-system*. New York: Academic Press.

9. See, for example, Frank, A. G. (1967). *Capitalism and underdevelopment in Latin America*. New York: Monthly Review Press.

10. Appadurai, A. (1996). *Modernity at large: Cultural dimensions of globalization*. Minneapolis: University of Minnesota Press.

11. Beck, U. (in press). Cosmopolitanism: A critical theory for the 21st century. In G. Ritzer (Ed.), *The Blackwell companion to globalization*. Oxford, UK: Blackwell.

12. Lechner, F. (2005). Globalization. In George Ritzer (Ed.), *Encyclopedia of Social Theory* (pp. 330–333). Thousand Oaks, CA: Sage.

13. It is worth pointing out that many in the world, especially in the third world, may have little or no global consciousness. Furthermore, when they do, it may well be primarily about how globalization adversely affects them in various ways.

14. For an excellent overview, see Antonio, R. J., & Bonanno, A. (2000). A new global capitalism? From "Americanism" and "Fordism" to "Americanization-Globalization." *American Studies 41*, 33–77; see also Lechner F., & Boli, J. (Eds.). (2004). *The globalization reader* (2nd ed.). Malden, MA: Blackwell.

15. Dicken, P. (in press). Economic globalization: Corporations. In G. Ritzer (Ed.), *The Blackwell companion to globalization*. Oxford, UK: Blackwell.

16. Delanty, G., & Rumford, C. (in press). Political globalization. In G. Ritzer (Ed.), *The Blackwell companion to globalization*. Oxford, UK: Blackwell; Rosenau, J. N. (1990). *Turbulence in world politics: A theory of change and continuity*. Princeton, NJ: Princeton University Press.

17. Dicken, P. (in press). Economic globalization: Corporations. In G. Ritzer (Ed.), *The Blackwell companion to globalization*. Oxford, UK: Blackwell.

18. Keane, J. (2003). *Global civil society?* Cambridge, UK: Cambridge University Press; Kaldor, M. (2003). *Global civil society: An answer to war*. Cambridge, UK: Polity Press.

19. Sassen, S. (1991). *The global city*. Princeton, NJ: Princeton University Press; Sassen, S. (2000). The global city: Strategic site/new frontier. *American Studies, 41*(2/3), 79–95; Timberlake, M., & Ma, X. (in press). Cities and globalization. In G. Ritzer (Ed.), *The Blackwell companion to globalization*. Oxford, UK: Blackwell.

20. Marcuse, P., & van Kempen, R. (Eds.). (2000). *Globalizing cities: A new spatial order*. Malden, MA: Blackwell.

21. The importance of the global cities could decline as the stock exchanges continue to move in the direction of electronic transactions (NASDAQ has always been electronic). Furthermore, ongoing efforts by the American exchanges to buy the London exchange could eventually lead to one huge global electronic market that girdles the globe, making the current global cities less important, at least in this realm.

22. DePalma, D. A. (2002). *Business without borders: A strategic guide to global marketing*. New York: John Wiley; Stegner, M. (2002). *Globalism: The new market ideology*. Lanham, MD: Rowman & Littlefield.

23. Kellner, D., & Pierce, C. (in press). Media and globalization. In G. Ritzer (Ed.), *The Blackwell companion to globalization*. Oxford, UK: Blackwell.

24. Yunker, J. (2002). *Beyond borders: Web globalization strategies*. Indianapolis, IN: New Riders; Porter, D. (Ed.). (1997). *Internet culture*. London: Routledge.

25. Hornborg, A. (in press). *The power of the machine: Global inequalities of economy, technology, and environment*. Walnut Creek, CA: AltaMira Press; Drori, G. (2004). The Internet as a global social problem. In G. Ritzer (Ed.), *Handbook of social problems: A comparative international perspective* (pp. 433–450). Thousand Oaks, CA: Sage; Drori, G.

(2006). *Global e-litism: Digital technology, social inequality, and transnationality*. New York: Worth.

26. Tumber, H., & Webster, F. (in press). Globalization and information and communications technologies: The case of war. In G. Ritzer (Ed.), *The Blackwell companion to globalization*. Oxford, UK: Blackwell.

27. Beyer, P. (1994). *Religion and globalization*. London: Sage; Beyer, P. (in press). Religion and globalization. In G. Ritzer (Ed.), *The Blackwell companion to globalization*. Oxford, UK: Blackwell.

28. Andrews, D., & Grainger, A. D. (in press). Sport and globalization. In G. Ritzer (Ed.), *The Blackwell companion to globalization*. Oxford, UK: Blackwell; Maguire, J. (1999). *Global sport: Identities, societies, civilizations*. Cambridge, UK: Polity Press.

29. Seago, A. (2000). "Where hamburgers sizzle on an open grill night and day": Global pop music and Americanization in the year 2000. *American Studies, 41*(2/3), 119–136.

30. Bhalla, S. S. (2002). *Imagine there's no country: Poverty inequality and growth in the era of globalization*. Washington, DC: Institute for International Economics.

31. Hashemian, F., & Yach, D. (in press). Public health in a globalizing world. In G. Ritzer (Ed.), *The Blackwell companion to globalization*. Oxford, UK: Blackwell.

32. Castells, M. (1998). *End of millennium*. Malden, MA: Blackwell.

33. Warner, C. (in press). Globalization and corruption. In G. Ritzer (Ed.), *The Blackwell companion to globalization*. Oxford, UK: Blackwell.

34. Altman, D. (2001). *Global sex*. Chicago: University of Chicago Press.

35. Farr, K. (2005). *Sex trafficking: The global market in women and children*. New York: Worth; Farr, K. (in press). Globalization and sexuality. In G. Ritzer (Ed.), *The Blackwell companion to globalization*. Oxford, UK: Blackwell.

36. Scruton, R. (2002). *The West and the rest: Globalization and the terrorist threat*. Wilmington, DE: Intercollegiate Studies Institute; Martin, G. (in press). Globalization and international terrorism. In G. Ritzer (Ed.), *The Blackwell companion to globalization*. Oxford, UK: Blackwell.

37. McMichael, P. (in press). Globalization and the agrarian world. In G. Ritzer (Ed.), *The Blackwell companion to globalization*. Oxford, UK: Blackwell.

38. Elliott, L. (1998). *The global politics of the environment*. London: Macmillan; Yearley, S. (in press). Globalization and the environment. In G. Ritzer (Ed.), *The Blackwell companion to globalization*. Oxford, UK: Blackwell.

39. Singer, P. (2002). *One world: The ethics of globalization*. New Haven, CT: Yale University Press.

40. Kahn, R., & Kellner, D. (in press). Resisting globalization. In G. Ritzer (Ed.), *The Blackwell companion to globalization*. Oxford, UK: Blackwell.

41. Tomlinson, J. (in press). Cultural globalization. In G. Ritzer (Ed.), *The Blackwell companion to globalization*. Oxford, UK: Blackwell; Tomlinson, J. (1999). *Globalization and culture*. Chicago: University of Chicago Press.

42. Goodman, D. (in press). Globalization and consumer culture. In G. Ritzer (Ed.), *The Blackwell companion to globalization*. Oxford, UK: Blackwell.

43. Caldwell, M. L., & Lozada, E., Jr. (in press). The fate of the local. In G. Ritzer (Ed.), *The Blackwell companion to globalization*. Oxford, UK: Blackwell.

44. See Ritzer, G. (2007). *Contemporary sociological theory and its classical roots* (2nd ed.). New York: McGraw-Hill.

45. See, for example, Robinson, W. I. (in press). Theories of globalization. In G. Ritzer (Ed.), *The Blackwell companion to globalization*. Oxford, UK: Blackwell.

46. MacPherson, C. B. (1962). *The political theory of possessive individualism.* Oxford, UK: Clarendon Press.

47. Harvey, D. (2005). *A brief history of neoliberalism.* Oxford, UK: Oxford University Press; Campbell, J., & Pederson, O. K. (Eds.). (2001). *The rise of neoliberalism and institutional analysis.* Princeton, NJ: Princeton University Press.

48. Williamson, J. (1990). What Washington means by policy reform. In J. Williamson (Ed.), *Latin American adjustment: How much has happened?* (pp. 7–20). Washington, DC: Institute for International Economics; Williamson, J. (1997). The Washington consensus reassessed. In L. Emmerij (Ed.), *Economic and social development into the XXI century* (pp. 48–61). Washington, DC: Inter-American Development Bank.

49. Antonio, R. (in press). The cultural construction of neoliberal globalization: "Honey . . . I think I shrunk the kids." In G. Ritzer (Ed.), *The Blackwell companion to globalization.* Oxford, UK: Blackwell.

50. Spegele. R. D. (1996). *Political realism in international theory.* Cambridge, UK: Cambridge University Press; Scholte, J. A. (2005). *Globalization: A critical introduction* (2nd ed.). Basingstoke, UK: Palgrave Macmillan.

51. It could also be argued that its political interests (in the Middle East) and its military interests (the positioning of troops and matériel in forward military bases throughout the world) were advanced by the war.

52. See, for example, Smouts, M.-C. (2001). *The new international relations: Theory and practice.* New York: Palgrave Macmillan; Rosenau, J. (2003). *Distant proximities: Dynamics beyond globalization.* Princeton, NJ: Princeton University Press.

53. Rosenberg, J. (2005). Globalization theory: A post mortem. *International Politics, 42,* 2–74.

54. In this section, the focus is not on the work of economists but rather that of other social scientists, especially sociologists, who have focused on economic issues.

55. Even though the theory's creator dismisses the idea of globalization; see Wallerstein, I. (2000). Globalization in the age of transition. *International Sociology, 15*(2), 249–265.

56. Wallerstein, I. (1974). *The modern world system* (Vol. 1). New York: Academic Press.

57. Sklair, L. (2002). *Globalization: Capitalism and its alternatives.* New York: Oxford University Press; see also Robinson, W. I. (2004). *A global theory of capitalism: Production, class and state in a transnational world.* Baltimore: Johns Hopkins University Press, although Robinson gives greater importance to the emergence of a transnational state.

58. Dicken, P. (in press). Economic globalization: Corporations. In G. Ritzer (Ed.), *The Blackwell companion to globalization.* Oxford, UK: Blackwell.

59. Hardt, M., & Negri, A. (2000). *Empire.* Cambridge, MA: Harvard University Press; see also Hardt, M., & Negri, A. (2004). *Multitude.* New York: Penguin.

60. Castells, M. (1996–1998). *The rise of the network society* (Vols. 1–3). Oxford, UK: Blackwell.

61. Ritzer, G. (2001). *Explorations in the sociology of consumption.* London: Sage.

62. At least to the economies of developed nations and to those better-off segments of their populations.

63. Pieterse, J. N. (2004). *Globalization and culture: Global melange.* Lanham, MD: Rowman & Littlefield.

64. Huntington, S. (1996). *Clash of civilizations and the remaking of the world order.* New York: Simon & Schuster.

65. Ritzer, G. (2004). *The McDonaldization of society* (Rev. New Century ed.). Thousand Oaks, CA: Pine Forge Press.

66. For example, Watson, J. L. (1997). *Golden arches east: McDonald's in East Asia.* Stanford, CA: Stanford University Press; Caldwell, M. (2004). Domesticating the French fry: McDonald's and consumerism in Moscow. *Journal of Consumer Culture, 4,* 5–26.

67. Among those who understand this are Bryman, A. (2003). Global implications of McDonaldization and Disneyization, *American Behavioral Scientist, 47,* 154–167; Ram, U. (2004). Glocommodification: How the global consumes the local; McDonald's in Israel. *Current Sociology, 52,* 11–31.

68. Ritzer, G. (1995). *Expressing America: A critique of the global credit card society.* Thousand Oaks, CA: Pine Forge Press.

69. Ritzer, G. (2005). *Enchanting a disenchanted world: Revolutionizing the means of consumption* (2nd ed.). Thousand Oaks, CA: Pine Forge Press.

70. DiMaggio, P., & Powell, W. W. (1983). The iron cage revisited: Institutional isomorphism and collective rationality in organizational fields. *American Sociological Review, 48,* 147–160.

71. Meyer, J. (1980). The world polity and the authority of the nation-state. In A. J. Bergesen (Ed.), *Studies of modern world-system* (pp. 109–137). New York: Academic Press; Meyer, J., Boli, J., Thomas, G. M., & Ramirez, F. O. (1997). World society and the nation-state. *American Journal of Sociology, 103,* 144–181; Meyer, J., Ramirez, F. O., & Soysal, Y. (1992). World expansion of mass education, 1870–1970. *Sociology of Education, 65,* 128–149; Lechner, F. J., & Boli, J. (2005). *World culture: Origins and consequences.* Malden, MA: Blackwell.

72. McGrew, A. (in press). Globalization in hard times: Contention in the academy and beyond. In G. Ritzer (Ed.), *The Blackwell companion to globalization.* Oxford, UK: Blackwell.

73. Robertson, R. (2001). Globalization theory 2000+: Major problematics. In G. Ritzer & B. Smart (Eds.), *Handbook of social theory* (pp. 458–471). London: Sage.

74. Appadurai, A. (1996). *Modernity at large: Cultural dimensions of globalization.* Minneapolis: University of Minnesota Press.

75. Anderson, B. (1983). *Imagined communities.* London: Verso.

76. This is part of a long-term interest of mine in theoretical and metatheoretical integration. See, for example, Ritzer, G. (1980). *Sociology: A multiple paradigm science.* Boston: Allyn & Bacon. (Original work published 1975); Ritzer, G. (1981). *Toward an integrated sociological paradigm.* Boston: Allyn & Bacon; Ritzer, G. (1991). *Metatheorizing in sociology.* Lexington, MA: Lexington Books.

77. Robertson, R. (2001). Globalization theory 2000+: Major problematics. In G. Ritzer & B. Smart (Eds.), *Handbook of social theory* (pp. 458–471). London: Sage. Glocalization is at the heart of Robertson's own approach, but it is central to that of many others. Among the most notable are Appadurai's view on the "Indianization of cricket" and his idea that the "new global cultural economy has to be seen as a complex, overlapping, disjunctive order." See Appadurai, A. (1996). *Modernity at large: Cultural dimensions of globalization* (pp. 32, 95). Minneapolis: University of Minnesota Press. While John Tomlinson uses other terms, he sees glocalization as "friendly" to his own orientation. See Tomlinson, J. (1999). *Globalization and culture.* Chicago: University of Chicago Press.

78. I am combining a number of different entities under this heading (nations, corporations, a wide range of organizations, etc.), but it should be clear that there are profound differences among them, including the degree to which, and the ways in which, they seek to grobalize. I feel the same way about grobalization as Charles Peirce did about the creation of the concept of "pragmaticism" to distinguish it from the way "pragmatism" had come to be used by others (especially William James). Peirce felt that pragmaticism was "ugly enough to be safe from kidnappers" (cited in Halton, E. [2005]. Pragmatism. In G. Ritzer [Ed.], *Encyclopedia of social theory* [pp. 595–599]. Thousand Oaks, CA: Sage).

79. Here we discuss McDonaldization as a process that is sweeping across the globe as a centrally important grobalization process.

80. States further the interests of capitalist organizations but also further their own interests, some of which are separable from the capitalist system.

81. Ritzer, G. (2005). *Enchanting a disenchanted world: Revolutionizing the means of consumption* (2nd ed.). Thousand Oaks, CA: Pine Forge Press.

82. DiMaggio, P. J., & Powell, W. W. (1983). The iron cage revisited: Institutional isomorphism and collective rationality in organizational fields. *American Sociological Review, 48,* 147–160.

83. Best, S., & Kellner, D. (1997). *The postmodern turn.* New York: Guilford; Ritzer, G. (1997). *Postmodern social theory.* New York: McGraw-Hill. For an explicit effort to link globalization and postmodern social theory, see Featherstone, M. (1995). *Undoing culture: Globalization, postmodernism and identity.* London: Sage. I should make it clear that I am *not* arguing that those who emphasize glocalizaton are postmodernists; in most cases they certainly are not! I am simply arguing that at least some of the views of those associated with the idea of glocalization are in tune with postmodern thinking and perhaps are affected by the mood and orientation emerging from the "postmodern turn."

84. Stiglitz, J. E. (2002). *Globalization and its discontents* (p. 34). New York: W. W. Norton.

85. Meyer, J., Boli, J. W., Thomas, G. M., & Ramirez, F. (1997). World society and the nation-state. *American Journal of Sociology, 103,* 144–181.

86. Barber's view of McWorld is not restricted to politics; he sees many other domains following the model of McWorld; Barber, B. (1995). *Jihad vs. McWorld.* New York: Times Books.

87. More broadly, there are those who focus not only on politics but on the global influence of a multiplicity of institutions. For example, few if any countries can afford the American system of health and medical care, but most have at least been influenced by it to some degree. While the grobalization of aspects of the U.S. health care system has led to some degree of homogeneity, glocalization resulting from the interpenetration of that system with folk remedies and systems has led to increases in heterogeneity.

88. See, for example, Cowen, T. (2002). *Creative destruction: How globalization is changing the world's cultures.* Princeton, NJ: Princeton University Press.

89. Watson, J. (Ed.). (1997). *Golden arches east: McDonald's in East Asia.* Stanford, CA: Stanford University Press.

90. Marx, K. (1967). *Capital: A critique of political economy* (Vol. 1). New York: International. (Original work published 1867)

91. This is part of what Marx called the general law of capitalist accumulation.

92. I could have easily added another section here on technology, which can be seen as a grobalizing force in its own right. However, it is also closely linked to capitalism, Americanization, and McDonaldization (nonhuman technology is, of course, one element of this process).

93. This is what Kellner calls "techno-capitalism." See Kellner, D. (1989). *Critical theory, Marxism and modernity.* Baltimore, MD: Johns Hopkins University Press. On the role of technology in globalization, see Hornborg, A. (2001). *The power of the machine: Global inequalities of economy, technology, and environment.* Walnut Creek, CA: AltaMira Press.

94. Wood, E. M., & Foster, J. B. (Eds.). (1997). *In defense of history: Marxism and the postmodern agenda* (p. 67). New York: Monthly Review Press.

95. Burawoy, M. (1990). Marxism as science: Historical challenges and theoretical growth. *American Sociological Review, 55,* 775–793.

96. It is possible, but not likely, that the recent move to the left by some Latin American governments—notably Venezuela and Bolivia—will come to be seen as initial 21st-century developments in this direction.

97. Hardt, M., & Negri, A. (2000). *Empire*. Cambridge, MA: Harvard University Press; Hardt, M., & Negri, A. (2004). *Multitude*. New York: Penguin.

98. Implied, at times, in Marx's work, and more explicit in the work of some neo-Marxists, is the idea that it is the economy that is of ultimate importance in society, and everything else (politics, religion, etc.) is merely "superstructure" that is erected on that all-important economic base. It should be clear why this is often associated with *economic determinism*, an idea that is anathema to most non-Marxists and even many neo-Marxists.

99. Although the United States has supported many authoritarian regimes when it is in its interest to do so.

100. Dicke, T. S. (1992). *Franchising in America: The development of a business method, 1840–1980*. Chapel Hill: University of North Carolina Press.

101. Weber, M. (1968). *Economy and society* (Vols. 1–3). Totowa, NJ: Bedminster Press. (Original work published 1921)

102. Weber, M. (1981). *General economic history*. New Brunswick, NJ: Transaction Books. (Original work published 1927)

103. Ritzer, G. (2004). *The McDonaldization of society* (Rev. New Century ed.). Thousand Oaks, CA: Pine Forge Press. It should be pointed out that McDonald's did not create these principles, many of which can be traced back to scientific management and the assembly line, but it did apply them in new and different ways.

104. Hayes, D., & Wynyard, R. (Eds.). (2002). *The McDonaldization of higher education*. Westport, CT: Bergin & Garvey.

105. Turner, B. (1999). McCitizens: Risk, coolness and irony in contemporary politics. In B. Smart (Ed.), *Resisting McDonaldization* (pp. 83–100). London: Sage; Beilharz, P. (1999). McFascism: Reading Ritzer, Bauman and the Holocaust. In B. Smart (Ed.), *Resisting McDonaldization* (pp. 222–233). London: Sage.

106. Drane, J. (2001). *The McDonaldization of the church*. London: Darton, Longman & Todd; Drane, J. (2006). From creeds to burgers: Religious control, spiritual search, and the future of the world. In G. Ritzer (Ed.), *McDonaldization: The reader* (2nd ed., pp. 197–202). Thousand Oaks, CA: Pine Forge Press.

107. Robinson, M. B. (2006). McDonaldization of America's police, courts, and corrections. In G. Ritzer (Ed.), *McDonaldization: The reader* (2nd ed., pp. 77–90). Thousand Oaks, CA: Pine Forge Press.

108. Ritzer, G. (with Ovadia, S.). (2000). The process of McDonaldization is not uniform, nor are its settings, consumers, or the consumption of its goods and services. In Gottdiener, M. (Ed.), *New forms of consumption: Consumers, cultures and commodification* (pp. 33–49). Lanham, MD: Rowman & Littlefield.

109. Ritzer, G. (1998). *The McDonaldization thesis*. London: Sage.

110. As I write this (early 2006), McDonald's has just announced the closing of 25 restaurants in Great Britain. Retrieved from news.bbc.co.uk/go/em/fr//1/hi/business/4759130.stm

111. Ritzer, G. (1998). *The McDonaldization thesis* (pp. 174–183). London: Sage.

112. While McDonald's is not likely to go out of business anytime soon, it does find itself in an already overcrowded, saturated market in which profits are being driven down by increasingly intense price competition. This problem is likely to be exacerbated as foreign competitors increasingly enter the American market. However, even if McDonald's were to disappear, the process of McDonaldization would continue apace, although we might need a new label for it.

113. Williams, F. (1962). *The American invasion*. New York: Crown Williams.

114. Murden, T., & Miller, P. (2002, April 28). Coke beats Irn-Bru to be top of the pops. *Sunday Times*.

115. Kael, P. (1985). Why are movies so bad? or, The numbers. In P. Kael (Ed.), *State of the art* (pp. 8–20). New York: E. P. Dutton.

116. Said, E. (1978). *Orientalism*. New York: Pantheon.

117. Chung, C. J., Inaba, J., Koolhaas, R., & Leong, S. T. (Eds.). (2001). *Harvard Design School guide to shopping*. Koln, Germany: Taschen.

118. Manicas, P. (in press). Globalization and higher education. In G. Ritzer (Ed.), *The Blackwell companion to globalization*. Oxford, UK: Blackwell.

119. Leiby, R. (2003, March 17). You want falafel with that? *Washington Post*, p. C1.

120. It is also possible that this turn inward could lead to less benign outcomes such as increases in xenophobia.

121. Bak, S. (1997). McDonald's in Seoul: Food choices, identity, and nationalism. In J. Watson (Ed.), *Golden arches east: McDonald's in East Asia* (pp. 136–160). Stanford, CA: Stanford University Press.

122. Grobalization tends to involve what Hansen calls "delocalization," or the deforming effects of the grobal on the local. See Hansen, C. E. (2002). *The culture of strangers: Globalization, localization and the phenomenon of exchange*. Lanham, MD: University Press of America. See also Stiglitz, J. E. (2002). *Globalization and its discontents*. New York: W. W. Norton.

Chapter 2

1. Barrow, J. D. (2000). *The book of nothing* (p. 1). New York: Pantheon Books.

2. For a discussion of nothing in these terms, see the Appendix to the original edition of this book.

3. As we will see, there are some forms of nothing that are locally conceived or controlled. While the reader should keep this caveat in mind throughout this book, it will not necessarily be repeated in later uses of nothing.

4. The use of the term *form* (and *content*) brings to mind the work of the philosopher Immanuel Kant and many neo-Kantians, especially within sociology, such as Georg Simmel. Their ideas are discussed in the Appendix to the original edition of this book, where it is clear that they use the terms differently than they are employed here.

5. Ritzer, G. (1995). *Expressing America: A critique of the global credit card society*. Thousand Oaks, CA: Pine Forge Press; Manning, R. (2000). *Credit card nation*. New York: Basic Books.

6. There are such things as "personality" cards, whereby a card might identify the holder as, for example, an Elvis fan or indicate one's astrological sign. Of course, there is then little to distinguish among the large numbers of holders of each of these types of cards.

7. Board of Governors of the Federal Reserve System. (2005, June). *The profitability of credit card operations of depository institution*. Annual report submitted to the Congress pursuant to Section 8 of the Fair Credit and Charge Card Disclosure Act of 1988. Washington, DC: Federal Reserve.

8. Board of Governors of the Federal Reserve System. (2006, July 10). *Consumer credit*. (Federal Reserve Statistical Release B19). Retrieved from www.federalreserve.gov/release/g19/current

9. Ibid.

10. I would like to thank Lois Vitt for assisting with the 2005 data.

11. Ritzer, G. (2001). *Explorations in the sociology of consumption*. London: Sage.

12. As in the case of the caveat about the definition of nothing, there are some forms of something (see discussion of muscle cars to follow) that are centrally conceived and controlled.

Once again, while the reader should keep this caution in mind throughout this book, it will not necessarily be repeated in future definitions of something.

13. The great German social theorist Max Weber praised rationalization in general, and the bureaucracy in particular, for greatly limiting such biases in decision making.

14. For a critique of dichotomous thinking, see Mudimbe-Boyi, E. (Ed.). (2002). *Beyond dichotomies: Histories, identities, cultures, and the challenge of globalization.* Albany: State University of New York Press.

15. Gottdiener makes this point, based on his discussion of airports, arguing that it is "wrong to create a dichotomy between place and placelessness because there are always elements of both in any milieu." See Gottdiener, M. (2001). *Life in the air: Surviving the new culture of air travel.* Lanham, MD: Rowman & Littlefield.

16. Zelizer, V. (1994). *The social meaning of money.* New York: Basic Books.

17. Ibid., 18.

18. However, it is not simply a matter of somehow just adding these positions together to come up with an overall score, and therefore placement, on the something-nothing continuum.

19. A caveat is needed here. These continua, taken individually and collectively, are not infallible in distinguishing something from nothing: there are anomalies. For example, as a general rule, they are better at distinguishing the man- (and woman-)made from that which is largely natural. Thus, while these continua work very well on shopping malls, credit card loans, Gap jeans, Valentino gowns, and the like, they work less well on things like diamonds, pets, and lettuce. For example, most would consider diamonds (and other precious stones) to be something, and I would not quarrel with that view, but diamonds lie toward the nothing end of several of the continua employed above. While diamonds clearly stand toward the something end of the unique-generic (every diamond is unique, although it would take an expert to find most differences) and the enchanted-disenchanted (a diamond, especially one that is of high quality, is quite magical) continua, it could be argued that they are closer to the nothing end of the other continua since they lack local ties, they are not specific to the times, and they are dehumanized. In spite of the fact that they stand toward the nothing end of more subcontinua than they do toward the something pole of others, the fact is that on the overarching something-nothing continuum, diamonds would stand toward the something end because of their distinctive substance. This includes not only the idiosyncratic characteristics of every stone but also the specific events and people involved in the giving and receiving of them.

At one level, the case of a diamond simply illustrates the utility of the various tools developed here and the subtleties involved in analyzing any given phenomenon. At another level, it could be interpreted as revealing limitations in the use of these tools. It may well be that there are phenomena like diamonds that are not well analyzed with this conceptual arsenal. It could be that there is something quite unusual about diamonds (and a limited number of other phenomena) that makes them different from most other phenomena. Or, it could be that they reveal some weaknesses in the concepts and flaws in the basic argument. However, it is clear that, in the main, the tools developed here do a good, though imperfect, job of analyzing that which is of concern in this book. In an era where the faith in modernity in general, and modern science in particular, has been undermined, if not destroyed, that may be the best we can do.

Nonetheless, overall, and especially in terms of the focal interests of this book, these continua are useful in making the general distinctions that lie at the base of this work and, more generally, in helping us to understand better the general trend toward the increase of nothing.

20. While it is obvious the other four subcontinua to be discussed below can be subsumed under the something-nothing continuum, that is not immediately obvious in this case. Unique-generic sounds very similar to, if not identical with, something-nothing. However, unique-generic is more specific than something-nothing. For example, unique (one of a kind) literally refers to something singular (e.g., Rembrandt's *Night Watch*), but that which is something can

be repeated (e.g., a particular style of vase preferred by a potter), perhaps even a number of times (although at some point we begin to move from something to nothing).

21.   Of course, it is true that even the most generic of products—say, a Big Mac—has subtle differences. Any given Big Mac may have a bit more lettuce, a few less sesame seeds on the bun, and so on. Nonetheless, it is clear that each Big Mac is far better described as being generic than unique.

22.   By the way, to avoid the charge of elitism (more on this as we proceed), the cook can either be a professional chef in an expensive restaurant or simply an amateur who uses local products with great skill to prepare homemade meals at low cost.

23.   Wilbur, T. (1993). *Top secret recipes: Creating kitchen clones of America's favorite brand-name foods.* New York: Plume.

24.   Pitzer, G. (2001). *Secret fast food recipes. The fast food cookbook.* Marysville, MI: Author.

25.   There are now a wide range of Lunchables available that include hamburgers, pizza, tacos, soft drinks, desserts, cookies, and many other things that most dieticians consider among the last things children, especially American children, need to eat.

26.   Few such lunches, however, could be considered gourmet.

27.   This section on space and the next on time deal with the two dimensions that have come to occupy the attention of many scholars, including social theorists, interested in an array of issues, including globalization.

28.   Although they may have complexity of another type derived from a multitude of inputs from many locales. For example, scholarly work often derives much of its complexity from the multitude of intellectual inputs and the idiosyncratic way in which a particular scholar puts them together. The currently popular "fusion" cuisine is another, more mundane example of complexity stemming from a variety of ingredients and recipes from many different parts of the world.

29.   Interestingly, not long ago Oaxaca voted to ban one of the major examples of nothing—McDonald's. See *McDonald's, rechazado por el munipio de Oaxaca, Mexico.* Retrieved December 12, 2002, from www.clarin.com/diario/hoy/t-488322.htm

30.   Retrieved from www.manos-de-oaxaca.com/jr_frmst.htm

31.   Retrieved from www.manos-de-oaxaca.com/intro.htm

32.   Thorstein Veblen pokes fun at the preference for handmade products and the kind of devaluation of mass-produced products found here. See Veblen, T. (1994). *The theory of the leisure class.* New York: Penguin Books. (Original work published 1899)

33.   Although the mixing might well produce a unique clay.

34.   Hunt, M. C. (2000, January 12). Beyond burritos: US cooks starting to appreciate bright flavors of authentic Mexican cooking. *San Diego Union-Tribune*, p. 1ff (FOOD).

35.   Retrieved from www.manos-de-oaxaca.com/intro.htm

36.   In the previous edition, I used the term *time-less*, but because of the ease with which it could be confused with what is its opposite, *timeless*, I decided to use *not specific to the times* (or *time-free*) in this edition. However, the two terms—*not specific to the times* (or *time-free*) and *time-less*—have the same meaning.

37.   Although it is true that it could be tied to the time period since the introduction of mass production and the Industrial Revolution. However, mass production is applied to an enormous range of products and has little to do with pottery per se. The real point is that mass-produced products in general, and pottery in particular, cannot easily be tied to any particular time period; they are more likely to seem time-free in the sense in which this term is defined below.

38.   Campisano, J. (1995). *American muscle cars.* New York: MetroBooks.

39. Other automobiles that lie toward the something end of the continuum reflect other eras of American history. Examples include the Stutz Bearcat (first produced in 1914), which reflects the exuberance and hubris of the United States about to emerge as a true world power in World War I, and the Jeep, whose enduring appeal is traceable to the mobility and triumph, through the mass manufacture of war matériel, of the United States in World War II.

40. Retrieved from www.geocities.com/thenewtbird

41. Retrieved from www.fordvehicles.com/cars/thunderbird/index.asp?bhcp=1

42. Retrieved from www.canadiandriver.com/articles/bv/convertible.htm

43. And this is not just a price issue.

44. Of course, mass manufacturing is not, in itself, the source of the difference, because muscle cars were mass-manufactured as well.

45. Iacocca, L., & Novak, W. (1986). *Iacocca: An autobiography*. New York: Bantam Books.

46. Of course, these are just tendencies. For a discussion of humanized relations in a *non-place*, the mall, see Lewis, G. H. (1990). Community through exclusion: The creation of social worlds in an American shopping mall. *Journal of Popular Culture, 24,* 121–136.

47. The University of Phoenix also offers more traditional classes in various locations.

48. Esquivel, L. (1992). *Like water for chocolate* (pp. 10–11). New York: Doubleday.

49. Ibid., 39.

Chapter 3

1. Crang, M. (1998). *Cultural geography*. London: Routledge; Foote, K. E., Hugill, P. S., Mathewson, K., & Smith, J. (1994). *Rereading cultural geography*. Austin: University of Texas Press.

2. Relph, E. (1976). *Place and placelessness*. London: Pion; see also Jacobson, D. (2002). *Place and belonging in America*. Baltimore, MD: Johns Hopkins University Press; Feld, S., & Basso, K. H. (Eds.). (1996). *Senses of place*. Santa Fe, NM: School of American Research Press.

3. Relph, E. (1976). *Place and placelessness* (p. 141). London: Pion.

4. Ibid., 143.

5. Augé, M. (1995). *Non-places: Introduction to an anthropology of supermodernity* (p. 79). London: Verso.

6. Ibid., 78.

7. Castells, M. (1996). *The rise of the network society*. Malden, MA: Blackwell.

8. One problem with Castells's conceptualization is that it tends to conflate space (*non-place*) and place.

9. Ironically, because it was the first of its kind, Levittown appears to have developed, at least in some ways, into something.

10. Exceptions are those communities—Disney's Celebration in Florida is the best example—that are purposely designed to simulate communities of a bygone era. However, as simulations, these communities cannot be considered unique; they are better seen as copies and as generic and therefore closer to the nothing, rather than the something, pole.

11. Kuntsler, J. H. (1994). *The geography of nowhere: The rise and decline of America's man-made landscape*. New York: Touchstone Books. Kuntsler gets at his idea of place in a later book; see Kuntsler, J. H. (1996). *Home from nowhere: Remaking our everyday world for the twenty-first century*. New York: Simon & Schuster. For an interesting view of nowhere (in this case those who live full time in motor homes and often park them in Wal-Mart parking lots when they are on the road), see *This is nowhere* (Missoula, MT: High Plains Film, 2002).

12. Retrieved from www.melsdiners.com/about/index.htm

13. Oldenburg, R. (1997). *The great good place*. New York: Marlowe. (Original work published 1989); Oldenburg, R. (Ed.). (2001). *Celebrating the third place*. New York: Marlowe.

14. Oldenburg, R. (1997). *The great good place* (p. 18). New York: Marlowe. (Original work published 1989)

15. Ibid., xvii.

16. May, R. A. B. (2001). *Talking at Trena's: Everyday conversation at an African American tavern* (p. 19). New York: New York University Press.

17. Neighborhood restaurants come to be "homes away from home." (1996). *Nation's Restaurant News, 30*(33), 66.

18. Ibid.

19. Watson, J. (1997). Transnationalism, localization, and fast foods in East Asia. In J. Watson (Ed.), *Golden arches east: McDonald's in East Asia*. Stanford, CA: Stanford University Press.

20. An interesting example of a *non*place is described in Diller, E., & Scofido, R. (2002). *Blur: The making of nothing*. New York: Harry N. Abrams. Diller and Scofido are architects who designed a structure for Swiss Expo 02 that, through the use of jets of water, was designed to appear to be a blur, nothing, in Lake Neuchatel.

21. Hurley, A. (2001). *Diners, bowling alleys and trailer parks*. New York: Basic Books; Jones, S. (2002, April 8). Back to basics: Silver Diner retreats from growth to focus on food and service. *Washington Post*, pp. E1, E12. Another example, this time in Great Britain, is the fish and chips shop; see Walton, J. K. (1992). *Fish and chips and the British working class, 1870–1940*. Leicester, UK: Leicester University Press.

22. Schlosser, E. (2000). *Fast food nation*. Boston: Houghton Mifflin; see also Ritzer, G. (2004). *The McDonaldization of society*. Thousand Oaks, CA: Pine Forge Press.

23. Hurley, A. (1997). From hash house to family restaurant: The transformation of the diner and post-World War II consumer culture. *Journal of American History, 83*, 1282–1308; Hurley, A. (2001). *Diners, bowling alleys and trailer parks*. New York: Basic Books.

24. One minor exception is the chain of 10 Mel's Diners in Southwest Florida, with 3 more to be added in 2006. Retrieved from www.melsdiners.com/

25. An obvious attempt to associate itself with a paradigmatic great good place.

26. Applebee's, "America's favorite neighbor," reopens its doors just blocks away from ground zero. (2002, July 22). *Business Wire*. Retrieved from ir.applebees.com/phoenix.zhtml?c=107582&p=irol-fastfacts

27. The movie *Diner* (1982) is a nostalgic look at the role that one diner played in the lives of young people in Baltimore in the late 1950s.

28. Jones, S. (2002, April 8). Back to basics: Silver Diner retreats from growth to focus on food and service. *Washington Post*, p. E12.

29. An exception might be a chain like Applebee's, but its efforts to adapt to the local environment seem more like simulations than authentic efforts to be local. Acting local, when it is a result of corporate dictates, is less convincing than those efforts that stem from truly being embedded in the local.

30. Kokopellis are replicas of ancient images of a humpbacked flute player. Malotki, E. (2000). *Kokopelli: The making of an icon*. Lincoln: University of Nebraska Press. Retrieved from www.acaciart.com/stories/archive10.html. Of course, some may be produced as local crafts.

31. Interestingly, there is an Atlanta restaurant by that name, a simulation based on a simulation found in a book and a movie.

32. One exception to this is Johnny Rockets, which seeks to re-create the 1940s hamburger and malt shop, down to the soda jerk outfits. However, the name communicates something very modern, perhaps to compensate for the chain's orientation to the past. The

very contemporary name and the old-fashioned orientation tend to cancel each other out, leaving one with a sense of time-freeness.

33. Interestingly, instead of seeking to appear time-free, there is a not insignificant number of McDonaldized settings that seek to simulate those of a particular time period. Good examples abound in Las Vegas, including the Excalibur Hotel-Casino, which simulates England of the 11th century, and New York, New York, which conjures up an image of pre-1950 New York City. We already mentioned the Applebee's chain that presents itself as an old-fashioned neighborhood restaurant. Then there are English pub chains (Inn Partnership, Scottish and Newcastle) that seek to export this phenomenon with deep roots in English history to many places around the world. All of these are, of course, simulations, and there is an enormous difference between a setting that emerges from a particular time (and place) and one that simulates a time period (and a place).

34. Jones, S. (2002, April 8). Back to basics: Silver Diner retreats from growth to focus on food and service. *Washington Post*, p. E12.

35. Ibid.

36. Ritzer, G. (2005). *Enchanting a disenchanted word: Revolutionizing the means of consumption* (2nd ed.). Thousand Oaks, CA: Pine Forge Press.

37. Petrini, C. (2001). *Slow food.* Chelsea, VT: Chelsea Green; Kummer, C. (2002). *The pleasures of slow food: Celebrating authentic traditions, flavors, and recipes.* San Francisco: Chronicle Books; Miele, M., & Murdoch, J. (2002). Slow food. In G. Ritzer (Ed.), *McDonaldization: The reader* (pp. 250–254). Thousand Oaks, CA: Pine Forge Press.

38. Although they could simply purchase, say, 100 grams of sliced Culatello ham and eat that, perhaps in a sandwich, as quickly as a Big Mac. This reminds us of the fact that the problem is not fast food but the kind of fast food sold by the chains and the way it is consumed.

39. McCracken, G. (1988). *Culture and consumption: New approaches to the symbolic character of consumer goods and activities.* Bloomington: Indiana University Press.

40. Schlosser, E. (2000). *Fast food nation.* Boston: Houghton Mifflin.

41. Ritzer, G. (2002). Revolutionizing the world of consumption: A review essay on three popular books. *Journal of Consumer Culture, 2,* 103–118.

42. Schlosser, E. (2000). *Fast food nation* (p. 171). Boston: Houghton Mifflin.

43. The study of things, bringing things into social analysis, has been popularized by actor-network theory. See Law, J., & Hassard, J. (Eds.). (1999). *Actor network theory and after.* Oxford, UK: Blackwell.

44. Following and extending Marx and neo-Marxian theorists, it could be argued that both workers and consumers are *alienated* from *non*things like Big Macs.

45. Goffman, E. (1959). *Presentation of self in everyday life.* Garden City, NY: Anchor Books; Ducharme, L., & Fine, G. A. (1995). The construction of nonpersonhood and demonization: Commemorating the traitorous reputation of Benedict Arnold. *Social Forces, 73,* 1309–1331; Davis, F. (1959). The cabdriver and his fare: Facets of a fleeting relationship. *American Journal of Sociology, 65,* 158–165.

46. Disney's worlds have been subjected to innumerable analyses. See, for example, Fjellman, S. (1992). *Vinyl leaves: Walt Disney World and America.* Boulder, CO: Westview; Bryman, A. (1995). *Disney and his worlds.* London: Routledge.

47. May, R. A. B. (2001). *Talking at Trena's: Everyday conversation at an African American tavern* (p. 14). New York: New York University Press.

48. Carlson, J. (2001, December 15). In a bar named after a mead hall, bartender talks to many. *Associated Press.*

49. Schutz, A. (1967). *The phenomenology of the social world.* Evanston, IL: Northwestern University Press. (Original work published 1931)

50. On the other hand, Disney, his movies, his characters, and his worlds have all become cultural icons.

51. Interestingly, there is now a cruise ship on which people are able to purchase very expensive condominiums and live in them full time as they circumnavigate the globe, perhaps over and over.

52. Klein, N. (2000). *No logo: Taking aim at the brand name bullies*. Toronto: Vintage Canada.

53. The search for origins is another modern idea that has fallen victim to the critiques of such new social theorists as the postmodernists.

54. Although, as we have seen, some mass-produced automobiles (muscle cars, the VW Beetle) come to be defined by some people as things. Even the Model T Fords that survive today would likely now be considered things by aficionados.

55. Goldman, S. L., Nagel, R. N., & Preiss, K. (1995). *Agile competitors and virtual organizations: Strategies for enriching the customer*. New York: Van Nostrand Reinhold.

56. Pine, J. (1993). *Mass customization: The new frontier in business competition*. Cambridge, MA: Harvard Business School Press.

57. It has also led to an increase in things, although the increase in things was minuscule in comparison to the increase in *non*things.

Chapter 4

1. I would like to thank Bob Antonio for suggesting these clarifications to me.

2. Baudrillard, J. (1983). *Simulations*. New York: Semiotext(e).

3. In a clever, satirical essay titled "Nothing: A Preliminary Account," Donald Barthelme endeavors to come up with a list of nothing, an effort that is doomed to failure, since everything he iterates turns out *not* to be nothing. To Barthelme, nothing is the opposite of that which exists; it is characterized by "non-appearances, no-shows, incorrigible tardiness." However, that is not quite what I mean by nothing here. The nothing of concern throughout this book—the credit card, the fast-food restaurant, the casino-hotel—clearly exists; there is no question about their existence. The issue, again, for us is the existence of centrally conceived and controlled forms that are to a large degree devoid of substance. Here, nothing (although it never exists in a pure form) clearly exists, indeed it is an increasingly dominating existence, but it is an existence that is largely empty of distinctive content.

4. Barrow, J. D. (2000). *The book of nothing* (p. 10). New York: Pantheon Books.

5. Even though it was composed of blank pages, *The Nothing Book*, published in 1974, went through several editions.

6. At another level, Wal-Mart is cram full of a wide array of products. Indeed, one of its great attractions is that so many different things are available under one roof. People go there because of this fact (as well as Wal-Mart's reputation—perhaps exaggerated—for low prices). However, a wide array of products that are nothing does not transform them into something.

7. Chung, C. J., Inaba, J., Koolhaas, R., & Leong, S. T. (Eds.). (2001). *Harvard Design School guide to shopping*. Koln, Germany: Taschen.

8. Chozick, A., & Inada, M. (2006, April 21). Tokyo loves New York food. *Wall Street Journal*, pp. B1, B5.

9. Small towns might be a different matter. Forms of something are likely to be well ensconced in such settings, and they are protected by the fact that the small population base

may make the towns unattractive and unprofitable to various forms of nothing (fast-food restaurants, ATMs). I would like to thank Mike Ryan, who grew up in such a town, for pointing this out to me.

10. Boas, M., & Chain, S. (1976). *Big Mac: The unauthorized story of McDonald's* (p. 117). New York: E. P. Dutton.

11. Georg Simmel is the classical social theorist who contributed most to our understanding of the role of quantitative factors in the social world.

12. Why we're so fat. (2002, October 21). *Business Week*, pp. 112–114; Spurlock, M. (2005). *Don't eat this book: Fast food and the supersizing of America.* Putnam.

13. Bad money drives out good money. See de Roover, R. (1949). *Gresham on foreign exchange.* Cambridge, MA: Harvard University Press.

14. Berger, P., & Luckmann, T. (1967). *The social construction of reality.* Garden City, NY: Anchor.

15. See the Appendix to the original edition of this book for a discussion of this issue.

16. For example, talking to one employee may reinforce a sense of nothing, while another employee may deal with us in a very human manner.

17. Although it may be that there is now something of a renaissance in farmers' markets and craft fairs.

18. While nothing has become increasingly common in the social world, in a way it has become less and less possible to offer nothing in the intellectual world, at least in the social sciences and humanities. That is, it is harder to offer abstract concepts, devoid of content, that purport to be accurate descriptions of the social world or that claim to be scientific tools that can be used in an objective, value-free analysis of that world. Scholars are increasingly questioning whether the objective creation and utilization of such substantively empty concepts are either possible or desirable. In addition, it is argued that it is illusory to think that scholars can do what others cannot do—be completely objective about their world and its activities. Instead, it is argued that it may be that highly subjective analyses, that is, those using concepts that are saturated with the realities of the social world (something) rather than being abstracted from that world, are not only inevitable but also preferable.

19. Diehl, L. B., & Hardart, M. (2002). *The automat: History, recipes and allure of Horn & Hardart's masterpiece.* New York: Clarkson N. Potter.

20. Chung, C. J., Inaba, J., Koolhaas, R., & Leong, S. T. (Eds.). (2001). *Harvard Design School guide to shopping.* Koln, Germany: Taschen.

21. Jakle, J. A., & Wilson, D. (1992). *Derelict landscapes.* Savage, MD: Rowman & Littlefield.

22. Retrieved from www.nikewages.org/FAQs.html

23. Stiglitz, J. E. (2002). *Globalization and its discontents.* New York: W. W. Norton.

24. Glantz, A. (2003, February 26). Jordan's sweatshops: The carrot or the stick of US policy? *Corpwatch.* Retrieved from http://www.corpwatch.org/article.php?id=5688

25. However, as pointed out in Chapter 2, some mass-produced objects (e.g., muscle cars, convertibles) can be considered something.

26. Molotki, E. (2000). *Kokopelli: The making of an icon.* Lincoln: University of Nebraska Press. Retrieved from www.acaciart.com/stories/archive10.html

27. Of course, some may still be produced as local crafts.

28. Retrieved from www.giftogive.com/doll.htm

29. Korchagina, V. (2002, September 11). Souvenir makers ride a wave of American pride. *Moscow Times.*

30. Schumpeter, J. (1950). *Capitalism, socialism and democracy* (3rd ed.). New York: Harper & Brothers.

31. Ritzer, G., & Lair, C. (in press). Outsourcing: Globalization and beyond. In G. Ritzer (Ed.), *The Blackwell companion to globalization*. Oxford, UK: Blackwell.

32. The theory was developed before the boom in globalization in the late 20th century.

33. Although it has many similarities to the diner, the greasy spoon is more associated with small, independently owned cafés and restaurants. For some contemporary examples that still resemble the old-fashioned greasy spoon, see Oldenburg, R. (Ed.). (2001). *Celebrating the third place*. New York: Marlowe.

34. Schumpeter, J. (1950). *Capitalism, socialism and democracy* (3rd ed.). New York: Harper & Brothers.

35. But not exclusively. There are certainly many forms of something—a homemade soup or stew, a hand-knitted ski cap, homemade ice cream—that are inexpensive, indeed far less costly than comparable store-bought products.

36. For example, elite cookery is subject to standardization.

37. Fake villages that derive their name from Grigori Aleksandrovich Potemkin, who had them built on an elaborate scale for Catherine the Great when she visited the Ukraine and the Crimea.

38. I will discuss below the fact that in actuality this may be more a perception than a reality; nothing is certainly not always inexpensive.

39. This is made possible by the fact that those who do not pay their bills in full, who regularly carry a balance and pay high fees, in effect, support those who pay their bills in full each month.

40. Gifton, L. (1995). Convenience and the moral status of consumer practices. In D. W. Marshall (Ed.), *Food choice and the consumer* (pp. 52–181). London: Blackie Academic & Professional.

41. This is consistent with many defenses of consumption. See, for example, Twitchell, J. (1999). *Lead us not into temptation: The triumph of materialism*. New York: Columbia University Press; also Lipovetsky, G. (1994). *The empire of fashion: Dressing modern democracy*. Princeton, NJ: Princeton University Press.

42. Lindley, D. (2002, September 8). Quaint's nice, but sprawl makes me weak at the knees. *Washington Post*, pp. A1, A4.

43. Ibid, A1.

44. Ibid.

45. Ibid, A4.

46. Ibid.

47. Ibid.

48. Ibid.

Chapter 5

1. And there is not an *elective affinity* between grobalization and something and glocalization and nothing.

2. Indeed, it is difficult to accept the view that there are *any* such relationships in the social world.

3. Howe, R. H. (1978). Max Weber's elective affinities: Sociology within the bounds of pure reason. *American Journal of Sociology, 84*, 366–385.

4. However, new, eclectic cuisines and cookery do involve the combination of the most unlikely of foods. Nonetheless, such combinations are unlikely to be attractive to a large, global population of consumers, or at least one as large and global as that for, say, Coca-Cola.

5. Pavitt, J. (2001, July 9). Branded: A brief history of brands: 1. Coca Cola. *The Guardian*, p. 4.

6. However, it is interesting to note that many Mexicans in America claim that the taste of the Coke sold in Mexico is different from, and preferable to, that sold in the United States. Furthermore, Mexicans seem to prefer the old-fashioned and worn bottles that are recycled in Mexico to the American cans and largely plastic bottles. As a result, a growing trade has developed in Mexican Coke being exported, contrary to the company's wishes, to the United States to be consumed by Mexican Americans. This would seem to contradict the idea that Coke is nothing, at least in terms of lacking in distinctive content.

7. Kuisel, R. (1993). *Seducing the French: The dilemma of Americanization*. Berkeley: University of California Press.

8. Bickerton, I., & Jones, A. (2002, April 25). Heineken plans to grow with a new generation at the helm. *Financial Times*, p. 30.

9. Mathiesen, C. (2002, March 4). Foster's no longer just about beer. *The Times*.

10. Daykin, T. (2002, October 7). Point Brewery uncaps root beer. *Milwaukee Journal Sentinel*, p. 2D.

11. Ritzer, G. (2004, November 4). *Art, McDonaldization, and the globalization of nothing*. Paper presented at the Aesthetic Object: Globalization, Commodification, and the Limits of Consumer Culture conference. Cleveland Institute of Art, Cleveland, OH.

12. Survey-Pharmaceuticals. (2001, April 30). *Financial Times*, p. 1.

13. Abate, T. (2002, June 10). Biotrends. *San Francisco Chronicle*, p. E1.

14. Delacoma, W. (2002, October 26). Silk Road, CSO explore the East. *Chicago Sun-Times*, p. 20.

15. Segal, D. (2006, May 20). Want that to Gogh? *Washington Post*, pp. C1, C2.

16. I would like to thank Professor Daina Iglitis for suggesting that I deal with this issue.

17. Wahab, S., & Cooper, C. (Eds.). (2001). *Tourism in the age of globalisation*. London: Routledge.

18. In fact, there are strong regional differences in the United States in the nature, style, and taste of Chinese food (e.g., rice is served free with meals in the East, but in Seattle one must pay extra for rice), even among particular styles of Chinese cooking (Cantonese, Hunan, Szechuan, etc.).

19. Interestingly, in spite of a number of efforts, there is no large, highly successful chain of Chinese restaurants. Tight structural models do not seem to be able to compete with loose structural models in this domain and others. Wu, D. Y. H., & Sidney, C. H. (Eds.). (2002). *The globalization of Chinese food*. Honolulu: University of Hawaii Press.

20. Indeed, the services of FedEx, DHL, and so on themselves take on the character of the grobalization of nothing.

21. Appadurai, A. (1996). *Modernity at large: Cultural dimensions of globalization*. Minneapolis: University of Minnesota Press.

22. Of course, returning to the grobalization of something, programs produced by PBS, and more important, BBC, are shown around the world. However, their global presence pales in comparison to that of sitcoms and soaps.

23. Interestingly, one reason given to support the euro was the nothingness resulting from the Americanization of Europe: a case of creating nothing to defend against nothing.

24. Of course, one could envision a time when the euro could become something to future residents of a more united Europe.

25. There are real national landmarks from European countries on one side of euro coins.

26. Chains and franchises can be thought of as technoscapes.

27. Ferri, J. (1996, October 27). Clubs help new arrivals to U.S. hold on to heritage. *Tampa Tribune*, p. 35.

28. In order to be widely accepted, these ideas are watered down and denuded so that they are often little more than pale imitations of the ideas that lie at their source.

Chapter 6

1. McGrew, A. (in press). Globalization in hard times: Contention in the academy and beyond. In G. Ritzer (Ed.), *The Blackwell companion to globalization*. Oxford, UK: Blackwell.

2. Some of the most important work of this genre is discussed below.

3. Many years ago I did this for sociology in general by identifying its three major paradigms and the theories associated with each. In addition, each paradigm has distinctive methods, a fundamental image of the subject matter, and an exemplar. Much the same thing would need to be done for paradigms in the study of globalization. See Ritzer, G. (1980). *Sociology: A multiple paradigm science* (2nd ed.). Boston: Allyn & Bacon.

4. See the Appendix to the original edition of this book for a discussion of this body of work on nothing.

5. Andrews, D., & Grainger, A. D. (in press). Sport and globalization. In G. Ritzer (Ed.), *Blackwell companion to globalization*. Oxford, UK: Blackwell.

6. Ibid.

7. Ibid.

8. Ibid.

9. Ibid.

10. Ibid.

11. Ibid.

12. Appadurai, A. (1996). *Modernity at large: Cultural dimensions of globalization*. Minneapolis: University of Minnesota Press.

13. And I think Appadurai greatly underestimates the role of grobalization in Indian cricket. While it is true that it has been glocalized in dramatic ways, in the end Indians (and others) are playing cricket, a sport grobalized by the British in the colonial era.

14. Andrews, D., & Grainger, A. D. (in press). Sport and globalization. In G. Ritzer (Ed.), *Blackwell companion to globalization*. Oxford, UK: Blackwell.

15. Ibid.

16. Ibid.

17. Ibid.

18. Ibid.

19. Ibid.

20. Ibid.

21. Ibid.

22. Watson, J. L. (Ed.). (1997). *Golden arches east: McDonald's in East Asia*. Stanford, CA: Stanford University Press.

23. Watson, J. L. (Ed.). (1997). Preface. In J. L. Watson (Ed.), *Golden arches east: McDonald's in East Asia* (p. vi). Stanford, CA: Stanford University Press.

24. Ibid., viii.

25. Ibid., ix.

26. Ibid., x.

27. Watson, J. L. (Ed.). (1997). Transnationalism, localization, and fast foods in Asia. In J. L. Watson (Ed.), *Golden arches east: McDonald's in East Asia* (p. 2). Stanford, CA: Stanford University Press.

28. Ibid., 6.
29. Ibid.
30. Ibid., 7.
31. Ibid., 36.
32. Ibid., 21.
33. Ibid., 37.
34. Although he lacks this term and in any case much prefers to think in terms of localization.
35. Watson, J. L. (1997). McDonald's in Hong Kong: Consumerism, dietary change, and the rise of a children's culture. In J. L. Watson (Ed.), *Golden arches east: McDonald's in East Asia* (p. 80). Stanford, CA: Stanford University Press.
36. Ibid., 92.
37. Ibid., 108.
38. Ohnuki-Tierney, E. (1997). McDonald's in Japan: Changing manners and etiquette. In J. L. Watson (Ed.), *Golden arches east: McDonald's in East Asia* (p. 173). Stanford, CA: Stanford University Press.
39. Ibid., 176–177.
40. Ibid., 178.
41. Ibid., 182.
42. Yan, Y. (1997). McDonald's in Beijing: The localization of Americana. In J. L. Watson (Ed.), *Golden arches east: McDonald's in East Asia* (pp. 72, 76). Stanford, CA: Stanford University Press.
43. Watson, J. L. (1997). McDonald's in Hong Kong: Consumerism, dietary change, and the rise of a children's culture. In J. L. Watson (Ed.), *Golden arches east: McDonald's in East Asia* (p. 80). Stanford, CA: Stanford University Press.
44. Wu, D. Y. H. (1997). McDonald's in Taipei: Hamburgers, betel nuts, and national identity. In J. L. Watson (Ed.), *Golden arches east: McDonald's in East Asia* (pp. 125–126). Stanford, CA: Stanford University Press.
45. Caldwell, M. (2004). Domesticating the French fry: McDonald's and consumerism in Moscow. *Journal of Consumer Culture, 4*(1), 5–26.
46. Ibid., 4(1), 20.
47. Ibid., 4(1), 21.
48. Bryman, A. (2003). Global implication of McDonaldization and Disneyization. *American Behavioral Scientist, 47*(2), 154–167.
49. Ibid., 47(2), 164.
50. Ram, U. (2004). Glocommodification: How the global consumes the local McDonald's in Israel. *Current Sociology, 52*(1), 11–31.
51. Fairclough, G., & Fowler, G. A. (2006, June 20). Drive-through tips for China. *Wall Street Journal,* pp. B1, B9.
52. Ibid., B9.
53. Caldwell, M., & Lozada, E. P., Jr. (in press). The fate of the local. In G. Ritzer (Ed.), *The Blackwell companion to globalization.* Oxford, UK: Blackwell.
54. Furthermore, the local can be seen as merely a vantage point from which to get at the fundamental issues of social analysis such as change, social structure, cultural practices, authenticity, and tradition.
55. Caldwell, M., & Lozada, E. P., Jr. (in press). The fate of the local. In G. Ritzer (Ed.), *The Blackwell companion to globalization.* Oxford, UK: Blackwell.
56. Rigsby, D. K., & Vishwanath, V. (2006, April). Localization: The revolution in consumer markets. *Harvard Business Review, 84,* 82–92.

Chapter 7

1. Although the nullities are not restricted to consumption.

2. Goodman, D. (2003). *Consumer culture: A reference handbook* (p. 4). Santa Barbara, CA: ABC-CLIO.

3. Slater, D. (1997). *Consumer culture and modernity*. Cambridge, UK: Polity Press.

4. Goodman, D. (2003). *Consumer culture: A reference handbook* (p. 4). Santa Barbara, CA: ABC-CLIO.

5. Douglas, M., & Isherwood, B. (1979). *The world of goods*. New York: Basic Books; Csikszentmihalyi, M., & Rochberg-Halton, E. (1981). *The meaning of things*. Cambridge, UK: Cambridge University Press; Appadurai, A. (Ed.). (1986). *The social life of things: Commodities in cultural perspective*. Cambridge, UK: Cambridge University Press.

6. Bauman, Z. (1997). *Postmodernity and its discontents*. New York: New York University Press; Ritzer, G. (2001). *Explorations in the sociology of consumption: Fast food, credit cards and casinos* (pp. 233–235). London: Sage.

7. Belk, R. (in press). Consumption, mass consumption, and consumer culture. In G. Ritzer (Ed.), *Encyclopedia of sociology*. Oxford, UK: Blackwell.

8. See, for example, Putnam, R. (2001). *Bowling alone: The collapse and revival of American community*. New York: Simon & Schuster.

9. Zukin, S. (2005). *Point of purchase: How shopping changed American culture*. New York: Routledge.

10. Urry, J. (1990). *The tourist gaze: Leisure and travel in contemporary societies*. London: Sage.

11. Interestingly, Marx also coined the term "means of consumption," and although it is defined in an unfortunate way by him, it provided the basis for some of my work, and part of the title of a book, in the realm of consumption. For a discussion of Marx's work on this, see Ritzer, G. (2005). *Enchanting a disenchanted world: Revolutionizing the means of consumption* (2nd ed.). Thousand Oaks, CA: Pine Forge Press.

12. Sklair, L. (2002). *Globalization: Capitalism and its alternatives*. New York: Oxford University Press.

13. Steger, M. (2002). *Globalism: The new market ideology*. Lanham, MD: Rowman & Littlefield.

14. Sklair, L. (2002). *Globalization: Capitalism and its alternatives*. New York: Oxford University Press.

15. Clammer, J. (1987). *Contemporary urban Japan: A sociology of consumption*. Oxford, UK: Blackwell.

16. Davis, D. (Ed.). (2000). *The consumer revolution in urban Japan*. Berkeley: University of California Press.

17. Neidhart, C. (2003). *Russia's carnival: The smells, sights, and sounds of transition*. Lanham, MD: Rowman & Littlefield.

18. Mazarella, W. (2003). *Shoveling smoke: Advertising and globalization in contemporary India*. Durham, NC: Duke University Press.

19. Marchand, R. (1986). *Advertising the American dream: Making way for modernity, 1920–1940*. Berkeley: University of California Press.

20. Ritzer, G. (2005). *Enchanting a disenchanted world: Revolutionizing the means of consumption*. Thousand Oaks, CA: Pine Forge Press.

21. By the way, almost all of the new means of consumption can be placed toward the *non*place end of the place-*non*place continuum.

22. The inclusion of McDonald's as one of the new means of consumption and as an example of Americanization makes it clear once again that Americanization and McDonaldization cannot be clearly and unequivocally distinguished from one another.

23. Scall, D. (2002, December 5). Coffee drinkers are not swallowing Starbucks line. *Irish Times*, p. 14.

24. It is worth remembering that it was not too long ago that the United States was the world leader in production. In many ways, consumption has replaced production as the focus of the American economy, and it has become the nation's prime export to the rest of world. It is interesting to ponder the implications of what it means to have gone from the world leader in the production of steel to, say, the world leader in the exportation of fast-food restaurants and shopping malls.

25. This, of course, is closely linked to the "epidemic" of obesity sweeping the nation.

26. See special mini-issue on branding: Holt, D. (Ed.). (in press). *Journal of Consumer Culture*; Holt, D. (2002). Why do brands cause trouble? A dialectical theory of consumer culture and branding. *Journal of Consumer Research, 29*, 70–90; Arvidsson, A. (2006). *Brands: Meaning and value in media culture*. London: Routledge.

27. Koehn, N. F. (2001). *Brand new: How entrepreneurs earned consumers' trust from Wedgwood to Dell*. Boston: Harvard Business School Press.

28. Baudrillard, J. (1998). *The consumer society*. London: Sage. (Original work published 1970)

29. The importance of emotions to brands is reflected in the fact that there are two books published about this issue with the same title, *Emotional Branding*. See Travis, D. (2000). *Emotional branding: How successful brands gain the irrational edge*. Roseville, CA: Prima Venture; Gobe, M. (2001). *Emotional branding: The new paradigm for connecting brands to people*. New York: Allworth Press.

30. Wilk, R. (in press). Bottled water: The pure commodity in the age of branding. *Journal of Consumer Culture*.

31. Trout, J. (2001). *Big brands, big trouble: Lessons learned the hard way* (pp. 6–7). New York: John Wiley.

32. By the way, this makes it clear that this critique of nothing, and *non*things in particular, is not to suggest that the solution involves some sort of return to an era before mass manufacturing. Clearly, our large and complex world cannot survive without mass production. However, must it dominate all sectors of our lives? Isn't there a place and a role for something in the contemporary world?

33. Although Nike played a key role in "branding" Michael Jordan once he became a spokesperson for the company. However, Jordan had long since acquired a brand among basketball fans who appreciated his unique and extraordinary abilities.

34. Baran, P., & Sweezy, P. (1966). *Monopoly capital: An essay on the American economic and social order*. New York: Monthly Review Press.

35. Retrieved from www.islam-online.net/English/News/2004–07/31/article08.shtml

36. Grimston, J. (2003, January 19). British Muslims find things go better with Mecca. *Sunday Times*, p. 12.

37. For example, college students these days think nothing of sending their professors numerous e-mails asking them to do various things for them (e.g., complete a homework assignment) that

they would have never asked for in the past. I often get e-mails from students around the world asking me to write at least part of their papers on topics like McDonaldization.

38. Ritzer, G. (1988). Problems, scandals and the possibility of TextbookGate: An author's view. *Teaching Sociology, 16,* 373–380.

39. One example in sociology is Giddens, A., & Duneier, M. (2003). *Introduction to sociology* (4th ed.). New York: W. W. Norton.

40. Robinson, M. B. (2006). McDonaldization of America's police, courts, and corrections. In G. Ritzer (Ed.), *McDonaldization: The reader* (2nd ed., pp. 88–101). Thousand Oaks, CA: Pine Forge Press.

41. Robinson, M. B. (2006). McDonaldization of America's police, courts, and corrections. In G. Ritzer (Ed.), *McDonaldization: The reader* (2nd ed., pp. 88–101). Thousand Oaks, CA: Pine Forge Press.

42. Drane, J. (2001). *The McDonaldization of the church.* London: Darton, Longman & Todd.

43. Turner, B. (1999). McCitizens: Risk, coolness and irony in contemporary politics. In B. Smart (Ed.), *Resisting McDonaldization* (pp. 83–100). London: Sage.

44. Bove, J., & DuFour, F. (2001). *The world is not for sale: Farmers against junk food.* London: Verso; Morse, D. (2006). Striking the golden arches: French farmers protest McD's globalization. In G. Ritzer (Ed.), *McDonaldization: The reader* (2nd ed., pp. 266–268). Thousand Oaks, CA: Pine Forge Press.

45. This is exemplified by the case of a Japanese Boy Scout who, on a trip to the United States, was surprised to find McDonald's in Chicago—he thought McDonald's was a Japanese chain. See Watson, J. (Ed.). (1997). *Golden arches east: McDonald's in East Asia.* Stanford, CA: Stanford University Press.

46. Keller, B. (1990, September 12). Of famous arches, beeg meks and rubles. *New York Times,* sec. 1, pp. 1, 12; Keller, B. (1990, September 12). Wedge of Americana: In Moscow, Pizza Hut opens two restaurants. *Washington Post,* p. B10.

47. Kincheloe, J. (2002). *The sign of the burger: McDonald's and the culture of power.* Philadelphia: Temple University Press.

48. Ross, S. (2002, December 4). Survey says: Foreigners like U.S. culture but not policies. *Boston Globe.* Retrieved from www.boston.com/dailynews/338/wash/Survey_says_Foreigners_like_U:.shtml

49. French, H. (2005, December 24). Spot the difference: France quarrels with America not because the pair are so different but because they are so alike. *The Economist,* pp. 75–77.

50. Kuisel, R. (1993). *Seducing the French: The dilemma of Americanization.* Berkeley: University of California Press.

51. For an alternate view, see James, H. (2001). *The end of globalization.* Cambridge, MA: Harvard University Press.

52. Derber, C. (2002). *People before profits: The new globalization in an age of terror, big money, and economic crisis* (p. 15). New York: St. Martin's Press.

53. Thus, for example, in international fine art sales, Great Britain is poised to supplant the United States as the world leader.

54. For example, in the realm of the military, American weaponry is far more sophisticated than that of any other nation in the world.

55. Loeb, V. (2002, December 15). Burst of brilliance. *Washington Post Magazine,* pp. 6ff.

56. Stiglitz, J. E. (2002). *Globalization and its discontents.* New York: W. W. Norton.

57. Faiola, A. (2002, August 6). Despair in once-proud Argentina. *Washington Post,* pp. A1, A9.

Chapter 8

1. As I pointed out previously, there are exceptions.

2. Leland, J. (2002, December 1). How the disposable couch conquered America. *New York Times,* sec. 6, p. 86.

3. Chung, C. J., Inaba, J., Koolhaas, R., & Leong, S. T. (2001). *Harvard Design School guide to shopping* (p. 135). Koln, Germany: Taschen.

4. However, once again it is important to point out that since something is not necessarily desirable (e.g., a pogrom is something according to our definition), the loss of it is not necessarily to be regretted (it might even be welcomed). However, regrettable or not, it still represents a loss.

5. Although there are grand narratives in his work as well as in that of other postmodern social theorists.

6. Stuever, H. (2002, June 16). Just one word: Plastic. *Washington Post Magazine,* p. 27.

7. Ibid., 28.

8. The implication is that Gucci is something and it is distinguished from the various forms of nothingness. However, given the definition employed in this book, Gucci would be considered nothing. As we have seen, there is a continuum from nothing to something, and while Gucci may be seen as being closer to the something end of the continuum than the other brands discussed here, it is still better thought of as nothing.

9. Many of the points to be made here apply, as well, to online casinos and many other large-scale online consumption sites.

10. Interestingly, racetracks have had to respond to this by offering televised races from other tracks and wagering on those races to supplement, and sometimes instead of, their live races.

11. Or, more recently, an offtrack betting site.

12. Sandoval, G., & La Canfora, J. (2003, March 13). Jagr: Gambling was a mistake. *Washington Post,* pp. D1, D6.

13. This is also true in the world of credit cards. See Ritzer, G. (1995). *Expressing America: A critique of the global credit card society.* Thousand Oaks, CA: Pine Forge Press; Klein, L. (1999). *It's in the cards: Consumer credit and the American experience.* Westport, CT: Praeger; Manning, R. (2000). *Credit card nation: The consequences of America's addiction to debt.* New York: Basic Books.

14. Gergen, K. (2000). *The saturated self.* New York: Basic Books.

15. As discussed above, there are, of course, satisfactions associated with consumption on the Internet.

16. Nelson, J. L. (2001). On mass distribution: A case study of chain stores in the restaurant industry. *Journal of Consumer Culture, 1,* 119–138.

17. Fast-food restaurants predate McDonald's, but they really came of age with the founding of that chain.

18. Of course, the increase in population plays a central role in this.

19. This argument has some similarities to that of Walter Benjamin and his view that while technological change leads to various advances, it is also associated with the loss of "aura"; see Benjamin, W. (1969). The work of art in the age of mechanical reproduction. In W. Benjamin, *Illuminations.* New York: Schocken.

20. Stuever, H. (2002, June 16). Just one word: Plastic. *Washington Post Magazine,* p. 18.

21. Ritzer, G., Stepnisky, J., & Lemich, J. (2005). The magical world of consumption: Transforming nothing into something. *Berkeley Journal of Sociology, 49,* 118–137.

22. In addition, little or nothing needs to be extracted from these empty forms because there is so little there to remove.

23. In contrast, designer clothes are likely to be discarded when they begin to show wear.

24. Campbell, C. (2005). The craft consumer: Culture, craft and consumption in a postmodern society. *Journal of Consumer Culture, 5,* 24.

25. Ibid., 27.

26. See Chapter 2 for a discussion of the earmarking of money.

27. For more on this theory, see the Appendix to the original edition of this book.

28. Florida, R. (2004). *The flight of the creative class: The new global competition for talent.* New York: HarperBusiness.

29. Kummer, C. (2002). *The pleasures of slow food* (p. 23). San Francisco: Chronicle Books.

30. Of course, there are numerous examples of groups that define themselves *in opposition to* the extant consumer culture. However, these groups do not address our principal interest: the transformation of nothing into something. For example, the Voluntary Simplicity movement advocates for a reduction in personal spending and a refusal of the excesses of consumer culture. Alternately, counterculture festivals such as Burning Man give rise to communities that oppose market consumption. Participants in the Burning Man festival are diverse in their beliefs and lifestyles, but for one week every year they form a community that is united in its attempt to develop forms of consumption that don't rely on the identities and exchange practices supplied through branding. These groups do not transform nothing into something; rather, they attempt to escape nothing.

31. Muniz, A. M., Jr., & O'Guinn, T. (2001). Brand community. *Journal of Consumer Research, 27,* 412–432; Muniz, A. M., Jr., & O'Guinn, T. (in press). Marketing communications in a world of consumption and brand communities. In R. Ratneshwar & D. Mick (Eds.), *Inside consumption: Frontiers of research on consumer motives, goals, and desires.* London: Routledge.

32. Muniz, A. M., Jr., & O'Guinn, T. (2001). Brand community. *Journal of Consumer Research, 27,* 418.

33. Walker, R. (2004, October 31). The old new thing. *New York Times.*

34. Kummer, C. (2002). *The pleasures of slow food* (p. 26). San Francisco: Chronicle Books.

35. Ibid., 23.

36. Ibid.

37. Ibid., 25.

38. Ibid.

39. Retrieved from www.terramadre2004.org/terramadre/eng/comunita.lasso

40. Ibid.

Index